THE CHANGING EUROPEAN UNION

It is widely recognised that international order is undergoing transformative change. This collection looks at the role of law and courts in the changing EU. On the one hand, it analyses how EU law and EU courts have reacted to the new developments and challenges that Europe and the world are facing, such as rising inequalities in and across societies, the rise of populism, the migration crisis, and technological developments. On the other hand, it investigates the transformative potential of EU law and the extent to which law can progressively be used to bring about social change. Taking a multifaceted approach, the book draws on voices from academia and the judiciary to suggest how the EU might respond effectively to the challenges faced

Volume 114 in the Series Modern Studies in European Law

Modern Studies in European Law

Recent titles in this series:

EU Citizenship at the Edges of Freedom of Movement
Katarina Hyltén-Cavallius

The Internal Market 2.0
Edited by Sacha Garben and Inge Govaere

New Directions in European Private Law
Edited by Mateja Durovic and Takis Tridimas

Standing to Enforce European Union Law before National Courts
Hilde Ellingsen

The Relative Authority of Judicial and Extra-Judicial Review: The EU Courts, the Boards of Appeal and the Ombudsman
Michal Krajewski

Responsive Human Rights: Vulnerability and the ECtHR
Corina Heri

The Architecture of Fundamental Rights in the European Union
Šejla Imamovic

The EU and its Member States' Joint Participation in International Agreements
Edited by Nicolas Levrat, Yuliya Kaspiarovich, Christine Kaddous and Ramses A Wessel

The UN Convention on the Rights of Persons with Disabilities and the European Union: The Impact on Law and Governance
Carmine Conte

EU Criminal Law, Second Edition
Valsamis Mitsilegas

The EU as a Global Digital Actor: Institutionalising Global Data Protection, Trade, and Cybersecurity
Elaine Fahey

Exporting the European Convention on Human Rights
Maria-Louiza Deftou

Judicial Authority in EU Internal Market Law: Implications for the Balance of Competences and Powers
Vilija Velyvyte

The Changing European Union: A Critical View on the Role of Law and the Courts
Edited by Tamara Ćapeta, Iris Goldner Lang and Tamara Perišin

For the complete list of titles in this series
see www.bloomsbury.com/uk/series/modern-studies-in-european-law/

The Changing European Union

A Critical View on the Role of Law and the Courts

Edited by
Tamara Ćapeta
Iris Goldner Lang
and
Tamara Perišin

• HART •
OXFORD • LONDON • NEW YORK • NEW DELHI • SYDNEY

HART PUBLISHING

Bloomsbury Publishing Plc

Kemp House, Chawley Park, Cumnor Hill, Oxford, OX2 9PH, UK

1385 Broadway, New York, NY 10018, USA

29 Earlsfort Terrace, Dublin 2, Ireland

HART PUBLISHING, the Hart/Stag logo, BLOOMSBURY and the Diana logo are trademarks of Bloomsbury Publishing Plc

First published in Great Britain 2022

A catalogue record for this book is available from the British Library.

Library of Congress Cataloging-in-Publication data

Names: Ćapeta, Tamara, editor. | Goldner Lang, Iris, editor. | Perišin, Tamara, editor.

Title: The changing European Union : a critical view on the role of law and the courts / edited by Tamara Ćapeta, Iris Goldner Lang, and Tamara Perišin.

Description: Oxford ; New York : Hart Publishing, an imprint of Bloomsbury Publishing, 2022. | Series: Modern studies in European law ; 114 | Includes bibliographical references and index. | Summary: "It is widely recognised that international order is undergoing transformative change and the old norms no longer apply. This collection looks at how the EU, specifically its judicial wing, is responding to these new challenges. It looks both externally at those internationally shared problems of unequal societies, the rise of populism and the migrant crisis and internally at Brexit, the differences between the EU centre and peripheries and the division of competences. Taking a multifaceted approach, it draws on voices from academia and the judiciary to suggest how the EU might respond effectively to the challenges faced"– Provided by publisher.

Identifiers: LCCN 2022036554 | ISBN 9781509937332 (hardback) | ISBN 9781509964888 (paperback) | ISBN 9781509937356 (pdf) | ISBN 9781509937349 (Epub)

Subjects: LCSH: Law—European Union countries. | Courts—European Union countries.

Classification: LCC KJE947 .C449 2022 | DDC 341.242/2—dc23/eng/20220921

LC record available at https://lccn.loc.gov/2022036554

ISBN: HB: 978-1-50993-733-2
ePDF: 978-1-50993-735-6
ePub: 978-1-50993-734-9

Typeset by Compuscript Ltd, Shannon

CONTENTS

1

The Changing European Union: A Critical View on the Role of Law and the Courts

TAMARA ĆAPETA,* IRIS GOLDNER LANG**
AND TAMARA PERIŠIN***

'One impossible thing at a time'

Jean Luc Picard[1]

The principal theme of this book is the relationship between societal change and the law. The law has transformative potential and can initiate change, or can simply react to it. The authors, thus, approach the notion of change in different ways and from different angles. They either adopt a descriptive approach, observing the changes that have occurred in society for different reasons and ask how the law and its principal actors, the courts, have reacted to such change. Alternatively, they adopt a normative attitude, criticising either how the law has reacted to change or claiming that the law has failed to cause the necessary change. Most of the analyses focus on the case law of the Court of Justice of the European Union (CJEU), that Court being the most important protagonist of 'transformation through law' in the European Union (EU).

The idea for the book arose during the conference 'The Role of Law and Courts in a Changing European Union' which took place in May 2018 in Zagreb, marking

* Tamara Ćapeta, Advocate General, Court of Justice of the European Union; Professor, University of Zagreb. All opinions expressed herein are personal to the author.

** Iris Goldner Lang, Jean Monnet Professor of EU Law, UNESCO Chairholder and Vice Dean, University of Zagreb – Faculty of Law.

*** Tamara Perišin, Judge, Court of Justice of the European Union – General Court; Professor, University of Zagreb. All opinions expressed herein are personal to the author.

[1] 'Absolute Candor', *Star Trek*: Picard Season 1 Episode 4 (2020) written by Michael Chabon © CBS Studios Inc.

five years of Croatian membership in the Union. Accessions always spur discussion on the changes they bring to the Union, but in the EU change has become a constant … or at least the need for change has.

In this regard, it should be noted that the editors were struggling to decide whether to title the book 'Changing the European Union' so as to suggest an active attempt to bring about change or to opt for the title 'The Changing European Union', implying that the EU is continuously changing even without any deliberate effort. We now believe that this second title is more reflective of reality – the EU is undergoing constant transformation due to societal developments or even due to events that are difficult to control by humans such as the global viral pandemic, climate change or by the outbreak of a war. In these circumstances, EU actors must be quick not only to respond to change and attempt to mitigate its negative effects, but to predict developments and imagine better solutions.

I. Challenges which the EU is Facing

Over recent years, the EU has faced one crisis after another, but it has to be recognised that the world as a whole has been in a turbulent period.

Thus, on the one hand, some of the challenges that the EU has been experiencing have been faced by many other global players: job losses of low-skilled workers, unequal social standards and economic opportunities, the rise of the ultra-conservative social and political movement, nationalism, populism paired with fake news, the migration influx followed by restrictive legal and political moves that challenge existing values and rules, the unequal speed of recovery from financial crises, the shaky position of national courts when trying to remedy questionable measures of the legislature or the executive, and the unprecedented development of technology in the Fourth Industrial Revolution that causes changes in production, trade and all aspects of life. The Covid-19 pandemic added more layers of complexity to the attempts to deal with all the above-mentioned issues.

On the other hand, there are also a number of challenges specific to the EU. First, the EU is not entirely homogeneous since there are significant differences between the EU's centre and its periphery. These differences might require different legal mechanisms. Second, the supranational set-up of the EU and the division of competences often make it more difficult to react to both internal and external crises. Third, Brexit has highlighted that the EU could dissolve if people remain unclear about the benefits of integration. Finally, the rule of law crisis has made the EU rethink the role of the institutions of government, both in its Member States and at the EU level. Discussions on the role of courts, even if evergreen in legal academia, have found their way into the judicial process itself.

II. Addressing the Challenges

The EU has two options on how to deal with all these challenges. It can either continue making small changes in the law aiming at marginally mitigating the adverse effects of new developments. Alternatively, it can take the position that new developments require more radical change in the set-up of the EU to allow its society to prosper in a new era. Perhaps the European project is unsustainable and the quality of life will start dropping unless law is used more proactively and with more imagination for the reshaping of the current social order (Society 5.0). This new arrangement could possibly go as far as to turn the EU upside down for the supranational level to focus on social rights, EU-wide critical education, equality of opportunity, the integration of third-country nationals, the equal rights of EU citizens and third-country nationals residing in the EU, etc, instead of basing the integration project on the market and rights reserved predominantly for EU citizens.

Addressing these challenges certainly implies closely examining particular triggers of change, including the tension between the market and social rights, unequal standards in the EU's centre and periphery, specifically unequal educational opportunities, the influx of migrants, the development of technology such as artificial intelligence, etc. The book does not have the ambition to tackle all these challenges. It has rather grouped a number of authors and invited them to assess what role the law and, in particular, the courts play in the changing EU, asking them to choose themselves the challenges they wish to focus on. In the traditional narrative of European integration, law has always been understood as the cornerstone of change. The CJEU has been seen to have a leading role in the transformation of Europe. However, the original context in which European transformation was possible has (arguably) changed. Nowadays, the EU is significantly larger and more heterogeneous than originally foreseen, and different political majorities in various Member States have opposing views on how the EU should evolve. What is seen as a legitimate division of power between EU and national institutions is constantly changing and differs throughout Europe. The EU is vested with relatively wide powers significantly exceeding the initial project of building a common market, so the Treaties allow for more EU law to be created through the European legislative process. However, new developments and crises might require even more power to be transferred to the EU despite opposition in some Member States. It might also require the rethinking of the role of EU law and its courts in reacting to these developments and, possibly, changing the EU as we know it today. Over the years, the balance of power between the branches of EU governance has shifted, as has, in particular, the relationship between the Court and the legislative institutions. This raises the question of the extent to which the EU judiciary can become involved in the changes in today's EU, but also in the possible necessary changes in the judiciary itself.

III. The Role of Courts in a Changing EU

The first part of this book titled 'The Role of Courts in a Changing European Union' focuses on the institutional balance that exists or ought to exist in the process of creating change in and through law. In particular, this part examines the possible role of the CJEU in bringing about future change in European society and its limits.

This part starts with the contribution of Koen Lenaerts which focuses on the pivotal role of judicial independence for the 'Union of democracies, rights and justice'. It explains the importance of judicial dialogue in a changing world and shows the dynamic relationship between courts of different Member States and the CJEU. The contribution puts into focus changes in national laws which in some Member States have endangered the independence of judges, judicial cooperation between Member States, and the EU value of the rule of law. It gives a detailed account of the case law in the field.

The following chapter, written by Tamara Ćapeta and Nika Bačić Selanec, puts forward a different, procedural concept of the rule of law and argues that an important change which needs to happen to safeguard the rule of law in the EU would be a change in the written reasoning of the CJEU's decisions. It is claimed that the formalist legal narrative, presenting only one solution to the dispute as the legally possible one, lacks persuasiveness and ought to be replaced with one recognising and explaining the reasons for the judicial choices made.

Alexander Somek's contribution suggests that the authoritative nature of the judgments of the CJEU and the Court's reliance on innovation and on pushing the boundaries of EU law are the chief means of what the Court perceives as 'being faithful to the law of European integration'. In this respect, the chapter encompasses new ideas on how to account for innovation in the CJEU's case law and offers an explanation of the surprising fidelity to law in cases moving beyond existing law.

The chapter co-authored by Samuel Dahan, Rohan Bhambhoria, Simon Townsend and Xiaodan Zhu offers insight into how technological developments are influencing the functioning of courts. By using the example of EU trademark rules, the authors seek to explain the relevance of artificial intelligence, machine learning and deep learning for access to justice and for decision-making processes. They argue that shifting the EU courts' operations online, though commendable, does not constitute a full-blown paradigmatic shift, as it cannot address the root causes of the access-to-justice crisis in the EU.

IV. Substantive Areas Triggering Structural Change in EU Law

The second part of this book under the title 'Substantive Areas Triggering Structural Change in European Union Law' examines substantive areas in which social tensions, new circumstances and crises mandate changes in the law. These triggers of change include the tension between the market and social rights, unequal standards in the EU's centre and periphery, particularly unequal educational opportunities, and migration crises. Most of the contributions in this part also focus on the role that courts, especially the CJEU have, or could/should have, in addressing the tensions at issue.

This part on substantive areas starts with Stephen Weatherill's examination of the constitutionalisation of the internal market. The author explores whether the CJEU should be accused of over-constitutionalisation of EU free movement law to the detriment of political contestation at both national and EU level. He argues that the Court usually knows its limits and that it should be trusted as long as it consistently interprets free movement law by respecting the vertical and horizontal distribution of competences in the EU.

Building upon the constitutionalisation of internal market rules and its spillover effects, Tamara Perišin's contribution examines whether the EU could undertake more measures in the field of education. It explains how the educational field has changed through CJEU case law and EU legislation, and shows in which areas further action might be possible. The chapter gives examples not only of what the EU could do in the field of education, but of the ways in which such measures would be beneficial to the EU and its citizens.

The contribution of Damjan Kukovec critically explains how the internal market has not lived up to its promise of improving and equalising the quality of life in the EU. It argues that the adverse effects of internal market rules on the EU periphery have led to *ressentiment* which lies in the background of the EU's rule of law crisis. The chapter argues that the EU can achieve stability only if it addresses the persisting inequalities by creating fair competitive opportunities to all its Member States and by promoting cohesion.

The last two chapters discuss developments relating to the 2015/2016 refugee influx into the EU. Iris Goldner Lang suggests that the behaviour of the CJEU in some of its most prominent judgments in this area can be labelled as 'judicial passivism' – a term she coins to apply to cases where the CJEU is consciously (actively) not using its powers where it should. According to the author, these judgments open up the question of the Court's role and responsibility in the context of the refugee influx into Europe and in terms of the consequent legal and policy developments.

Sam Koplewicz, Alfred Bridi and Mona Haghgou Strindber criticise the EU's growing practice of externalising immigration management to third countries. They argue that this shift has resulted in an unchecked and deteriorating humanitarian situation, with particular focus on Libya. They assess how migration has been dealt with through the interaction of all EU institutions, Member States and third countries, and advocate more control over these processes by the CJEU. The authors review potential routes that can be taken to remedy these violations before the CJEU and argue that the CJEU should not shy away from its constitutional and humanitarian imperative.

To conclude, this book seeks to examine the role of law and courts in the changing EU. On the one hand, it analyses how EU law and EU courts have reacted to the new developments and challenges that Europe and the world are facing and questions whether EU law is equipped to master these challenges. On the other hand, it investigates the transformative potential of EU law and the extent to which law can progressively be used to bring about social change.

PART I

The Role of Courts in a Changing European Union

2

Judicial Dialogue in a Changing World: Preserving Judicial Independence

KOEN LENAERTS*

I. Introduction

The very nature of European Union (EU) law is inherently linked to the preliminary reference mechanism that, in the words of the Court of Justice of the European Union (the Court of Justice), is the 'keystone' of the EU system of judicial protection. The Court of Justice has, time and again, held that that mechanism provides for a dialogue between the Court of Justice and national courts, the object of which is to ensure the uniform interpretation of EU law. In so doing, the preliminary reference mechanism serves to ensure the consistency, the full effect and the autonomy of EU law.[1]

Since the dialogue between national courts and the Court of Justice is based on the law – and nothing but the law – access to the preliminary reference mechanism is only open to courts that are independent. Judicial independence is required because it guarantees that the national court referring a question to the Court of Justice will not take political considerations into account when making the reference and when implementing the Court's judgment.

Moreover, in the EU legal order, the enforcement of EU law is largely decentralised. It is not only for the Court of Justice but also for national courts to guarantee that the rights that EU law confers on individuals are effectively protected. In that regard, the Court of Justice has ruled that only independent national courts may

* President of the Court of Justice of the European Union and Professor of European Union Law, Leuven University. All opinions expressed herein are personal to the author.

[1] See, eg, Opinion 2/13 (Accession of the European Union to the ECHR) EU:C:2014:2454 para 176. See also Case C-284/16 *Achmea* EU:C:2018:158 para 37; Case C-234/17 *XC and Others* EU:C:2018:853 para 41; and Case C-619/18 *Commission v Poland (Independence of the Supreme Court)* EU:C:2019:531 para 45. On the autonomy of EU law, see K Lenaerts, JA Gutiérrez-Fons and S Adam, 'Exploring the Autonomy of the European Union Legal Order' (2021) 8 *ZaöRV* 47.

ensure compliance with the principle of effective judicial protection enshrined in Article 47 of the Charter of Fundamental Rights of the EU (the Charter).

European integration has long since moved on from the internal market paradigm. It now seeks to establish an Area of Freedom, Security and Justice (the AFSJ) without internal frontiers, where citizens may move freely and securely. In an area without internal frontiers, the exercise of free movement should not undermine the jurisdiction of national courts and the effectiveness of national law operating on a territorial basis. The 'long arm of the law' should therefore acquire a transnational dimension, so that, for example, criminals are prevented from relying on free movement as a means of pursuing their activities with impunity. Accordingly, the authors of the EU Treaties reasoned that the free movement of persons should be accompanied by the free movement of judicial decisions. By virtue of the principle of mutual recognition, judicial decisions adopted in the Member State of origin are to be recognised and enforced in the Member State of enforcement as if they were its own.

In order for that principle to operate properly, national courts must trust that courts from other Member States are equally committed to upholding the values on which the EU is founded and, in particular, to protecting the fundamental rights of the persons concerned. As the principle of judicial independence constitutes the essence of the fundamental right to effective judicial protection, respect for that principle is of paramount importance in order to underpin the free movement of judicial decisions.

It follows from the foregoing that in the EU legal order, judicial independence is called upon to fulfil a triple function: it operates as a prerequisite for judicial dialogue between the Court of Justice and national courts to take place; it guarantees that EU rights are afforded effective judicial protection; and it facilitates mutual trust between national courts in the AFSJ. The purpose of this contribution is to look at that triple function more closely. To that end, it unfolds as follows. Section II explains that the entire system of EU judicial protection was originally built on the assumption that a Member State would never adopt measures curtailing the independence of national courts.[2] In section III, the concept of 'courts or tribunals', within the meaning of EU law, is explored, paying special attention to the requirement for such courts or tribunals to be independent. The question whether EU law protects the independence of those 'courts or tribunals' is also examined in the light of the seminal ruling of the Court in *Associação Sindical dos Juízes Portugueses*.[3] Section IV looks at judicial independence from a transnational perspective and posits that there cannot be mutual trust between courts of different Member States that are not independent. Finally, a brief conclusion supports

[2] See K Lenaerts, 'New Horizons for the Rule of Law within the EU' (2020) 21 *German Law Journal* 29.

[3] Case C-64/16 *Associação Sindical dos Juízes Portugueses v Tribunal de Contas* EU:C:2018:117.

the contention that the principle of judicial independence must be preserved so that the EU remains a 'Union of democracies', a 'Union of rights', and a 'Union of justice'.

II. The Rule of Law as the Law of Remedies

More than 50 years ago, the Court of Justice famously held in *Van Gend en Loos* that the judicial protection of EU rights is based on a system of 'dual vigilance': in addition to the supervision carried out by the European Commission and the Member States, individuals are entitled to rely on their EU rights in the national courts.[4] The enforcement of EU law is largely decentralised, in so far as the Treaties – and in particular Article 19 of the Treaty on European Union (TEU) – entrust 'the responsibility for ensuring the full application of EU law in all Member States and judicial protection of the rights of individuals under that law to national courts and tribunals and to the Court of Justice'.[5] It is for the Court of Justice to say what the law of the EU is, and for national courts – as courts of general jurisdiction – to apply that law.

National courts have thus played a leading role in upholding the rule of law within the EU. In cooperation with the Court of Justice, they have relied on EU law in order to provide effective remedies to enforce the rights that that law confers on individuals. By virtue of EU law, national courts have provided access to justice where national law prevented those courts from examining the legality of decisions adopted by public authorities.[6] They have set aside conflicting legal norms, including those of constitutional rank.[7] They have also granted interim, declaratory and monetary relief, even where national law failed to provide those remedies.[8]

Until recently, providing effective remedies was deemed sufficient in itself to secure the primacy, the unity and the effectiveness of EU law. With effective remedies, European integration was able to move forward. The case law of the Court of Justice focused on the effectiveness of the remedies to be provided by national courts rather than on protecting the independence of the national courts providing those remedies. Academic discussions as well as references to the Court of

[4] Case 26/62 *van Gend & Loos* EU:C:1963:1.

[5] See, eg, Case C-619/18 *Commission v Poland (Independence of the Supreme Court)* (n 1) para 47. See also Opinion 1/09 *(Agreement creating a Unified Patent Litigation System)* EU:C:2011:123 para 66; Case C-583/11 P *Inuit Tapiriit Kanatami and Others v Parliament and Council* EU:C:2013:625 para 90; Case C-456/13 P *T & L Sugars and Sidul Açúcares v Commission* EU:C:2015:284 para 45.

[6] See, eg, Case 222/84 *Johnston* EU:C:1986:206.

[7] See, eg, judgment of 8 September 2010, Case C-409/06 *Winner Wetten* EU:C:2010:503 para 61 (holding that '[r]ules of national law, even of a constitutional order, cannot be allowed to undermine the unity and effectiveness of Union law') See also Case 11/70 *Internationale Handelsgesellschaft* EU:C:1970:114 para 3.

[8] See Case C-213/89 *Factortame and Others* EU:C:1990:257; Case 106/77 *Simmenthal* EU:C:1978:49; and Joined Cases C-46/93 and C-48/93 *Brasserie du pêcheur and Factortame* EU:C:1996:79.

Justice dealt with the complex question of how to strike the right balance between the principle of national procedural autonomy and the twin principles of equivalence and effectiveness.[9] It is true that 'judicial independence' has been examined by the Court of Justice in the past when a body – which did not belong to the national judiciary – sought to make a reference to that Court, as a requirement that the referring body has to meet in order to have access to the preliminary reference mechanism.[10] However, that case law did not relate to concerns that the judicial independence of a national court, within the meaning of EU law, was in doubt.

Perhaps, given that the principle of judicial independence stems from the constitutional traditions common to the Member States as one of the founding tenets of any democratic system of governance, it was assumed that national governments would not threaten it. That principle was 'uncontested and incontestable'.[11] It was taken as read that national governments would encourage citizens to trust the courts as the ultimate arbiters of any legal dispute, including in situations where a court ruling was decided against the wishes of the political majority of the day.

The motto 'in the courts we trust' also applied to matters falling within the scope of EU law. The internal market could not have been built without the role played by national courts in guaranteeing the full effect of the fundamental freedoms. Since 'free movers' do not, in principle, enjoy political representation in the host Member State, upholding their rights may require access to a court of law that must be able to provide effective remedies. Where those rights enter into conflict with the views of the political majority of the day, respect for the rule of law requires that majority to comply with the judgments of the courts. National courts have thus contributed to dismantling protectionist laws, either by enforcing the Treaty provisions on free movement or by applying secondary EU law giving concrete expression to those provisions. The same was true in other areas of law where the EU has conferred rights on individuals. EU anti-discrimination law and EU environmental law are key examples of fields where national courts have made a critical contribution to delivering justice throughout the EU.

In the same way, the Court of Justice has stressed the fact that independent courts are crucial for ensuring the protection of the EU budget and its financial interests. In two recent judgments it dismissed as unfounded the actions for annulment brought respectively by Hungary and Poland ([12]) against Regulation 2020/2092

[9] See, eg, C Kakouris, 'Do the Member States Possess Judicial Procedural "*Autonomy*"' (1997) 34 *Common Market Law Review* 1389, 1389–1412; S Prechal, 'Community Law in National Courts: The Lessons from *Van Schijndel*' (1998) 35 *Common Market Law Review* 681, 681–706; and W van Gerven, 'Of Rights, Remedies and Procedures' (2000) 37 *Common Market Law Review* 501, 501–36. See also M Dougan, *National Remedies before the Court of Justice: Issues of Harmonisation and Differentiation* (Oxford, Hart Publishing, 2004).

[10] See section III below.

[11] T von Danwitz, 'Values and the Rule of Law: Foundations of the European Union: An Inside Perspective from the ECJ' (2018) 21 *PER/PELJ* 1, 1–17.

[12] To that effect, Case C-156/21 *Hungary v Parliament and Council* EU:C:2022:97, and Case C-157/21 *Poland v Parliament and Council* EU:C:2022:98.

on a general regime of conditionality for the protection of the Union budget.[13] In those two cases, the question arose, in particular, whether the EU was competent to adopt such a regulation which, as a financial rule, is intended to protect the EU budget, by making the benefit of EU financing conditional upon compliance with the principles of the rule of law, including access to independent and impartial courts.[14] The Court of Justice replied in the affirmative, stating that that regulation does not apply to all infringements of the rule of law, but only to those which adversely affect – or present a serious risk of adversely affecting – in a sufficiently direct manner, the sound financial management of the EU budget or the protection of its financial interests.[15]

The question also arose whether the EU could adopt a horizontal conditionality mechanism, applicable across all sectors, or whether its powers were confined to sector-specific conditionality as the applicants had argued. On the one hand, in accordance with Regulation 2020/2092, the condition of access to the EU financing at issue may consist in respecting the value of the rule of law in all areas of EU action. On the other hand, applicants contended that that condition should have been closely linked either to one of the objectives of a programme or to specific action of the EU or to sound financial management. The Court of Justice upheld the lawfulness of the regulation in that respect. First of all, it recalled that

> once a candidate State becomes a Member State, it joins a legal structure that is based on the fundamental premiss that each Member State shares with all the other Member States, and recognises that they share with it, the common values contained in Article 2 TEU, on which the European Union is founded.[16]

'That premiss', the Court wrote, 'implies and justifies the existence of mutual trust between the Member States that those values will be recognised and, therefore, that the EU law that implements them will be respected'.[17] Next, the Court emphasised that those values 'define the very identity of the European Union as a common legal order' and that, consequently, 'the European Union must be able to defend those values, within the limits of its powers as laid down by the Treaties'. In those circumstances, respect for the value of the rule of law is capable of forming

[13] Regulation 2020/2092 of the European Parliament and of the Council of 16 December 2020 on a general regime of conditionality for the protection of the Union budget, [2020] L 433I/ 1, and corrigendum [2021] OJ L 373/94.

[14] See Art 2 (a) of Regulation 2020/2092.

[15] See Case C-156/21 *Hungary v Parliament and Council* (n 12) para 117, and Case C-157/21 *Poland v Parliament and Council* (n 12) para 137. In that regard, the Court noted that, in accordance with the contested regulation, if there is no longer any adverse effect or serious risk of adversely affecting the sound management of the EU budget or the protection of its financial interests, such a circumstance would entail the lifting of the measures adopted on the basis of that regulation (eg, the suspension of payments), even if the infringements of the rule of law which have been established persist. To that effect, Case C-156/21 *Hungary v Parliament and Council* (n 12) para 113, and Case C-157/21 *Poland v Parliament and Council* (n 12) para 135.

[16] See Case C-156/21 *Hungary v Parliament and Council* (n 12) para 125, and Case C-157/21 *Poland v Parliament and Council* (n 12) para 143.

[17] ibid.

the basis of a horizontal conditionality mechanism such as that established by Regulation 2020/2092.[18] Finally, the Court noted that the EU budget is one of the principal instruments for giving practical effect to the principle of solidarity referred to in Article 2 TEU, a principle on which the EU is founded and which is based on mutual trust between the Member States as to the responsible use of the common resources included in that budget. The sound financial management and the financial interests of the EU are liable to be seriously compromised by breaches of the principles of the rule of law committed by the authorities of a Member State, if they are not subjected to effective judicial review. Without independent and impartial courts to carry out such a review, it cannot be guaranteed that the expenditure covered by the EU budget satisfies all the financing conditions laid down by EU law and, therefore, meets the objectives pursued by the EU when it finances such expenditure. Such an infringement of the value of the rule of law undermines mutual trust between the Member States and constitutes an obstacle to the application of the principle of solidarity at EU level.[19]

In order to act as a check on the political majority of the day, national courts had to enjoy a series of guarantees that enabled them to operate without fear or favour. Undercutting the authority of their own courts was seen as a red line that no democratic government of a Member State would dare to cross. Any European State wishing to become a member of the EU must adhere unequivocally to the constitutional traditions common to the Member States by ensuring compliance with democratic principles, fundamental rights and the rule of law. As the Court of Justice made clear in the seminal *Wightman and Others* case,[20] joining the EU (as well as leaving it) is a free and voluntary act of national sovereignty. However, once a candidate State becomes a member of the EU, it must comply with a set of common values.

In that regard, the Court of Justice has made crystal clear that an ongoing commitment to democratic principles, fundamental rights and the rule of law is what being a Member State is all about. Becoming a Member State is a 'constitutional moment' for a candidate Member State since at that very moment, the legal order of that Member State is deemed by the 'Masters of the Treaties' to uphold the values on which the EU is founded. From that moment onwards, interlocking that legal order with the EU legal order and the other Member States' legal orders takes place. The Member State in question commits itself to respecting those values for as long as it remains a member of the EU. That ongoing commitment means that there is 'no turning back the clock' when it comes to respecting those values. The level of value protection provided for by a Member State when it joins

[18] To that effect, see Case C-156/21 *Hungary v Parliament and Council* (n 12) paras 127 and 128, and Case C-157/21 *Poland v Parliament and Council* (n 12) paras 145 and 146.

[19] To that effect, Case C-156/21 *Hungary v Parliament and Council* (n 12) para 129, and Case C-157/21 *Poland v Parliament and Council* (n 12) para 147.

[20] Case C-621/18 *Wightman and Others* EU:C:2018:999 para 63. See also Case C-619/18 *Commission v Poland (Independence of the Supreme Court)* (n 1) para 42.

the EU is a starting point and the trend of constitutional reforms must always be towards strengthening that protection. As the Court of Justice held in *Repubblika*, '[a] Member State cannot therefore amend its legislation in such a way as to bring about a reduction in the protection of the value of the rule of law, a value which is given concrete expression by, inter alia, Article 19 TEU'.[21] It follows from that judgment that the EU legal order prohibits 'value regression'. Authoritarian drifts have simply no room in the EU legal order, since they would call into question the effectiveness of Articles 2, 19(1) and 49 TEU.

It is thus assumed – and most importantly, required by the Treaties – that after taking up EU membership such a State will remain committed to defending liberal democracy, fundamental rights and a government of laws, not men. Recent developments show, however, that this assumption cannot simply be taken for granted, since Member States may, in breach of EU law, still depart from their original commitment to upholding the rule of law within the EU.[22]

III. Judicial Independence, the Preliminary Reference Mechanism and the Effective Protection of EU Rights

In order to have access to the preliminary reference procedure, national courts must be independent because only independent courts can be trusted with applying loyally the law of the EU, as interpreted by the Court of Justice. The effective protection of EU rights indeed requires that the competent national court should be insulated from any political pressure, not least on the part of the public authorities that brought about the breach of these rights.

The fact that the preliminary reference procedure is open only to independent courts stems from the fact that Article 267 of the Treaty on the Functioning of the European Union (TFEU) refers explicitly to 'any court or tribunal of a Member State'.[23] As understood by the Court of Justice, the notion of 'court or tribunal' is an autonomous concept of EU law.[24] This means that national law is not decisive in order to determine whether the body making a preliminary reference qualifies as a 'court or tribunal' under that Treaty provision. It is, however, highly relevant in verifying whether the factors by reference to which EU law defines the notion of 'court or tribunal' are present. It follows from settled case law that the Court of Justice 'will take account of a number of factors, such as whether the body is

[21] Case C-896/19 *Repubblika* EU:C:2021:311 para 63.

[22] See D Adamski, 'The Social Contract of Democratic Backsliding in the "New EU" Countries' (2019) 56 *Common Market Law Review* 623, 623–66.

[23] See, generally, M Broberg and N Fenger, *Preliminary References to the European Court of Justice* (Oxford, Oxford University Press, 2014).

[24] See, eg, Case C-396/14 *MT Højgaard and Züblin* EU:C:2016:347 para 23.

established by law, whether it is permanent, whether its jurisdiction is compulsory, whether its procedure is *inter partes*, whether it applies rules of law and whether it is independent'.[25]

The concept of judicial independence requires, in the administrative law context, that judicial power should be exercised by a body that acts as a third party in relation to the authority which adopted the contested decision. Thus, for example, in *Devillers*, the Court of Justice ruled that the Belgian Regional Council of the Society of Veterinary Doctors was not a third party for the purposes of making a preliminary reference, since it was the body responsible for imposing disciplinary sanctions against the applicant in the main proceedings, ie, a veterinary surgeon who had allegedly violated the relevant rules of professional conduct.[26]

In addition, the concept of judicial independence, as developed in the seminal *Wilson* judgment,[27] has both an internal and an external dimension. Internally, judicial independence is intended to ensure a level playing field for the parties to proceedings and for their competing interests. In other words, independence requires courts to be impartial.

In *Banco Santander*, for example, the Court of Justice departed from its previous findings in *Gabalfrisa*, decided in 2000, holding that Spanish Tax Tribunals (Tribunales Economicos Administrativos, TEAs) are not 'courts or tribunals' for the purposes of Article 267 TFEU. In *Gabalfrisa*, the Court of Justice found that the TEAs met the requirement of impartiality, given that the relevant Spanish legislation ensured a separation of functions within the Ministry of Economy between, on the one hand, the departments of the tax authority responsible for adopting decisions relating to the management, clearance and recovery of tax and, on the other, the TEAs which rule on complaints brought against those decisions.[28]

However, 'in the light of the most recent case-law … concerning, in particular, the criterion of independence',[29] the Court of Justice took a different view in *Banco Santander*. It held that such a separation of functions did not guarantee that the Spanish Central Tax Tribunal (the TEAC) acted as a third party in relation to the administration. This was because the Director-General for Taxation of the Ministry of Economy acted as both 'judge and interested party' in cases where an extraordinary appeal for the unification of precedent was brought against a decision of the TEAC. That Director-General acted as the appellant and, at the same time, was part of the eight-person panel that was to hear the appeal. In addition, the Director-General (or Director) of the competent Department of the State Tax

[25] See, eg, Case 61/65 *Vaassen-Göbbels* EU:C:1966:39; Case C-205/08 *Umweltanwalt von Kärnten* EU:C:2009:767 para 35; Case C-203/14 *Consorci Sanitari del Maresme* EU:C:2015:664 para 17; Case C-396/14 *MT Højgaard and Züblin* (n 24) para 23.

[26] The Court of Justice noted that, whilst the member of that Council in charge of investigating the case did not participate in the deliberations, nor took part in the adoption of the final decision, there was a close functional link between him and that Council. See order of 28 November 2013, Case C-167/13 *Devillers* not published, EU:C:2013:804 para 19.

[27] Case C-506/04 *Wilson* EU:C:2006:587 paras 49–52.

[28] Joined Cases C-110/98 to C-147/98 *Gabalfrisa and Others* EU:C:2000:145 para 39.

[29] Case C-274/14 *Banco de Santander* EU:C:2020:17 para 55.

Administration Agency was also part of that panel, despite the fact that the object of that extraordinary appeal was a ruling of the TEAC on the validity of a decision adopted by the body to which that Director-General (or Director) belonged.[30] This led the Court of Justice to rule that the TEAC was not impartial.

Externally, judicial independence establishes the dividing line between the political process and the courts. Courts must be shielded from any external influence or pressure that might jeopardise the independent judgement of their members as regards proceedings before them.[31] That protection must apply to the members of the judiciary, by, for example, laying down guarantees against removal from office.[32]

Thus, in *Syfait* the Court of Justice held that in the absence of adequate safeguards in respect of the dismissal or termination of the appointment of 'judges' belonging to the Greek competition authority, the rules governing their tenure did not appear to provide effective protection against undue intervention or pressure from the executive.[33] Accordingly, that authority could not be seen as a 'court or tribunal' within the meaning of Article 267 TFEU.

Similarly, in *Banco Santander* the Court of Justice held that '[t]he principle of irremovability … requires, in particular, that judges may remain in post provided that they have not reached the obligatory retirement age or until the expiry of their mandate, where that mandate is for a fixed term'.[34] It is true that the principle of irremovability is not absolute. However, exceptions to that principle must be warranted by legitimate and compelling grounds, subject to the principle of proportionality. Accordingly, the Court held that 'judges may be dismissed if they are deemed unfit for the purposes of carrying out their duties on account of incapacity or a serious breach of their obligations, provided the appropriate procedures are followed'.[35] As to the case at hand, the Court of Justice found that the removal of the President of the TEAC and of other members of the other TEAs did not comply with the principle of irremovability, since such removal was not limited to certain exceptional cases reflecting legitimate and compelling grounds.[36]

Furthermore, the external aspect of judicial independence also requires the absence of any 'hierarchical constraint or subordination to any other body that could give … orders or instructions' to the body making the reference. Therefore, in *Margarit Panicello* the Court of Justice ruled that the Registrar (Secretario Judicial) of a Spanish court did not constitute a 'court or tribunal' within the meaning of Article 267 TFEU, since he or she was required to comply with instructions

[30] ibid para 74.

[31] Case C-506/04 *Wilson* (n 27) para 51.

[32] See Joined Cases C-9/97 and C-118/97 *Jokela and Pitkäranta* EU:C:1998:497 para 20; Case C-103/97 *Köllensperger and Atzwanger* EU:C:1999:52 para 21.

[33] Case C-53/03 *Syfait and Others* EU:C:2005:333 para 31.

[34] Case C-274/14 *Banco de Santander* (n 29) para 59 (referring to Case C-619/18 *Commission v Poland (Independence of the Supreme Court)* (n 1) para 76).

[35] Case C-274/14 *Banco de Santander* (n 29) para 59.

[36] ibid para 67.

from a hierarchical superior when making a reference in the context of an action for the recovery of fees due for legal services.[37]

Moreover, in *Land Hessen* the Court of Justice stated that it would only look at factors that may call into question the independence of the judges that made the reference, but not at those that are irrelevant for the case at hand.[38] For example, the referring court questioned whether 'temporary judges', ie civil servants with a legal background who covered temporary staff requirements in the judiciary of Land Hessen, were independent. However, 'since such judges [were] not members of the formation of the [referring] court', the Court of Justice found that question to be manifestly irrelevant.[39]

Most importantly for present purposes, in *Getin Noble Bank* the Court of Justice held that

> [in] so far as a request for a preliminary ruling emanates from a national court or tribunal, it must be presumed that it satisfies [the requirements by reference to which EU law defines the notion of 'court or tribunal'], irrespective of its actual composition.[40]

However, that presumption

> may … be rebutted where a final judicial decision handed down by a national or international court or tribunal leads to the conclusion that the judge constituting the referring court is not an independent and impartial tribunal previously established by law for the purposes of the second subparagraph of Article 19(1) TEU, read in the light of the second paragraph of Article 47 of the Charter.[41]

That said, that presumption only applies for the purposes of Article 267 TFEU: it does not follow from that presumption that the conditions for appointment of the judges that make up the referring court necessarily satisfy the guarantees of access to an independent and impartial tribunal previously established by law.[42]

Once it has been established that the body making a reference qualifies as a 'court or tribunal' within the meaning of Article 267 TFEU, that body may engage in a dialogue with the Court of Justice. As mentioned above, that dialogue is of paramount importance since it ensures the uniform application of EU law. The question thus arises whether, once it has been established that a body qualifies as a 'court or tribunal' within the meaning of Article 267 TFEU, EU law may also protect that body against a national measure that threatens its independence.

It follows from the case law of the Court of Justice that EU law protects the two different, albeit complementary, dimensions of judicial independence.[43] On the

[37] Case C-503/15 *Margarit Panicello* EU:C:2017:126 para 41.
[38] Case C-272/19 *Land Hessen* EU:C:2020:535 paras 46 and 47.
[39] ibid para 49.
[40] Case C-132/20 *Getin Noble Bank* EU:C:2022:235, para 69.
[41] ibid para 72.
[42] ibid para 74.
[43] K Lenaerts, 'The Two Dimensions of Judicial Independence in the EU Legal Order' in R Spano, P Pinto de Albuquerque, IA Motoc, B Lubarda and M Tsirli (eds), *Fair Trial: Regional and International Perspectives* (Limal, Anthemis-Nemesis, 2020).

one hand, EU law and, in particular, Article 47 of the Charter recognises 'the rights of persons involved in court proceedings' to an 'independent judge or tribunal'. Judges acting as applicants may benefit from the protection of that provision of the Charter (the 'fundamental rights dimension'). On the other hand, EU law also protects national judges in their institutional capacity as members of the courts of general jurisdiction for the application and enforcement of that law. In that regard, judicial independence is seen as a structural principle of constitutional importance that guarantees the proper functioning of the EU system of judicial protection (the 'rule of law dimension').

A. National Judges as Individuals

Just like any other EU citizen or third-country national, national judges are protected by EU law in their individual capacity. Where a national measure that implements EU law adversely affects their fundamental rights, national judges may bring proceedings before the competent court, basing their application on the relevant provisions of the Charter. Notably, for present purposes, a national judge who challenges his or her dismissal has a right of access to justice before another judge who is both independent and impartial. The ruling of the Court of Justice in *AK and Others (Independence of the Disciplinary Chamber of the Supreme Court)* illustrates that point.[44]

In that case, the applicants in the main proceedings were judges of the Polish Supreme Court who were forced to retire after the entry into force of a law that reformed the Supreme Court (the Law on the Supreme Court of 2017). Whilst that law lowered the retirement age from 70 to 65, it allowed the President of Poland to decide, on a discretionary basis, to extend the thus-shortened period during which a judge could perform his or her judicial functions. The Law on the Supreme Court of 2017 also provided for the creation of a new Disciplinary Chamber of the Supreme Court (the Disciplinary Chamber) enjoying exclusive jurisdiction over proceedings concerning the compulsory retirement of a Supreme Court judge. The President of Poland was given power to appoint the members of that Chamber acting on a proposal from the National Council of the Judiciary (known as the KRS).

Under the Polish Constitution, the KRS is the guardian of the independence of courts and judges. In 2017, Poland passed a law reforming the KRS (the Law on the KRS of 2017). Prior to the entry into force of that law, 15 out of the 25 members of the KRS were judges elected by their peers. That is no longer the case, since the Law on the KRS of 2017 states that those 15 members are to be judges elected by the Sejm (the Lower House of the Polish Parliament). It also provides that the

[44] Joined Cases C-585/18, C-624/18 and C-625/18 *AK and Others (Independence of the Disciplinary Chamber of the Supreme Court)* EU:C:2019:982.

four-year mandate of incumbent members of the KRS ends – before its normal date of expiry – upon the entry into office of the 'new' KRS.

Before the beginning of the term of office of the Disciplinary Chamber of the Supreme Court, the applicants brought proceedings before the Chamber of Labour Law and Social Security of the Supreme Court (the Supreme Court) that had enjoyed jurisdiction over labour law matters relating to Supreme Court judges until the adoption of the Law on the Supreme Court of 2017. They argued that their compulsory retirement was incompatible with EU law, in particular with the principle of non-discrimination on grounds of age enshrined in Directive 2000/78.[45]

The Supreme Court had doubts as to whether the Disciplinary Chamber – to which the case was supposed to be transferred after its taking office – qualified as 'an independent and impartial tribunal' within the meaning of Article 47 of the Charter and thus provided effective judicial protection of the rights conferred on the applicants by Directive 2000/78. It therefore referred a number of preliminary questions to the Court of Justice regarding the principle of judicial independence.

At the outset, the Court of Justice examined whether Poland was implementing EU law within the meaning of Article 51(1) of the Charter. If so, Article 47 of the Charter – and in particular, the principle of judicial independence – would apply to the case at hand. The Court of Justice observed that, since the applicants contended that the Law on the Supreme Court of 2017 discriminated against them on grounds of age in the context of their employment relationship, Directive 2000/78 applied to them. This meant that Article 9 of Directive 2000/78, which gives concrete expression to the principle of effective judicial protection, obliged Poland to ensure that persons such as the applicants who consider themselves to be the victims of discrimination are able to assert their rights.[46] Accordingly, by adopting the Law on the Supreme Court of 2017, Poland was implementing EU law within the meaning of Article 51(1) of the Charter.

The Court of Justice went on to interpret the notion of 'an independent and impartial tribunal', within the meaning of Article 47 of the Charter, in order to provide guidance to the Supreme Court as to whether the Disciplinary Chamber was such a tribunal. The Court held that the principle of judicial independence within the meaning of EU law provides a level of protection at least equivalent to that guaranteed by the European Convention on Human Rights (ECHR).[47] It therefore referred extensively to the case law of the European Court of Human Rights (ECtHR) when making its findings.[48]

[45] Council Directive 2000/78/EC of 27 November 2000 establishing a general framework for equal treatment in employment and occupation [2000] OJ L303/16.

[46] ibid paras 79–81.

[47] ibid paras 117 and 118.

[48] ibid paras 127 and 128. As to the notion of 'independent tribunal' within the meaning of Art 6 ECHR, the Court of Justice referred to ECtHR, judgments of 6 November 2018, *Ramos Nunes de Carvalho e Sá v Portugal* [Grand Chamber] App nos 55391/13, 57728/13 and 74041/13 para 144; and of 21 June 2011, *Fruni v Slovakia* App no 8014/07 para 141. As to the notion of impartiality within the meaning of Art 6 ECHR, it referred to ECtHR, judgments of 6 May 2003, *Kleyn and Others v the Netherlands* App nos 39343/98, 39651/98, 43147/98 and 46664/99 para 191; and of 6 November 2018, *Ramos Nunes de Carvalho e Sá v Portugal*, above, paras 145, 147 and 149.

On the basis of the concerns expressed by the Supreme Court, the Court of Justice focused its attention on a series of issues pertaining to the conditions as well as to the context governing the appointment of the judges called upon to sit in the Disciplinary Chamber, to its jurisdiction, and to the composition and functioning of that Chamber.

Drawing on the case law of the ECtHR,[49] the Court of Justice held, first, that the fact that the President of Poland appointed the judges of the Disciplinary Chamber was not, as such, capable of creating a relationship of dependency between him and that Chamber, provided that, once in office, those judges were insulated from external pressure and received no instructions from the executive.[50] However, the Court of Justice also ruled that the Supreme Court would need to examine whether the procedure leading to the decision of the President could create doubt in the minds of individuals as to the imperviousness of that Chamber to external factors and its neutrality with respect to the interests before it.[51]

In that connection, the role played by the KRS, as the constitutional body entrusted with protecting judicial independence, was thus of paramount importance since it could serve to limit the margin of discretion of the President.[52] This meant that in submitting its proposal to the President, the KRS itself had to be independent from both the executive and the legislature.[53] Accordingly, the Supreme Court was also required to examine the conditions under which the members of the KRS were appointed and exercised their functions. In particular, the Court of Justice drew the attention of the Supreme Court to a series of elements on the basis of which it could carry out its assessment. Notably, it had to examine the fact that the Law on the KRS had shortened the mandate of incumbent members, that 22 out of 25 members of the KRS were directly elected by the Sejm, and that some of the new members of the KRS had, according to the Supreme Court, been appointed in spite of significant irregularities.[54]

Second, as to the jurisdiction of the Disciplinary Chamber, the Court of Justice observed that it had been established concomitantly with the provisions of the Law on the Supreme Court of 2017 that lowered the retirement age from 70 to 65 and forced the sitting judges who were already 65 years old – or older – to retire.[55] Those provisions had already been declared incompatible with EU law in *Commission v Poland (Independence of the Supreme Court)*.[56]

[49] The Court of Justice referred to ECHR, judgments of 28 June 1984, *Campbell and Fell v the UK* App nos 7819/77 and 7878/77 para 79; of 2 June 2005, *Zolotas v Greece* App no 38240/02 paras 24 and 25; of 9 November 2006, *Sacilor Lormines v France* App no 65411/01 para 66; and of 18 October 2018, *Thiam v France* App no 80018/12 para 80.

[50] Joined Cases C-585/18, C-624/18 and C-625/18 *AK and Others (Independence of the Disciplinary Chamber of the Supreme Court)* (n 44) para 133.

[51] ibid para 134.

[52] ibid para 137.

[53] ibid para 138.

[54] ibid para 143.

[55] ibid paras 147–49.

[56] Case C-619/18 *Commission v Poland (Independence of the Supreme Court)* (n 1).

Third and last, the Court of Justice noted that the Disciplinary Chamber was not composed of sitting judges but only of newly appointed judges, and that that Chamber enjoyed a particularly high level of autonomy within the Supreme Court.[57]

Whilst none of those elements was sufficient on its own to call into question the independence and impartiality of the Disciplinary Chamber, it was for the Supreme Court to determine, in the context of an overall assessment, whether a combination of those elements could cast doubt in the minds of individuals as to the imperviousness of that Chamber to external factors and its neutrality with respect to the interests before it.[58] The Court of Justice held that if that were to be the case then, given that both Article 47 of the Charter and Article 9 of Directive 2000/78 produce direct effect,[59] it would be for the Supreme Court to set aside the conflicting provisions of the Law on the Supreme Court of 2017 and for its Chamber of Labour Law and Social Security to examine the claims put forward by the applicants.

In that regard, the Supreme Court found that that was indeed the case, since the members of the KRS were not independent either from the executive or from the legislature. This meant, in turn, that the Disciplinary Chamber did not offer the guarantees of an 'independent and impartial tribunal' within the meaning of Article 47 of the Charter.[60]

B. National Judges as the Arm of EU Law

As regards the protection of national judges in their role as the arm of EU law (or, put more simply, as 'European judges'), the Court of Justice held in *Associação Sindical dos Juízes Portugueses* that the second subparagraph of Article 19(1) TEU may be relied upon in order to set aside national measures that call into question the independence of the national judiciary.[61] The facts of that case were as follows.

In response to the EU programme of financial assistance and with a view to curtailing its excessive budget deficit, Portugal passed a law in 2014 that sought to cut public spending by reducing the salaries of various public office holders and employees, including members of the legislature, the executive and the judiciary. Such salary-reduction measures also applied to the members of the Portuguese Court of Auditors (Tribunal de Contas). The Union of Portuguese Judges, acting on behalf of those members, brought legal proceedings against the administrative acts implementing that law, arguing that those salary-reduction measures threatened

[57] Joined Cases C-585/18, C-624/18 and C-625/18 *AK and Others (Independence of the Disciplinary Chamber of the Supreme Court)* (n 44) paras 150 and 151.

[58] ibid para 153.

[59] ibid paras 162–66.

[60] See *Sąd Najwyższy* (Supreme Court), judgment of 5 December 2019, III PO 7/18.

[61] Case C-64/16 *Associação Sindical dos Juízes Portugueses* (n 3). See also Case C-824/18 *AB and Others (Appointment of judges to the Supreme Court – Actions)* EU:C:2021:153.

the judicial independence of the said members, as guaranteed by Article 19 TEU and Article 47 of the Charter.

At the outset, the Court of Justice stressed that the second subparagraph of Article 19(1) TEU applies *ratione materiae* to '*the fields covered by EU law*', irrespective of whether the Member States are implementing EU law within the meaning of Article 51(1) of the Charter.[62] Next, the Court of Justice went on to explain the relationship between the rule of law, Article 19 TEU, the principle of effective judicial protection and national courts. It held that the EU is founded on the values set out in Article 2 TEU, such as respect for the rule of law. Article 19 TEU gives concrete expression to that founding value by entrusting 'the responsibility for ensuring judicial review in the EU legal order not only to the [Court of Justice] but also to national courts and tribunals'.[63] Accordingly, the Member States are under the obligation 'to establish a system of legal remedies and procedures ensuring effective judicial protection in [the fields covered by EU law]'.[64] In that regard, the Court of Justice found that there is an unbreakable link between compliance with the rule of law and the principle of effective judicial protection: one cannot exist without the other. The bodies entrusted with responsibility for upholding the rule of law within the EU – ie 'courts or tribunals' – must meet the requirements of effective judicial protection. This means, in essence, that such protection must be provided for by a body that falls within the notion of 'court or tribunal' as defined by EU law. In particular, referring to its case law on Article 267 TFEU and on Article 47 of the Charter, the Court of Justice held that that notion requires courts to be independent.[65] After recalling what judicial independence means for the purposes of that case law, the Court of Justice found that 'the receipt by those members of a level of remuneration commensurate with the importance of the functions they carry out constitutes a guarantee essential to judicial independence'.[66]

As to the case at hand, the Court of Justice found, subject to final verification by the referring court, that the Tribunal de Contas could fall within the notion of 'court or tribunal' as defined by EU law.[67] Regarding the compatibility with the second subparagraph of Article 19(1) TEU of the salary-reduction measures at issue, the Court of Justice held, first, that those measures were adopted as a response to mandatory requirements linked to eliminating the Portuguese State's

[62] Case C-64/16 *Associação Sindical dos Juízes Portugueses* (n 3) para 29.

[63] ibid para 32.

[64] ibid para 34.

[65] ibid paras 42, 43 and 44. Regarding Art 47 of the Charter – which contains the notion of 'independent and impartial tribunal', the Court of Justice referred to judgments of 14 June 2017, Case C 685/15 *Online Games and Others* EU:C:2017:452 para 60; and of 13 December 2017, Case C-403/16 *El Hassani* EU:C:2017:960 para 40. As to the notion of 'court or tribunal' set out in Art 267 TFEU, it referred to judgments of 19 September 2006, Case C-506/04 *Wilson* (n 27) para 49; and of 16 February 2017, Case C-503/15 *Margarit Panicello* (n 37) para 37.

[66] Case C-64/16 *Associação Sindical dos Juízes Portugueses* (n 3) para 45.

[67] ibid para 40.

excessive budget deficit and in the context of an EU programme of financial assistance to Portugal.[68] Second, the reduction of the amount of remuneration was limited to a percentage varying in accordance with the level of salary.[69] Third, they were temporary in nature since by 2016, the full reinstatement of the rights to remuneration at issue in the main proceedings had already taken place.[70] Most importantly, the salary-reduction measures did not target the members of the Tribunal de Contas specifically, but applied to various public office holders as part of a comprehensive effort to cut spending in the public sector at a time of economic crisis.[71] As a result, the Court of Justice ruled that those measures could not be considered to impair the independence of the members of the Tribunal de Contas.

Three direct implications flow from the judgment of the Court of Justice in *Associação Sindical dos Juízes Portugueses*. First, that judgment is a positive development in the law on judicial remedies. It shows that national courts are called upon to play a pivotal role as 'EU Courts', and that the Court of Justice is committed to the protection of that role as the core element of upholding the rule of law within the EU.

Second, the judgment of the Court of Justice in *Associação Sindical dos Juízes Portugueses* shows that judicial independence may, by virtue of Article 19(1) TEU, be protected without having to examine whether the fundamental rights of the judges concerned, as individuals, have been violated. Where a national court qualifies as a 'court or tribunal' as defined by EU law and such a court therefore enjoys jurisdiction to rule on questions of EU law, that court acts as a court of general jurisdiction for the application and enforcement of EU law and, accordingly, that law protects its independence.[72]

That said, the case law has subsequently shown that one must draw a distinction between infringement actions and the preliminary reference mechanism. In the context of infringement actions, the application of Article 19(1) TEU only requires the independence of the courts of the defendant Member State which may be called upon to rule on questions relating to the interpretation of EU law to be adversely affected by the national measure(s) or practice(s) challenged by the Commission or another Member State. If that is the case, the Court of Justice will find that Article 19(1) TEU applies and proceed to examine the merits of the action.[73] Given that infringement actions seek to determine whether the defendant Member State infringes EU law in general, there is no need for there to be a relevant dispute before the national courts.[74]

[68] ibid para 46.
[69] ibid para 47.
[70] ibid para 50.
[71] ibid para 49.
[72] See, in this regard, C-430/21 *RS (Effects of the decisions of a constitutional court)* EU:C:2022:99.
[73] See Case C-619/18 *Commission v Poland (Independence of the Supreme Court)* (n 1) paras 55–59, and Case C-192/18 *Commission v Poland (Independence of ordinary courts)* EU:C:2019:924 paras 104–07.
[74] Joined Cases C-558/18 and C-563/18 *Miasto Łowicz and Prokurator Generalny* EU:C:2020:234 para 47.

Article 19(1) TEU may not, however, be construed in such a way as to change the function of the Court of Justice in the context of the preliminary reference mechanism, which 'is … to help the referring court to resolve the specific dispute pending before that court'.[75] As the Court of Justice observed in *Miasto Łowicz*, access to the preliminary reference mechanism is made conditional upon the existence of a connecting factor between the interpretation of Article 19(1) TEU sought by the referring court and the dispute before it.[76] That connecting factor may be of a substantive or procedural nature.

For example, in *Associação Sindical dos Juízes Portugueses*, it was substantive since the referring court had to decide whether it annulled administrative decisions reducing the salaries of members of the Tribunal de Contas on the ground that the national legislation providing for such reduction was incompatible with Article 19(1) TEU.[77]

In *IS (Illegality of the order for reference)*, the connecting factor was of a procedural nature.[78] In that case, the Kúria (the Supreme Court of Hungary) decided, upon an appeal brought in the interest of the law by the Prosecutor General, that a request for a preliminary ruling which had been submitted to the Court of Justice by a first instance court, sitting as a single-judge formation, was unlawful on the ground that the questions referred were not necessary for that court to give judgment, without, however, altering the legal effects of that request. Following this decision of the Kúria, the referring court added new questions to its initial request, asking, in essence, whether EU law was to be interpreted as opposing that decision. The Court of Justice replied in the affirmative, holding that the decision of the Kúria encroached upon the exclusive jurisdiction of the Court to rule on the admissibility of the questions referred for a preliminary ruling.[79] The referring court also drew the attention of the Court of Justice to the fact that disciplinary proceedings had been brought against the judge sitting as a single-judge court following the decision of the Kúria and on the same grounds. Accordingly, the referring judge asked whether EU law precluded those proceedings from being brought against him on the ground that he had made a reference to the Court of Justice. Hungary contested the admissibility of that question, since those disciplinary proceedings had subsequently been brought to an end. However, the Court of Justice upheld the admissibility of that question, given that the referring judge needed to know

> whether he will be able to refrain from complying with the *Kúria* decision when he rules on the substance of the case in the main proceedings without having to fear that, in so doing, the disciplinary proceedings that were brought against him, based on the *Kúria* decision, will be reopened.[80]

[75] ibid. See also Case C-896/19 *Repubblika* (n 21) para 48.

[76] Joined Cases C-558/18 and C-563/18 *Miasto Łowicz and Prokurator Generalny* (n 74) para 48.

[77] Case C-64/16 *Associação Sindical dos Juízes Portugueses* (n 3) para 12. See, in the same way, Case C-49/18 *Escribano Vindel* EU:C:2019:106.

[78] Case C-564/19 *IS (Illegality of the order for reference)* EU:C:2021:949.

[79] ibid para 72.

[80] ibid para 86.

Thus, the referring judge needed to resolve a procedural question before being able to rule on the substance of the dispute before him.

By contrast, in *Miasto Łowicz*, the connecting factor was missing, since an answer to the questions referred by the national courts was not objectively needed for the resolution of the disputes in the main proceedings.[81] Those questions, which were of a general nature, sought to determine whether the legislative reforms affecting the disciplinary proceedings applicable to judges called into question the principle of judicial independence within the meaning of Article 19(1) TEU. It is worth noting that the judges who made the references were, as a result of making them, the subject of an investigation prior to the possible initiation of disciplinary proceedings against them. However, the dispute in the main proceedings did not relate to that investigation which was, in any event, closed since no disciplinary misconduct was found.[82]

It is rather straightforward to establish the connecting factor between Article 19(1) TEU and the dispute in the main proceedings in cases where the judges whose independence is being threatened are parties to those proceedings. In order to ensure compliance with the rule of law, those judges must have access to justice. The Court of Justice has been categorical in that respect, holding that an independent court of law must provide them with effective remedies.

Conversely, the connecting factor is missing where the referring court seeks to have access to the preliminary reference mechanism in order to question, in a general fashion, whether legislative reforms comply with the principle of judicial independence, in so far as that question has no bearing on the main proceedings. The reason for imposing such a connecting factor lies again in structural considerations that seek to draw a clear distinction between the preliminary reference mechanism and infringement actions.

Third and last, the judgment of the Court of Justice in *Associação Sindical dos Juízes Portugueses* shows that the scope of application of the second subparagraph of Article 19(1) TEU is not the same as that of Article 47 of the Charter. The former applies to '*the fields covered by EU law*', whilst the latter applies to national measures *implementing EU law* within the meaning of Article 51(1) of the Charter.

That last distinction is important for present purposes as it draws the dividing line between the 'fundamental rights' and the 'rule of law' dimensions of judicial independence.[83]

[81] See also Case C-256/19 *SAD Maler und Anstreicher* EU:C:2020:684 para 49. In that case, the referring court took the view that the case at issue in the main proceedings was not properly allocated to it. It thus asked the Court of Justice whether such allocation complied with Art 19(1) TEU. However, the Court of Justice declared the reference inadmissible, since a connecting factor between the dispute in the main proceedings and that Treaty provision was missing. Substantively, Art 19(1) TEU was not required to solve the merits of the dispute in the main proceedings. Procedurally, there was no connecting factor either: the referring court could not call into question the lawfulness of the allocation in the context of the main proceedings, but that question fell within the jurisdiction of a superior court in the event of an appeal.

[82] Joined Cases C-558/18 and C-563/18 *Miasto Łowicz and Prokurator Generalny* (n 74) paras 56–59.

[83] That said, when the Member State concerned is implementing EU law within the meaning of Art 51 of the Charter, those two dimensions may overlap. See, in this regard, Case C-49/18 *Escribano Vindel* (n 77); Joined Cases C-585/18, C-624/18 and C-625/18 *AK and Others (Independence of the*

IV. Judicial Independence and Mutual Trust

The EU has clearly evolved beyond the internal market paradigm. Currently, it seeks to offer its citizens an Area of Freedom, Security and Justice (AFSJ) without internal frontiers, where citizens may move freely and securely.

In an area without internal borders, the exercise of free movement should not undermine the powers of the competent Member State court and the effectiveness of the applicable Member State laws, which operate on a territorial basis. As internal borders disappear in Europe, the *long arm of the law* should acquire a transnational dimension, so that, for example, criminals are prevented from relying on free movement as a means of pursuing their activities with impunity.

Accordingly, the authors of the EU Treaties took the view that the free movement of persons should be accompanied by the free movement of judicial decisions. By virtue of the principle of mutual recognition, judicial decisions adopted in the Member State of origin are to be recognised and enforced in the Member State of enforcement as if they were its own.

The European Arrest Warrant mechanism (the EAW mechanism) illustrates this point. This mechanism aims to replace the multilateral system of extradition between Member States with a simplified and more effective system of surrender between judicial authorities which facilitates and accelerates judicial cooperation.[84] In that regard, the Court of Justice has held that 'while execution of the [EAW] constitutes the rule, refusal to execute is intended to be an exception which must be interpreted strictly'.[85]

It follows that, in order to establish an AFSJ, judicial cooperation in civil and criminal matters must be facilitated to the greatest extent possible. Such cooperation is based on the fundamental premise that Member State courts trust each other and see each other as equals. Thus, in the light of the principle of mutual trust, 'each of [the Member] States, save in exceptional circumstances, [is] to consider all the other Member States to be complying with EU law and particularly with the fundamental rights recognised by EU law'.[86]

This shows that, whilst the principle of mutual trust is of paramount importance for the creation and maintenance of the AFSJ, 'mutual trust is not to be confused with blind trust'.[87] This means that, in exceptional circumstances, that fundamental premise may be set aside.

Disciplinary Chamber of the Supreme Court) (n 44) paras 167–69; Case C-192/18 *Commission v Poland (Independence of ordinary courts)* (n 73); and Joined Cases C-357/19, C-379/19, C-547/19, C-811/19 and C-840/19 *Euro Box Promotion and Others* EU:C:2021:1034.

[84] See, eg, Case C-168/13 PPU *F* EU:C:2013:358 para 57; Case C-237/15 PPU *Lanigan* EU:C:2015:474 para 27; Joined Cases C-404/15 and C-659/15 PPU *Aranyosi* and *Căldăraru* EU:C:2016:198 para 76; Case C-452/16 PPU *Poltorak* EU:C:2016:858; and Case C-216/18 PPU *Minister for Justice and Equality (Deficiencies in the system of justice)* EU:C:2018:586 para 25.

[85] See, eg, Case C-270/17 PPU *Tupikas* EU:C:2017:628 paras 49 and 50.

[86] Opinion 2/13 *(Accession of the European Union to the ECHR)* (n 1) para 192.

[87] See K Lenaerts, '*La vie après l'avis*: Exploring the Principle of Mutual (Yet Not Blind) Trust' (2017) 54 *Common Market Law Review* 805.

As to the principles of mutual trust and judicial independence, two lines of case law are relevant for present purposes, both of which concern the EAW Framework Decision.

A. The Two-Step Examination

As to the first line of case law, in *Minister for Justice and Equality (Deficiencies in the system of justice)*, the Court of Justice held that the executing judicial authority must refuse to execute an EAW where there is 'a real risk that the person [concerned] will, if surrendered to the issuing judicial authority, suffer a breach of his fundamental right to an independent tribunal'.[88] Therefore, the existence of such a real risk constitutes an 'exceptional circumstance' that limits the operation of the principles of mutual trust and mutual recognition.

In assessing the existence of that risk, the Court of Justice pointed out that the referring court must carry out a two-step examination.[89] The first step focuses on the situation of the justice system of the Member State concerned as a whole.[90] The executing judicial authority must, in the light of objective, reliable, specific and properly updated material, find that there is such a real risk on account of systemic or generalised deficiencies in the justice system of the issuing Member State. As a second step, the executing judicial authority must assess the circumstances of the case at hand. Having regard to the personal circumstances of the individual concerned, as well as to the nature of the offence for which he is being prosecuted and the factual context that forms the basis for the EAW, the executing judicial authority must determine whether the systemic or generalised deficiencies in the justice system of the issuing Member State are liable to call into question the independence of the court that actually issued the EAW in question.[91]

Again, one of the reasons for this two-step examination rests on structural considerations. If the executing judicial authorities were entitled to refuse to execute an EAW on the sole account of systemic or generalised deficiencies in the justice system of the issuing Member State, such refusal would amount to a de facto suspension of the EAW mechanism for that Member State. However, the prerogatives to declare such a suspension are vested in the Council acting upon a decision of the European Council grounded in Article 7 TEU, according to which the issuing Member State has committed a serious and persistent breach of the rule of law. Whilst most scholars agree that Article 7 TEU is not an effective tool that prevents the rule of law from backsliding in the issuing Member State, the truth is that it would be wrong for the Court of Justice to change the rules of the

[88] Case C-216/18 PPU *Minister for Justice and Equality (Deficiencies in the system of justice)* (n 84) para 59.

[89] Lenaerts, 'The Two Dimensions of Judicial Independence in the EU Legal Order' (n 43) 336 et seq.

[90] Case C-216/18 PPU *Minister for Justice and Equality (Deficiencies in the system of justice)* (n 84) para 61.

[91] ibid paras 74–77.

game. Article 7 TEU is what it is and it is not for the Court of Justice but for the Member States – acting as Masters of the Treaties – to change it. Subsequently, the Court of Justice has put forward two additional justifications for the application of the two-step examination, despite calls from referring courts to limit their assessment to finding systemic or generalised deficiencies. First, in *Openbaar Ministerie (Independence of the issuing judicial authority)*, the Court recalled that the EAW mechanism seeks to combat the impunity of a requested person who is present in a territory other than that in which he or she has allegedly committed an offence. In its view, if the second step were to be abandoned, this would allow those persons to go free, 'even if there is no evidence, relating to the personal situation of those individuals, to suggest that they would run a real risk of breach of their fundamental right to a fair trial' if the EAW is executed.[92] Second, in *Openbaar Ministerie (Tribunal established by law in the issuing Member State)*, the Court of Justice added that the EAW framework decision had to be interpreted not only in light of the rights of the person concerned by the EAW, but also in light of those 'of the victims of the offences concerned'. This means that a finding that the person concerned faces a real risk of breach of his or her fundamental right to a fair trial must have 'a sufficient factual basis'.[93]

Furthermore, in *Openbaar Ministerie (Tribunal established by law in the issuing Member State)*, the referring court asked, in essence, whether the two-step examination was also applicable where the fundamental right to 'a tribunal previously established by law' is at issue. To that end, it drew the attention of the Court of Justice to the fact that in the issuing Member State, the KRS – a body that proposes to the President of Poland the name of candidates for judicial office – was no longer independent. This was because, following the adoption of a new law reforming it, the KRS is, for the most part, made up of members chosen by the legislature. If the KRS proposed the appointment of one or more of the judges who had imposed the custodial sentence or detention order in the issuing Member State, the referring court reasoned that this could give rise to doubts as to whether those judges were members of 'a tribunal previously established by law'. The same doubts could also arise in relation to the judges who would conduct criminal proceedings following the execution of the EAW at issue.

At the outset, the Court of Justice confirmed the application of the two-step examination, highlighting

> the inextricable links which … exist, for the purposes of the fundamental right to a fair trial, within the meaning of [Article 47 of the Charter], between the guarantees of judicial independence and impartiality as well as that of access to a tribunal previously established by law.[94]

[92] Joined Cases C-354/20 PPU and C-412/20 PPU *Openbaar Ministerie (Independence of the issuing judicial authority)* EU:C:2020:1033 paras 62–63.

[93] Joined Cases C-562/21 PPU and C-563/21 PPU *Openbaar Ministerie (Tribunal established by law in the issuing Member State)* EU:C:2022:100 paras 60 and 61.

[94] ibid para 56.

In particular, regarding the judicial appointment procedure, those links exist because that procedure constitutes an inherent element of the concept of a 'tribunal previously established by law', whilst also being a factor by which the independence of the judges appointed 'may be measured'.[95]

As to the first step, drawing on its case law on the rule of law,[96] the Court of Justice held that not every irregularity in the judicial appointment procedure constitutes a breach of the fundamental right to 'a tribunal previously established by law', but only those 'of such a kind and of such gravity as to create a real risk that other branches of the State, in particular the executive, could undermine the integrity of the outcome of the appointment procedure'.[97] Finding such a breach requires 'an overall assessment of a number of factors which, taken together, serve to create in the minds of individuals reasonable doubt as to the independence and impartiality of the judges'.[98] This meant, for present purposes, that the fact that a judge is appointed by the KRS is not sufficient in itself to call into question his or her independence, nor to refuse to execute the EAW in question. That overall assessment is to be carried out on the basis of objective, reliable, specific and properly updated information, which may be obtained from the case law of the courts in the issuing Member State, of the Court of Justice and of the ECtHR. In our view, the requirement of an overall assessment fits well with the need to establish systemic or generalised deficiencies in the justice system of the issuing Member State. Indeed, it is only by carrying out an overall assessment that one may identify those deficiencies.

As to the second step, it is for the executing judicial authority to examine whether the systemic and generalised deficiencies found are likely to materialise if the person concerned is surrendered to the issuing Member State. It is for that person to adduce specific evidence that those deficiencies had or are liable to have 'a tangible influence on the handling of his or her criminal case'. That evidence may, for example, relate to the secondment of a particular judge within the panel that imposed the custodial sentence that the EAW seeks to execute, where that secondment was made by the Minister for Justice on the basis of arbitrary criteria. Similarly, that evidence may also include statements made by public authorities which could have an influence on the specific case in question. That said, the Court of Justice again stressed the importance of judicial cooperation: if the person concerned puts forward evidence that is relevant but not sufficient to demonstrate the existence of a real risk of breach of his or her fundamental right to a tribunal previously established by law, the executing judicial authority is required to ask the issuing judicial authority to provide it with supplementary information. Failure to

[95] ibid para 57.

[96] See generally L Pech and D Kochenov, *Respect for the Rule of Law in the Case Law of the European Court of Justice* (SIEPS, Stockholm, 2021).

[97] Joined Cases C-562/21 PPU and C-563/21 PPU *Openbaar Ministerie (Tribunal established by law in the issuing Member State)* (n 93) para 73.

[98] ibid para 74.

cooperate may be taken into account by the executing judicial authority for the purposes of establishing the existence of such a real risk.[99]

B. The Notion of Judicial Authority

As to the second line of case law, in *Poltorak* and the cases that followed,[100] the Court of Justice has been called upon to interpret the notion of 'judicial authority' within the meaning of the EAW Framework Decision. In that regard, the Court of Justice has pointed out that that notion is broader than that of 'court or tribunal' within the meaning of EU law, since it may include other judicial authorities involved in the administration of criminal justice, which are distinct from, inter alia, ministries or police services which are part of the executive.[101] Given that the EAW mechanism imposes limitations on the exercise of the fundamental rights of the persons concerned, in particular on the right to liberty, its proper functioning requires a high level of trust between the Member States. That high level of trust may only be provided by authorities that are independent from the legislator and the executive.[102]

> That independence requires that there are statutory rules and an institutional framework capable of guaranteeing that the issuing judicial authority is not exposed, when adopting a decision to issue such an arrest warrant, to any risk of being subject, inter alia, to an instruction in a specific case from the executive.[103]

[99] ibid paras 84 and 85.

[100] Case C-452/16 PPU *Poltorak* (n 84). See also Case C-453/16 PPU *Özçelik* EU:C:2016:860; Case C-477/16 PPU *Kovalkovas* EU:C:2016:861; Case C-508/18 *OG and PI (Public Prosecutor's Offices, Lübeck and Zwickau)* EU:C:2019:456; Case C-509/18 *PF (Prosecutor General of Lithuania)* EU:C:2019:457; Joined Cases C-566/19 PPU and C-626/19 PPU *Parquet général du Grand-Duché de Luxembourg and Openbaar Ministerie (Public Prosecutors of Lyons and Tours)* EU:C:2019:1077; Case C-625/19 PPU *Openbaar Ministerie (Swedish Public Prosecutor's Office)* EU:C:2019:1078; and Case C-627/19 PPU *Openbaar Ministerie (Public Prosecutor, Brussels)* EU:C:2019:1079. For an analysis of that line of case law, see K Lenaerts, 'On Judicial Independence and the Quest for National, Supranational and Transnational Justice' in G Selvik, M-J Clifton, T Haas, L Lourenço and K Schwiesow (eds), *The Art of Judicial Reasoning: Festschrift in Honour of Carl Baudenbacher* (Cham, Springer, 2019) 155, 170 et seq.

[101] Case C-452/16 PPU *Poltorak* (n 84) paras 33 and 35; Case C-477/16 PPU *Kovalkovas* (n 100) paras 34 and 36; Case C-508/18 *OG and PI (Public Prosecutor's Offices, Lübeck and Zwickau)* (n 100) para 50; and Case C-509/18 *PF (Prosecutor General of Lithuania)* (n 100) para 29.

[102] Case C-452/16 PPU *Poltorak* (n 84) para 35. However, textual, contextual and teleological differences between the EAW Framework Decision and other EU law instruments pertaining to the AFSJ may justify a different interpretation of the notion of 'judicial authority'. This is the case of that notion within the meaning of Parliament and Council Directive 2014/41 regarding the European Investigation Order (EIO) in criminal matters [2014] OJ L130/1. See Case C-584/19 *Staatsanwaltschaft Wien (Falsified transfer orders)* EU:C:2020:1002. Moreover, another distinguishing factor to be taken into account is whether there are limitations on the right to liberty. In that regard, the Court of Justice pointed out that 'except in the specific case of the temporary transfer of persons already held in custody for the purpose of carrying out an investigative measure … the [EIO], unlike [an EAW], is not such as to interfere with the right to liberty of the person concerned, enshrined in Article 6 of the Charter'. See ibid para 73.

[103] Case C-508/18 *OG and PI (Public Prosecutor's Offices, Lübeck and Zwickau)* (n 100) para 74; and Case C-509/18 *PF (Prosecutor General of Lithuania)* (n 100) para 72.

Accordingly, neither ministers nor police services which are part of the executive may be considered to be 'issuing judicial authorities'.[104] Similarly, in *OG and PI (Public Prosecutor's Offices, Lübeck and Zwickau)*, the Court of Justice found that the notion of 'issuing judicial authority' must be interpreted as not including public prosecutors' offices of Germany which are exposed to the risk of being subject, directly or indirectly, to directions or instructions in a specific case from the executive, such as a Minister for Justice, in connection with the adoption of a decision to issue [an EAW].[105] By contrast, in the light of the applicable statutory rules and institutional framework, the Court of Justice found that Lithuanian, French, Swedish and Belgian public prosecutors' offices enjoy the status of 'judicial authority'.[106]

C. When Two Lines of Case Law Intersect

Logically, the question that arises is what happens when the *Poltorak* and *Minister for Justice and Equality (Deficiencies in the system of justice)* lines of case law intersect. May the executing judicial authority deny the status of 'issuing judicial authority' to the courts belonging to the judicial system of the issuing Member State, where there is evidence of systemic or generalised deficiencies concerning the independence of the judiciary in that Member State? In *Openbaar Ministerie (Independence of the issuing judicial authority)*, the Court of Justice was confronted with that very question and replied in the negative.[107] It found that denying such status would extend the limitations on the operation of the principles of mutual trust and mutual recognition beyond 'exceptional circumstances', within the meaning of its case law, since such denial would lead to a general exclusion of those principles in respect of all judges or all courts of the issuing Member State. Moreover, those systemic or generalised deficiencies do not necessarily affect every decision that the courts of the issuing Member State may adopt in a particular case. Most importantly, the criteria developed in the *Poltorak* line of case law with respect to the public prosecutor's offices do not apply mutatis mutandis to courts, within the meaning of EU law. The reason is twofold. First, with regard to the public prosecutor's offices, the requirement of independence looks at the

[104] Case C-452/16 PPU *Poltorak* (n 84); and Case C-477/16 PPU *Kovalkovas* (n 100).

[105] Case C-508/18 *OG and PI (Public Prosecutor's Offices, Lübeck and Zwickau)* (n 100) para 90. However, those same authorities would be considered to be 'judicial authorities' for the purposes of issuing an EIO. See, in this regard, Case C-584/19 *Staatsanwaltschaft Wien (Falsified transfer orders)* (n 102) para 74.

[106] Case C-509/18 *PF (Prosecutor General of Lithuania)* (n 100); Joined Cases C-566/19 PPU and C-626/19 PPU *Parquet général du Grand-Duché de Luxembourg and Openbaar Ministerie (Public Prosecutors of Lyons and Tours)* (n 100); Case C-625/19 PPU *Openbaar Ministerie (Swedish Public Prosecutor's Office)* (n 100); and Case C-627/19 PPU *Openbaar Ministerie (Public Prosecutor, Brussels)* (n 100).

[107] Joined Cases C-354/20 PPU and C-412/20 PPU *Openbaar Ministerie (Independence of the issuing judicial authority)* (n 92).

applicable statutory rules and institutional framework, and not at the existence or absence of systemic or generalised deficiencies. Second, since courts, within the meaning of EU law, are required to be independent, they are not subordinated to the executive. An executing judicial authority may not therefore deprive those courts of their status of 'issuing judicial authorities', even if their independence is being threatened by those deficiencies.

That does not mean, however, that the right to a fair trial of the person concerned is left unprotected, since the executing judicial authority may still refuse to execute the EAW by applying the two-step examination set out in *Minister for Justice and Equality (Deficiencies in the system of justice)*. In *Openbaar Ministerie (Independence of the issuing judicial authority)*, the Court of Justice confirmed that two-step examination, drawing, nonetheless, a distinction between EAWs issued for the purpose of conducting a criminal prosecution and those issued for the purpose of executing a custodial sentence or detention order, both types being at issue in that case. In relation to the former type, the executing judicial authorities must take into account whether the systemic or generalised deficiencies – including those arising after the issuing of the EAW – may adversely affect the trial to be held in the issuing Member State.[108] In relation to the latter type, the executing judicial authority should focus solely on whether those deficiencies – at the time of the issuing of the EAW – affected the independence of the court that imposed the custodial sentence or detention order.[109]

It is worth mentioning that both referring courts in *Minister for Justice and Equality (Deficiencies in the system of justice)* and in *Openbaar Ministerie (Independence of the issuing judicial authority)* – respectively the High Court of Ireland and the District Court of Amsterdam – applied that two-step examination, reaching, however, different outcomes in relation to the EAWs issued by the Polish judicial authorities for the purpose of conducting a criminal prosecution. Whilst the High Court decided to execute the EAW,[110] the District Court of Amsterdam refused to do so.[111] By contrast, in relation to the EAW issued

[108] ibid para 66.

[109] ibid para 68.

[110] Following the ruling of the Court of Justice in *Minister for Justice and Equality (Deficiencies in the system of justice)*, the High Court of Ireland decided to execute the warrants at issue. It reasoned that 'although recent reforms had brought about systemic deficiencies in the Polish justice system, there [was] no evidence showing that any other aspect of the fair trial right – such as the right to know the nature of the charge, the right to counsel, the right to challenge evidence and the right to present evidence – [was] at risk in Poland'. *The Minister for Justice and Equality v Celmer* No 5 [2018] IEHC 639 para 103. Subsequently, that ruling was upheld by the Irish Supreme Court in *Minister for Justice & Equality v Celmer* [2019] IESC 80.

[111] The District Court of Amsterdam found that Polish laws reforming the judicial system had had a 'chilling effect' on the members of the judiciary, who now feared being sanctioned in the event of adopting a decision running against the interests of the executive. As to the case at hand, the District Court observed that two Polish judges, who sit in the court having jurisdiction for the trial of the person concerned by the EAW at issue, had been the subject of disciplinary proceedings before the Disciplinary Chamber of the Supreme Court. The District Court called into question the independence and impartiality of that Chamber. Moreover, it pointed out that the case at hand had attracted the attention of

for the purpose of executing a custodial sentence at issue in *Openbaar Ministerie (Independence of the issuing judicial authority)*, the District Court of Amsterdam decided to execute it.[112]

V. Concluding Remarks

Through these recent developments in the case law on the rule of law, the Court of Justice has further clarified the guarantees that EU law requires in order for a national court to be – or to remain – independent. This is undoubtedly a positive development because it gives the Court of Justice the opportunity to consolidate the foundations of the EU system of judicial protection. When the Court of Justice rules that a national measure is incompatible with the principle of judicial independence, it is imperative that the Member State concerned implements that Court's judgment in a loyal manner, given that such implementation will bear witness to its ongoing commitment to the values on which the EU is founded.[113]

Today, Europeans are facing a defining moment in the history of integration. They must stand up for the values – most particularly democracy, the rule of law and fundamental rights – that we share in order to emphasise the point that what brings us together remains stronger than what might pull us apart. This is why the principle of judicial independence must be preserved so that the EU remains a 'Union of democracies', a 'Union of rights' and a 'Union of justice'. If the next generation of Europeans is to explore new horizons for an ever-closer Union where citizens may continue to enjoy a sphere of individual liberty free from state interference, integration through the rule of law is the only way forward.

the media, and that the Polish Public Prosecutor's office had given instructions to scrutinise the EAWs issued by Dutch judicial authorities in order to find grounds for mandatory non-execution. In the light of the foregoing considerations, the District Court decided not to execute the EAW at issue in Case C-345/20 PPU. See Rechtbank Amsterdam, order of 10 February 2021, ECLI:NL:RBAMS:2021:420.

[112] The District Court found that the systemic deficiencies in the Polish justice system had not adversely affected the independence of the Polish court that imposed the custodial sentence and, accordingly, did not call into question the right to a fair trial of the person concerned. See Rechtbank Amsterdam, order of 27 January 2021, ECLI:NL:RBAMS:2021:179.

[113] The fact that Poland repealed the law that was under consideration in Case C-619/18 *Commission v Poland (Independence of the Supreme Court)* (n 1) before the Court of Justice ruled on that case is a positive sign in that regard. See paras 27–31. See in this regard, Order of 17 December 2018, Case C-619/18 R *Commission v Poland* EU:C:2018:1021.

3

The Rule of Law and Adjudication of the Court of Justice of the European Union

NIKA BAČIĆ SELANEC AND TAMARA ĆAPETA

I. Introduction

In this chapter, we discuss how the concept of rule of law can be employed to assess the adjudication of the Court of Justice of the European Union (hereinafter: Court of Justice or Court).

The chapter is divided into two parts.

First, we aim to conceptualise the rule of law as applied to courts more generally. After assessing the two most common concepts of the rule of law – formal and substantive – we conclude that they do not respond adequately to the question of our research: what requirements does the rule of law impose on courts to control judicial discretion? We therefore propose a different, procedural concept of the rule of law. Such a concept entails upholding the effectiveness of judicial review by an independent judiciary, which also demands from the judiciary a standard of judicial responsiveness to legal argument and quality of legal reasoning. Approaching the process of adjudication as an argumentative discipline, the procedural rule of law necessitates a reasoned elaboration of judicial choices and justifications of a judgment compared with alternative outcomes.

Second, we assess the case law of the Court of Justice in relation to these procedural requirements. Finally, we suggest that certain aspects of the judicial method used by the Court of Justice should change in order to satisfy the proposed requirements of the rule of law. In particular, the Court of Justice should abandon the formalist narrative of 'one correct legal answer' in its judgments, with no mention of conflicting interpretations of the applicable law, and start adequately addressing the submissions of the parties, the new developments of the law or departures from previous case law.

II. Conceptualising the Rule of Law

The rule of law has in recent times become one of the central topics of contemporary constitutional discourse in the European Union (EU). In the EU's legal framework, the rule of law is often understood very broadly. For instance, the European Commission understands a system based on the rule of law as requiring that

> all public powers always act within the constraints set out by law, in accordance with the values of democracy and fundamental rights, and under the control of independent and impartial courts. The rule of law includes principles such as legality, implying a transparent, accountable, democratic and pluralistic process for enacting laws; legal certainty; prohibiting the arbitrary exercise of executive power; effective judicial protection by independent and impartial courts, effective judicial review including respect for fundamental rights; separation of powers; and equality before the law.[1]

Such an extensive description of the rule of law, encompassing many other constitutional meta-principles enumerated in Article 2 of the Treaty on European Union (TEU), inevitably brings into question its functionality as an analytical legal concept.

In legal theory, the rule of law is first and foremost understood as a political ideal or, more specifically, an ideal underpinning a liberal political morality.[2] Allan called it 'an ideal of constitutionalism' providing for an 'integrated theory of constitutional government'.[3] Beyond such generalities, there is controversy over what the rule of law as a legal concept precisely requires.[4] How we, as jurists, conceptualise the rule of law as a normative ideal is to a large extent linked to our understanding of what 'the law' even is.[5] Our fundamental disagreements about the concept of law in legal theory, including the theories of adjudication and the proper role of courts, extend to discussions on the rule of law. For this reason, assessing the features of the rule of law is impossible without referencing them to their respective jurisprudential foundations.

This is reflected in the most common distinction between different concepts of the rule of law, distinguishing between formalist and substantive theories.[6]

[1] Communication from the Commission to the European Parliament, the Council, the European Economic and Social Committee and the Committee of the Regions, 2020 Rule of Law Report: The rule of law situation in the European Union, COM/2020/580 final.

[2] J Waldron, 'The Concept and the Rule of Law' (2008) 43 *Georgia Law Review* 1, 1.

[3] TRS Allan, *Constitutional Justice: A Liberal Theory of the Rule of Law* (Oxford, Oxford University Press, 2003) 6 and 4.

[4] The reason for this inevitable controversy is partly because, as Waldron said, 'the Rule of Law is a working political idea, as much the property of ordinary citizens, lawyers, activists and politicians as of the jurists and philosophers who study it'. See J Waldron, 'The Rule of Law' in EN Zalta (ed), *The Stanford Encyclopedia of Philosophy* (Summer 2020 edn), available at: plato.stanford.edu/archives/sum2020/entries/rule-of-law/.

[5] Waldron, 'The Concept and the Rule of Law' (n 2) 53. See also RH Fallon Jr, 'The Rule of Law as a Concept in Constitutional Discourse' (1997) 97 *Columbia Law Review* 1, 10; P Craig, 'Formal and Substantive Conceptions of the Rule of Law: An Analytical Framework' [1997] *Public Law* 467, 487.

[6] Craig, 'Formal and Substantive Conceptions of the Rule of Law' (n 5) 467.

Roughly speaking, these concepts correspond to jurisprudential theories of legal formalism (often closely related to legal positivism) and 'substantive' or critical theories (such as legal realism or particular variants of natural legal thought). Legal formalism, insisting that the law is determinate, tends to focus on the clarity and generality of legal norms as the core elements of the rule of law. Formalist accounts of the rule of law address the process of promulgating law, its requisite clarity to guide individual conduct, and its prospective application, refraining from passing judgment on the actual content of the law.[7] Substantive accounts of the rule of law, in contrast, reject that law is determinate in advance. Such accounts also insist that law is not value neutral, but includes substantive elements of social justice, democracy, individual liberty, dignity or the protection of fundamental rights. An inherent feature of the rule of law is, therefore, standards of substantive rights, distinguishing between 'good' and 'bad' laws which, in turn, necessarily depend on one's account of justice and political theory.[8]

Neither a formal nor substantive account of the rule of law, as our contribution will demonstrate, can adequately respond to the question about what constraints the rule of law imposes on judges. We will therefore argue that a third, procedural understanding of the rule of law is more appropriate to examine this concept when applied to courts. Such a procedural outlook focuses on legal processes and the specific characteristics of institutions administering the law, in particular courts, requiring them to uphold certain standards in adjudication.

These three concepts of the rule of law (formalist, substantive and procedural), as well as their implications, will now be analysed in turn.

A. The Formal Concept of the Rule of Law

Formal conceptions of the rule of law entail an expectation that society is 'ruled by and through rules'.[9] These rules have to possess certain formalist features. Probably the most common list of essential characteristics is one offered by Lon Fuller: rules need to be general; public; prospective; intelligible; consistent; practical; stable; and congruent.[10] Similar requirements have been proposed by other scholars supporting the formalist concept of the rule of law.[11]

Rules should possess the desired formalist characteristics of preventing arbitrary power with one main aim – to guarantee predictability to human behaviour.[12] According to Joseph Raz, one of the most famous proponents of the formalist outlook of the rule of law, the basic idea of this concept is that 'the law should be

[7] ibid.
[8] ibid.
[9] FC DeCoste, 'Redeeming the Rule of Law' (2002) 39 *Alberta Law Review* 1004, 1004–06.
[10] Lon Fuller, *The Morality of Law* (New Haven, CT, Yale University Press, 1969).
[11] Joseph Raz, 'The Rule of Law and Its Virtue' (1977) 93 *Law Quarterly Review* 195; reprinted in Joseph Raz, *The Authority of Law: Essays on Law and Morality* (Oxford, Clarendon Press, 1979) 210.
[12] FA Hayek, *The Constitution of Liberty* (Chicago, IL, University of Chicago Press, 1960) 156–57.

capable of providing effective guidance'.[13] This 'has two aspects: (1) that people should be ruled by the law and obey it, and (2) that the law should be such that people will be able to be guided by it'.[14]

At the same time, under the formal concepts of the rule of law, it is irrelevant whether the substance of the law is perceived as just and acceptable. Formal accounts of the rule of law refrain from 'passing judgment upon the actual content of the law'.[15]

According to Raz, the rule of law is a formal conception, saying 'nothing about how the law is to be made: by tyrants, democratic majorities, or any other way'.[16] Such understanding of the rule of law 'naturally fits together' with theories of legal positivism, which refuse to equate determining what the law is with issues of morality or considerations of substantive justness and political theory.[17]

The formal concept of the rule of law is linked to formalist legal thought, which, understanding law as determinate, insists that judicial decision-making requires only the application of norms and does not allow judges to engage in law-creating activities. Richard H Fallon, for example, relates it to originalism and formalism specific to American jurisprudence.[18] These theories associate the rule of law with 'rule by norms laid down by legitimate lawmaking authorities prior to their application to particular cases'.[19] Judges thereby retain a mechanical role of merely applying the law, being 'ruled by the law, rather than creating it in adjudication', while law-making is, as a political activity, considered legitimate only if there is democratic accountability.[20] Idealising a clear-cut distinction between the legislative and the judicial function, such an account maintains that judges are strictly bound by the law as a system of rules.[21]

To that extent, the formalists offer an easy answer to the question of how the rule of law constrains and controls judicial discretion. Given that legal rules are generally clear, the role of courts is simply to apply them, or, in rare cases when the rules are not clear, their role is to engage in legal interpretation that will guide them to the correct legal answer.

The crucial problem of the formalist outlook is, therefore, denying that judicial discretion even exists. The concept only works if the law is value neutral and determinate, and judges can mechanically apply the legal rules.

As Fallon noted, legal realists and their followers, such as those in critical legal studies (CLS), 'have advanced powerful claims that there is broad room for judicial

[13] Raz (n 11) 218.
[14] ibid 213.
[15] Craig, 'Formal and Substantive Conceptions of the Rule of Law' (n 5) 467.
[16] Raz (n 11) 214.
[17] Craig, 'Formal and Substantive Conceptions of the Rule of Law' (n 5) 477. See also DeCoste (n 9) 1006.
[18] Fallon (n 5) 5–6.
[19] ibid 11.
[20] ibid.
[21] ibid 15. Fallon notes that Scalia is the most prominent formalist, as well as originalist. See A Scalia, 'The Rule of Law as a Law of Rules' (1989) 56 *University of Chicago Law Review* 1175, 1178–80.

choice about which rule to apply to particular facts and about how rules should be formulated'.[22] Legal realism propelled a wave of criticism against the purported determinacy of legal rules, maintaining that, in reality, the law was neither as clear nor value neutral as formalist legal theory would seem to suggest. Instead, because of the inherent indeterminacy of legal rules, principles or concepts, especially those to be applied or interpreted at the appellate or constitutional level, courts are necessarily engaged in law-making and policymaking activities. By interpreting what the law is, courts are, in effect, making new law.[23]

It is true that contemporary legal formalists are 'soft formalists',[24] as they admit some indeterminacy, or at least under-determinacy, of legal rules.[25] However, they believe that this problem is resolved by the application of second order rules, which we may call clarifying rules (such as cannons of interpretation, different techniques for filling legal gaps and resolving contradictions, and different principles guiding interpretation). With the application of such rules, courts can always find the 'true' meaning of the applicable rule. Insistence on clarity can, therefore, still limit judicial discretion.

The realists' response to this is that these second-level clarifying rules are also not clear themselves, and that courts enjoy discretion in choosing which clarifying rule to apply. Different choices lead to different results.[26] Realists also challenge the idea that such rules actually guide courts in solving cases. They rather, the claim goes, have only justificatory purpose.[27]

Roberto Unger rightly pointed out that formalist legal reasoning can hardly be used by the judiciary unless the rules are clear and general enough to be applied mechanically.[28] In a 'post-liberal society', characterised by increased governmental regulation of the economy and societal regulation in general, legislation necessarily becomes more open-textured to reflect the complexity of aims to be attained, aims which cannot be achieved through clear and precise rules.[29] The style of reasoning progresses from being formalist to being purposive, placing increased attention on the aims of the law, weighing a number of substantive factors, and

[22] Fallon (n 5) 3.

[23] For a comprehensive account of the theory of legal realism and how it applies to the EU context, see N Bačić Selanec, 'A Realist Account of EU Citizenship' (PhD dissertation, University of Zagreb, 2019) 71–95.

[24] ibid 361: 'Under a soft formalist approach, textual indeterminacy is compensated for by determinacy in adjudication, achieved through legal reasoning extrapolating correct legal readings of the text from the existing sources within the legal system'.

[25] See, eg, LB Solum, 'On the Indeterminacy Crisis: Critiquing Critical Dogma' (1987) 54 *University of Chicago Law Review* 462; K Kress, 'Legal Indeterminacy' (1989) 77 *California Law Review* 283.

[26] KN Llewellyn, 'Remarks on the Theory of Appellate Decisions and the Rules or Canons about How Statutes Are To Be Construed (1950) 3 *Vanderbilt Law Review* 395; R Guastini, 'Rule-Scepticism Restated' in L Green and B Leiter (eds), *Oxford Studies in Philosophy of Law*, vol 1 (Oxford, Oxford University Press, 2011) 148–49.

[27] Llewellyn (n 26) 401.

[28] R Unger, *Law in Modern Society* (New York, The Free Press, 1976) 176–81, 192–223. See also Craig, 'Formal and Substantive Conceptions of the Rule of Law' (n 5) 475.

[29] M Cappelletti, *The Judicial Process in Comparative Perspective* (Oxford, Clarendon Press, 1989).

necessarily 'placing a higher premium' on substantive, not formal, justice, making judicial decision-making resemble political forums. As a result, the 'traditional attributes of the rule of law', such as the clarity of legal rules or the generality of laws, seem to be undermined.[30] As a matter of legal theory, this makes reliance on purely formal accounts of the rule of law, especially with regard to the constraints imposed on the judiciary, utterly problematic.

B. The Substantive Concept of the Rule of Law

Substantive conceptions of the rule of law entail the expectation that society is not only ruled by law, but that it is ruled by just law. This understanding is usually related to legal theories which reject that the law is value neutral, and which consider that law consists not only of legal rules, but also legal principles.

Proponents of substantive theories of the rule of law include, notably, Ronald Dworkin, Lord Thomas Bingham and Trevor Allan. Lord Bingham differentiated between a 'thin' and a 'thick' concept of the rule of law. He rejected a thin one, equated with formalist requirements in the likes of those pronounced by Dicey[31] or Raz, favouring instead a 'thick' version which necessitated an element of values through the protection of fundamental rights of individuals.[32] Allan's account of the rule of law, though 'primarily an ideal of procedural fairness, governing the manner in which laws and policies should be applied … also has important *implications* for the permissible content of such laws and policies'.[33] To that extent, Allan starts from a Dworkinian perspective, going beyond a positivist account of 'the law' as a system of legal rules, claiming it is a more nuanced system comprised also of principles. In his view, adjudication, in the application of not only legal rules, but also principles, requires courts to have recourse to substantive considerations of justice.[34]

Allan's theory strongly relies on the writings of Dworkin, who is perhaps the most well-known proponent of the substantive concept of the rule of law. In his theory of adjudication, Dworkin famously posited that 'what the law is' stems from the judges' constructive interpretation of the law which, on the one hand, 'fits' the institutional legal history and the principles the legal order expounds and, on the other, also has the best moral value in capturing the legal system's political

[30] Unger (n 28) 176–81, 192–223. See also Craig, 'Formal and Substantive Conceptions of the Rule of Law' (n 5) 475.

[31] AV Dicey, *An Introduction to the Study of the Law of the Constitution*, 5th edn (London, Macmillan, 1897).

[32] T Bingham, *The Rule of Law* (London, Allen Lane, 2010) loc 1150–59.

[33] Allan, *Constitutional Justice* (n 3) 1 (emphasis added).

[34] TRS Allan, *Law, Liberty and Justice: The Legal Foundations of British Constitutionalism* (Oxford, Oxford University Press, 1993) 28, 39. See also Craig, 'Formal and Substantive Conceptions of the Rule of Law' (n 5) 481.

morality. Dworkin, therefore, accepts the law-creating role of judges, considering at the same time that only such an approach to judicial decision-making which construes the law as the 'best' it can be, while pursuing coherence of the legal system, constitutes the 'law as integrity'.[35] Dworkin's account of adjudication and his theory of law in the wider sense are, in turn, translated into how he perceives the concept of the rule of law.

Dworkin differentiates between the 'rule book' and the 'rights' conception of the rule of law, endorsing the latter. The 'rule book' concept is effectively equated with the formalist account of the rule of law. It requires that rules, set out in advance and available to all, should provide limits to governmental action.[36] And under this account, 'substantive justice is an independent ideal, in no sense part of the ideal of the rule of law'.[37] The 'rights' conception of the rule of law, in turn, precisely includes considerations of substantive justice and individual moral and political rights inherent in positive law, such as liberty, equality and the like.[38]

The principal objection to substantive accounts is that they turn the concept of the rule of law into a 'partisan ideal', joining the disagreements about what the rule of law requires with 'substantive disagreements about what the law ought to be'.[39] And indeed, Dworkin's central argument essentially comes down to relating the meaning of the rule of law to one's concept of the law and the proper role of adjudication in a legal system. Craig criticised it as making the rule of law 'nothing more or less than a synonym for a rights based theory of law and adjudication'.[40] Substantive theories, in that sense, deprive the rule of law of its usefulness as a self-standing analytical tool.

While substantive rule of law accounts, in contrast to formalist ones, recognise that judicial discretion exists, they still maintain that applying substantive standards distinguishing between 'good' and 'bad' laws is an inherent feature of the rule of law. Therefore, this concept cannot be used in any neutral way to answer the question whether a court has in a particular situation exceeded the limits of its discretion as required by the standards of the rule of law. In these circumstances, approval or disagreement with a court's decision all necessarily depends on one's account of justice. Such an understanding of the rule of law motivates discussions on judicial activism,[41] but is hardly useful in assessing the limits of judicial discretion.

[35] See R Dworkin, *Law's Empire* (Cambridge, MA, Harvard University Press, 1986) 12–18.
[36] R Dworkin, *A Matter of Principle* (Cambridge, MA, Harvard University Press, 1985) 11.
[37] ibid.
[38] ibid 11–12.
[39] Fallon (n 5) 23.
[40] Craig, 'Formal and Substantive Conceptions of the Rule of Law' (n 5) 479.
[41] On judicial activism, see I Goldner Lang, 'Towards "Judicial Passivism" in European Union Migration and Asylum Law?', ch 9 in this volume.

C. The Rule of Law as a Liberal Concept

Despite their differences, formalist and substantive understandings of the rule of law have something in common: they are both entrenched in liberalism.

There are, indeed, scholars who negated the importance of the theoretical divide between the formalist and substantive concepts of the rule of law, seeing it as somewhat misleading.[42] Fallon, for example, observed that 'virtually every self-proclaimed adherent of a "thin" conception has been charged with covertly importing a substantive component'.[43] Laurent Pech noticed that in contrast to scholars

> who tend to favor formal conceptions over substantive ones … most if not all constitutions or courts in Europe view the formal and substantive components of the rule of law as interdependent and not mutually exclusive. Indeed, the formal and procedural components of the rule of law in liberal and democratic European polities (proportionality, non-retroactivity, access to courts, fundamental rights protection, etc.) are supposed to serve the substantive values (human dignity, individual autonomy, social justice, etc.) upon which these societies are founded.[44]

The quoted observations suggest that the two concepts cannot be entirely separated. What is common to both formal and substantive concepts of the rule of law is the necessity to limit the discretion possessed by the institutions of government. Such a need is grounded in theories of liberalism. The very concept of the rule of law is, therefore, an expression of liberal values. As noted by DeCoste, the rule of law sits 'at the core of liberal political morality' devoted to the equality of individuals as state subjects; it is 'the defining element of liberal political theory … [A]bsent an institutional practice to constrain power, political practice becomes inegalitarian and government becomes tyrannic or despotic'.[45]

Despite having a common background, the two concepts of the rule of law propose to safeguard liberal values in different ways. In order to secure individual liberty, the formal outlook insists on the clarity and prospectivity of legal norms. Individuals can better organise their lives if they know in advance which norms apply to their choices.[46] What, however, formalists neglect is that, while clarity may and possibly even should be present as an ideal, disputes often arise precisely because of the lack of clarity of the applicable norms. This does not mean that society should not aim for clear rules as an ideal, but rather that the protection of individual liberty as a requisite for the rule of law cannot be achieved merely by such a normative ideal.

[42] L Pech, 'The Rule of Law as a Constitutional Principle of the European Union' (2009) Jean Monnet Working Paper 04/09, 28.
[43] Fallon (n 5) 54.
[44] Pech, 'The Rule of Law as a Constitutional Principle of the European Union' (n 42) 44.
[45] DeCoste (n 9) 1025.
[46] Hayek (n 12) 152–57.

Substantive understandings of the rule of law try to maximise individual freedom by insisting that principles protecting individual fundamental rights are an inseparable part of the law. This, however, neglects the fact that precise consequences flowing from fundamental rights in each individual case may be, and often are, disputed. It leaves open the question of what the rule of law demands from courts to respect individual freedoms in situations of disagreement about their permissible limits.

The procedural concept of the rule of law, also grounded in liberalism, offers, in our view, an answer to the latter question.

D. The Procedural Concept of the Rule of Law

Apart from the two conceptions we have discussed so far, there is, as explained by Jeremy Waldron, 'another current in our Rule-of-Law thinking which emphasizes argument, procedure, and reason, as opposed to rules, settlement, and determinacy'.[47] This procedural understanding of the rule of law builds on the foundations of legal realism, accepting that judges, when interpreting the law, construe its meaning.

The law is, under the procedural concept, construed through an argumentative process, including in courts. Such an understanding comes into conflict with formal understandings, which, as the most important quality of the rule of law, posit an 'in advance' predictability achieved through the clarity of legal rules that precedes judicial decision-making. By accepting the law-creating activity of courts, the procedural concept is, instead, highly compatible with the substantive outlook to the rule of law. This similarity and simultaneous conflict with the (still dominant) formal concepts might be the reason why the procedural concept is usually not recognised in legal theory as a separate train of thought about the rule of law.[48]

However, its value is specific and particularly important for understanding the rule of law as applied to courts. Unlike the substantive one, the procedural outlook to the rule of law concentrates on institutions and procedures rather than on substantive political morality in relation to which the law was construed. More particularly, it focuses on the accessibility and institutional capacity of courts, above all their independence and effective operation, and on distinctive argumentative features of judicial processes. These two elements are the central features of the procedural concept of the rule of law.

[47] Waldron, 'The Concept and the Rule of Law' (n 2) 53.

[48] But see J Waldron, 'The Rule of Law and the Importance of Procedure' (2010) New York University School of Law, Public Law & Legal Theory Research Paper Series, Working Paper No 10-73. See also Fallon (n 5) 30 et seq, describing the legal process conception as one of the ideal types of the rule of law.

The first and most often referred to aspect of procedural rule of law deals with the right to access courts and to effective judicial review performed by an independent judiciary.

Waldron notes that

> [t]he most common political complaint about the Rule of Law is that governments have interfered with the operation of the courts, compromised the independence of the judiciary, or made decisions affecting people's interests or liberties in a way that denies them their day in court – their chance to make on their own behalf an argument.[49]

In the EU, as well, developments in Poland and Hungary, referred to as the rule of law crisis, were predominantly connected with government attacks on the independence of the judiciary.[50] Therefore, the public and institutional understanding of the rule of law (including in the EU) is associated with political values such as the separation of powers and the independence of the judiciary. EU scholars also often perceive procedural guarantees, such as the right to access independent and impartial courts, and the right to an effective judicial remedy, as the most important aspects of the rule of law.[51] The same is true for the case law of the Court of Justice, as will be demonstrated in the following part of this chapter.

The second constitutive feature of the procedural rule of law, as we see it, is the requirements imposed on the courts in relation to the quality of adjudication understood as an argumentative process.

The formulation of these requirements is inspired by the jurisprudential school of legal process,[52] and by the writings of other scholars who understand the interpretation of law as an argumentative endeavour, primarily Waldron[53] and MacCormick.[54]

As explained earlier, legal realism deconstructed the myth that legal rules exclusively determine legal outcomes. The legal process school accepted this main criticism of legal formalism, but focused on its institutional aspects, looking for possible constraints on judicial discretion. This school moved away from a concept of law as consisting solely of pre-existing rules which courts apply mechanically, and recognised that courts do weigh policy arguments, principles and values. Legitimation for their judgments was found in constitutional consensus with

[49] Waldron, 'The Concept and the Rule of Law' (n 2) 53.

[50] D Kochenov and P Bárd, 'Rule of Law Crisis in the New Member States of the EU. The Pitfalls of Overemphasising Enforcement' (July 2018) Reconnect Working Paper No 1; L Pech, 'Protecting Polish Judges from Poland's Disciplinary "Star Chamber"' (2021) 58 *Common Market Law Review* 137.

[51] See K Lenaerts, 'Judicial Dialogue in a Changing World: Preserving Judicial Independence', ch 2 in this volume. See also Pech, 'The Rule of Law as a Constitutional Principle of the European Union' (n 42) 27.

[52] Perhaps the most well-known proponents of the legal process theory are Hart and Sacks. See HM Hart Jr and AM Sacks, *The Legal Process: Basic Problems in the Making and Application of Law* (New York, Foundation Press, 1994).

[53] Waldron, 'The Concept and the Rule of Law' (n 2) 53; J Waldron, 'The Rule of Law and the Importance of Procedure' (n 48).

[54] N MacCormick, *Rhetoric and the Rule of Law* (Oxford, Oxford University Press, 2005).

which institutions are entrusted to render specific types of decisions. Such consensus only 'roughly frames' the substantive and procedural demands of the judicial decision-making process. The legal process school views all subjects of legal justice, including the judiciary, as 'reasonable persons, open to argument and persuasion, and deserving of reasoned explanations that the law should aspire to provide'.[55]

This theory, in a nutshell, considers that procedural fairness must be guaranteed through the requirements of judicial review and rational deliberation.[56] 'Rationality' in discourse effectively requires that judicial decisions elaborate on how new developments of the law relate to or depart from the pre-existing sources of law. This entails the assumption of an inherent connection between the law as an argumentative practice and reasonableness as a standard of argument. Admittedly, there might be disagreements as to what a reasonable elaboration justifying judicial outcomes is.[57] Nonetheless, we consider that the legal process theory was right to suggest that 'reasoned deliberation' could result in a normative consensus on what is *plausibly* lawful, while 'the outcomes of such deliberative processes might be [considered] as inherently legitimate and deserving of respect, even in the absence of clear rules specified in advance'.[58]

To further elaborate what this means for the purpose of answering how the rule of law constrains the judiciary, it is particularly useful to address Waldron's account of the procedural values of the rule of law. Waldron suggested that grasping the meaning of the rule of law may be easier if we understand its procedural themes which include and are intrinsically related to the law's argumentative nature. This implies that legal norms, rules and principles are not just obeyed and applied, but that 'we argue over them adversarially … and we engage in elaborate interpretive exercises about what it means to apply them faithfully'.[59] Such an account insists on the 'opportunities for argumentation' and, equally important, the 'responsiveness to argument' that courts should provide. What is crucial for Waldron is to recognise the 'presence and importance' of the argumentative nature of the law benefiting citizens as a guarantee of the rule of law.[60] What is even more crucial for the purposes of this chapter is to recognise that the rule of law as applied to courts mandates judges to respond to argument and elaborate their judicial choices.

The procedural concept is, as yet another understanding of the rule of law, entrenched in liberal theory. However, its understanding of freedom is different from the more passive Hayekian vision of freedom, safeguarded through certainty which allows an individual to plan her or his life. The procedural

[55] See Fallon (n 5) 19.

[56] ibid 18.

[57] ibid 20. See also MV Tushnet, 'Following the Rules Laid Down: A Critique of Interpretivism and Neutral Principles' (1983) 96 *Harvard Law Review* 781, 805.

[58] Fallon (n 5) 20. See also FI Michelman, 'Law's Republic' (1988) 97 *Yale Law Journal* 1493, 1510–15.

[59] Waldron, 'The Concept and the Rule of Law' (n 2) 56.

[60] ibid 58–59.

concept abandoned legal formalism by recognising the multiplicity of possible legal answers.[61] This results in insistence that individual freedom is respected by enabling individuals to contest proposals about the law. The procedural idea of freedom is 'more like positive freedom: active engagement in the administration of public affairs, the freedom to participate actively and argumentatively in the way that one is governed'.[62] In Waldron's words:

> To say that we should value aspects of governance that promote the clarity and determinacy of rules for the sake of individual freedom, but not the opportunities for argumentation that a free and self possessed individual is likely to demand, is to truncate what the rule of law rests upon: respect for the freedom and dignity of each person as an active center of intelligence.[63]

In judicial proceedings, individuals have an interest in judges accepting their position about the meaning of the legal rule in the circumstances of their case. In this way, they are able to offer their own position about the limits through which the law safeguards their individual freedom. The opposing arguments heard in the judicial process may reflect different political theories behind individual freedom and, in turn, force the deciding court to endorse one or the other, or indeed neither of the two, but to offer a third solution. The court's choice between different, but opposing arguments about the law is a law-creating activity. A court's choice, expressed in a judgment, becomes legally binding. However, this does not mean that other options presented to and considered by the court, but not relied on in the end, were legally not possible or of themselves 'incorrect'.

To show respect for these opposing arguments, the court must necessarily not only hear them, but address them. Explaining reasons for accepting some and rejecting other arguments not only respects the individual freedom of parties to the dispute at hand, but of future parties. Namely, understanding the reasons for a court's decision enables individuals to either adjust their behaviour or to challenge such reasons in future disputes or, indeed, in the political process with the aim of changing judicially construed meaning of the law. Stating reasons for the judicial choice is thus important from the perspective of the rule of law as it provides for individual freedom. At the same time, this allows for the functioning of the argumentative process through which the law is created.

Therefore, an important requirement which flows from the rule of law for the process of adjudication is the need for courts to hear different arguments and give reasons for accepting or rejecting them as part of the justification for their decisions.

[61] Pieter Van Malleghem described legal formalism as a belief that legal reasoning has the power 'to yield interpretive closure in the form of correct legal answers'. P-A Van Malleghem, 'Reflections on European Legal Formalism' in S Rodin and T Perišin (eds), *Transformation or Reconstitution of Europe: The Critical Legal Studies Perspective on the Role of Courts in the European Union* (Oxford, Hart Publishing, 2018) 204.

[62] Waldron, 'The Rule of Law and the Importance of Procedure' (n 48) 18.

[63] Waldron, 'The Concept and the Rule of Law' (n 2) 53.

Indeed, in judicial proceedings parties must not only be able to make submissions and be 'listened to' by a court, they must also be 'treated respectfully', which means that a court must be bound to respond to their submissions while explaining the reasons for its judicial decision.[64] In other words, taking into account its procedural and argumentative values, the rule of law requires reasoned elaboration of judicial decisions which necessarily includes judicial explanation why one possible argument or canon of interpretation was chosen over the alternative.

A problem arises, however, because courts often perform their inevitable law-making functions non-transparently, and under the pretence that the law is merely being 'discovered, not made or changed'.[65] Judges never admit they make new law. When courts do engage in law-making, their decisions are presented as inevitable results of purely legal reasoning, not an exercise in judicial discretion. Martin Shapiro called this the ultimate judicial paradox. According to him 'judges lie': 'although every court makes law in a few of its cases, judges must always deny that they make law'.[66] Why is this so? Why do judges hide their choice-making activity from the public? Most likely, this is the inheritance of legal formalism, which, maintaining the myth that law contains predesigned answers to legal problems, shaped public understanding according to which any law-making activity by courts is illegitimate. However, a different paradigm offered by the procedural conception of the rule of law frees judges from blind insistence on the pure discovery of pre-existing law, as this is no longer understood as a condition for the legitimacy of courts. On the contrary, when choices are made, an adequate explanation of the rationale of the decisions becomes a source of the court's legitimacy.

The procedural concept of the rule of law thus demands judges to abandon the current 'judicial lie' of not engaging in a law-making activity and to explain their choices. However, this still does not mean that judicial decision-making can be equated with the pure exercise of political will as in legislative law-making. Judges do operate under the constraint of an existing, even if indeterminate, system of rules and principles. Even CLS scholars admit that '[t]he rule of law requires that judges understand themselves to be bound by a norm of interpretive fidelity to the body of legal materials that are relevant to whatever dispute is before them'.[67] The call for a reasonable elaboration of the justification of judgments does not, therefore, relieve judges from linking their choices to existing legal rules or from trying to secure the coherence of the legal system. Judicial law-making, however, as a minimum, requires a reasoned elaboration of how the existing law as text (constitutional, legislative or judicial precedent) connects to the chosen meaning of the law, and why arguments to the contrary were rejected.

[64] Waldron, 'The Concept and the Rule of Law' (n 2) 53.

[65] ibid 53.

[66] M Shapiro, 'Judges as Liars' (1994) 17 *Harvard Journal of Law & Public Policy* 155, 156.

[67] D Kennedy, *A Critique of Adjudication (fin de siècle)* (Cambridge, MA, Harvard University Press, 1997) 13.

III. Adjudication of the Court of Justice

In the remainder of this chapter, we aim to examine how the standards of the procedural rule of law apply to the adjudication of the Court of Justice. By analysing its case law on the accessibility of judicial review, we will demonstrate that the Court's vision of the rule of law is indeed procedural in nature. The main requirement of the rule of law has so far been the right to access a court with the capacity of performing effective judicial review.

We will further argue that the Court's proactive style of decision-making goes beyond the expectations of legal formalism. In these circumstances, the Court should be required itself to uphold the procedural guarantees of the rule of law and adhere to the standards of argumentative adjudication. However, the Court still maintains the formalist 'one legal truth' narrative. For this reason, it does not adequately elaborate on other possible solutions to legal disputes, including those raised by the parties, apart from the one it has chosen to endorse. In conclusion, we will, therefore, argue that the Court of Justice should change this aspect of its decision-making method.

A. The Concept of the Rule of Law as Understood by the Court of Justice

As will be explained in more detail below, the Court of Justice is not a formalist court. Unsurprisingly, the requirements stressed by the formal understanding of the rule of law, such as clarity, generality or non-retroactivity, play a less important role in the Court's case law on the rule of law. This is not to say that the formal requirements are never used by the Court in reviewing or interpreting legislation,[68] but rather that the Court would not use and describe the concept of the rule of law primarily through these values. An analysis of the Court's case law demonstrates that the Court mostly focuses on values stressed by the procedural understanding of the rule of law, particularly the right to access courts, judicial independence or the existence (or effectiveness) of judicial review. In the vast majority of cases, the expression 'rule of law'[69] is indeed used to justify access to judicial review through

[68] The Court sometimes relies on the principle of legal certainty to justify its choice in the interpretation of EU law (eg, Case C-717/18 *X – European arrest warrant – Double criminality* EU:C:2020:142 para 38) or to justify or reject temporal limitations of its interpretation of EU law (eg, Case C-477/16 PPU *Kovalkovas* EU:C:2016:861 para 52). The Court also invokes legal certainty as well as clarity of rules to explain how directives have to be implemented (eg, Case C-808/18 *Commission v Hungary – Accueil des demandeurs de protection internationale* EU:C:2020:1029 para 288) or to impose limits to the national courts' obligation to interpret national law in conformity with EU law (for example, Case C-573/17 *Popławski* EU:C:2019:530 para 75). Even if such cases demonstrate that the Court understands that legal certainty and the clarity of rules are important qualities of law, the Court has used these requirements independently from the concept of the rule of law.

[69] About linguistic differences in the use of this notion, *cf* Pech, 'The Rule of Law as a Constitutional Principle of the European Union' (n 42) 6 et seq.

which courts (either European or national) can effectively control other branches of government.[70]

One of the first mentions of the concept of the rule of law by the Court of Justice was in *Les Verts*.[71] The case was decided in 1986, before the rule of law was mentioned in the text of the Treaties. In this celebrated judgment, the Court of Justice stated the EU 'is a community based on the rule of law, inasmuch as neither its Member States nor its institutions can avoid a review of the question whether the measures adopted by them are in conformity with the basic constitutional charter, the Treaty'.[72]

In this case, the Court of Justice relied on the rule of law concept to justify its own jurisdiction to review acts of the European Parliament, which, at the time, was not expressly mentioned as a possible defendant in annulment actions. Thus, the concept was used to justify widening the Court's jurisdiction beyond the text of the Treaty. The purpose of such widening was to respond to requirements, dictated by the rule of law, to make available judicial review of all measures adopted by EU institutions which produce legal effect.

The important condition for enabling judicial review is that individuals are able to access courts. To stress this requirement, the Court of Justice usually relies on the principle of effective judicial protection, as embodied today in Article 47 of the Charter. The example of the Court's usual reasoning are the following two paragraphs from the *UPA* case:

> The European Community is, however, a community based on the rule of law in which its institutions are subject to judicial review of the compatibility of their acts with the Treaty and with the general principles of law which include fundamental rights.
>
> Individuals are therefore entitled to effective judicial protection of the rights they derive from the Community legal order, and the right to such protection is one of the general principles of law stemming from the constitutional traditions common to the Member States. That right has also been enshrined in Articles 6 and 13 of the European Convention for the Protection of Human Rights and Fundamental Freedoms.[73]

Therefore, because the EU is based on the rule of law in the sense that its institutions are subject to judicial review, individuals enjoy the right to effective judicial protection.

However, even though the existence of judicial review of EU institutions requires that individuals may initiate such review, this does not mean that access

[70] We have reached this conclusion on the basis of the research of the Court's case law since 2010. The search was performed through the search engine of the Court, at curia.europa.eu, by using three different wordings. In English, we looked for the expression 'governed by the rule of law' and 'based on the rule of law' and in French, we looked for the expression 'Etat de droit', both in the description and the text of the judgments.

[71] Case 294/83 *Parti écologiste 'Les Verts' v European Parliament* EU:C:1986:166.

[72] ibid para 23.

[73] Case C-50/00 P *Unión de Pequeños Agricultores v Council* EU:C:2002:462 paras 38–39.

is always allowed directly to the Court of Justice (including the General Court). The courts of the Member States are also part of the EU judiciary, and they, in the Court's words, 'in collaboration with the Court of Justice, fulfil a duty entrusted to them jointly of ensuring that in the interpretation and application of the Treaties the law is observed'.[74] Therefore, the requirement of the availability of judicial review of EU acts is fulfilled either by the possibility to introduce a challenge directly to the EU court (the Court of Justice or, for individuals, the General Court of first instance), or indirectly, through an action initiated in a Member State's court, which should then, in accordance with the *Foto-Frost* judgment,[75] refer the question of validity of an EU measure to the Court of Justice under Article 267 of the Treaty on the Functioning of the European Union (TFEU). The described scheme results from the Court's understanding that the Treaties have created a coherent set of legal remedies against possible violations of rights by EU institutions.[76] However, this 'complete system' places the burden on the Member States' courts to create an avenue for access if such an avenue is lacking at the EU level.[77] The Court of Justice thus refused to widen direct access to EU courts in actions for annulment, but has, at the same time, in the name of the rule of law, demanded that national courts widen theirs. Interestingly, the Court of Justice has justified such a decision by relying heavily on the text of the Treaties, which insists that individuals show 'individual concern' in order to introduce an annulment action directly before the Court of Justice.[78] It has, at the same time, ignored (which could not be other than on purpose) that the meaning of the term 'individual concern' was crafted in its own case law, starting with *Plaumann*.[79] A change did not, therefore, necessarily demand Treaty amendments as claimed by the Court,[80] but only a different interpretation of the existing text of the Treaty, as proposed by its Advocate General.[81] This position is open to criticism, especially since the Court has clearly demanded that national courts be ready to change their own previous interpretations of law if necessary for the protection of EU-based rights, but did not impose the same requirement on itself.[82] And this was criticised both from within the Court[83] and by the academic community.[84] This resulted in a

[74] Case C-64/16 *Associação Sindical dos Juízes Portugueses v Tribunal de Contas* EU:C:2018:117 para 33.

[75] Case 314/85 *Foto-Frost v Hauptzollamt Lübeck-Ost* EU:C:1987:452.

[76] Case C-50/00 P *Unión de Pequeños Agricultores v Council* (n 73) para 40.

[77] ibid para 41.

[78] Art 263(4) TFEU.

[79] Case 25/62 *Plaumann & Co v Commission of the European Economic Community* EU:C:1963:17.

[80] Case C-50/00 P *Unión de Pequeños Agricultores v Council* (n 73) para 45.

[81] Case C-50/00 P *Unión de Pequeños Agricultores v Council* EU:C:2002:197, Opinion of AG Jacobs.

[82] In this respect, see Case C-414/16 *Egenberger* EU:C:2018:257 para 72; Case C-573/17 *Popławski* (n 68) para 78.

[83] AG Jacobs in *Unión de Pequeños Agricultores v Council* EU:C:2002:197 and the General Court (then Court of First Instance) in Case T-177/01 *Jégo-Quéré v Commission* EU:T:2002:112.

[84] eg, P Craig, 'Standing, Rights, and the Structure of Legal Argument' (2003) 9 *European Public Law* 493; JA Usher, 'Direct and Individual Concern: An Effective Remedy or a Conventional Solution?' (2003) 28 *European Law Review* 575.

Treaty change (which might have happened precisely because of the Court's refusal to address the rule of law demand through (re)interpretation). The Lisbon Treaty has, therefore, strengthened the right to access the Court of Justice by extending the possibilities to introduce actions for the annulment of an EU measure under Article 263 TFEU.[85]

The Court's reluctance to extend its own jurisdiction, but only provided that another available avenue exists to raise the question of the validity of an EU measure, has been constant ever since the *UPA* case. Thus, in a recent ruling in *Chrysostomides*,[86] the Court, contrary to the General Court, refused to allow an action for damages on the basis of Article 340 TFEU against Eurogroup. The General Court considered that the rule of law demands that such action be allowed.[87] However, the Court did not agree. The important reason offered to justify its position that the rule of law is not violated if Eurogroup cannot stand as a defendant was the possibility to introduce an action for damages against EU institutions – the Council, Commission or the European Central Bank – which would translate political agreements within Eurogroup into legal norms.[88] A wide reading of the Treaties to allow for the passive legitimation of Eurogroup was therefore not necessary, as an avenue existed to reach the Court which would indirectly allow the review of decisions initiated within that forum.[89]

Despite ample room for criticism of the case law developed since *UPA*, what seems important for the purposes of this contribution is that insistence on a judicial avenue for the control of an EU measure, whether through a national court coupled with the preliminary ruling procedure, or directly in front of the Court of

[85] The Lisbon Treaty, as a legacy of the unsuccessful Constitutional Treaty, introduced the amendment into Art 263 TFEU, according to which the standing of individuals in annulment actions was extended against regulatory acts which do not demand implementing measures if they are of direct but not individual concern for them. The case law explaining the amendment is still developing. See, in this respect, Case C-583/11 P *Inuit and Others v European Parliament and Council* EU:C:2013:625 and Case C-274/12 P *Telefónica v Commission* ECLI:EU:C:2013:852.

[86] Case C-597/18 P *Council v Chrysostomides et al* EU:C:2020:1028.

[87] ibid para 92.

[88] ibid para 93.

[89] The Court has yet to explain whether an action lies against decisions of the Conference of States appointing Judges and Advocates General to the Court of Justice. The appeal against the decision of the General Court which dismissed the action introduced by former Advocate General Sharpston was still pending at the time this contribution was being written. See Order of the General Court in *Eleanor Sharpston v Council of the European Union and Conference of the Representatives of the Governments of the Member States* EU:T:2020:473 and the appeal pending under number C-684/20 P. This case raised criticism from part of the academic community, questioning whether the Court had breached the rule of law requirements. *cf* Daniel Halberstam, 'Could There Be a Rule of Law Problem at the EU Court of Justice? The Puzzling Plan to Let UK Advocate General Sharpston Go After Brexit' (*Verfassungsblog*, 23 February 2020), available at: verfassungsblog.de/could-there-be-a-rule-of-law-problem-at-the-eu-court-of-justice/; and DV Kochenov and G Butler, 'The Independence and Lawful Composition of the Court of Justice of the European Union: Replacement of Advocate General Sharpston and the Battle for the Integrity of the Institution' (2020) Jean Monnet Working Paper 2/20.

Justice, was motivated by rule of law concerns.[90] The possibility of initiating judicial control of an EU measure is thus clearly understood as an essential component of the rule of law.[91]

The right to initiate judicial review of the acts of EU institutions and other EU bodies belongs not only to individuals, but also to public actors. Even though the rule of law creates the presumption that acts of EU institutions are lawful,[92] such a presumption can be rebutted in the judicial process. Therefore, if infringement proceedings are instituted against a Member State for violating an EU rule of general application, the State can raise a plea of illegality of such a rule, which the Court of Justice has to examine.[93] Member States also have a right, as privileged applicants, to challenge the validity of any act of EU institutions. Relying on the value of the rule of law, the Court of Justice has allowed for such a right for acceding States, by considering that the two-month time-limit for introducing an annulment action against acts adopted or amended between the period of the conclusion of negotiations and the moment of membership starts running only from the moment at which such a State has acceded to the EU.[94]

The Court of Justice insists on the availability of judicial review against measures taken not only by EU institutions and bodies, but by national authorities when they act within the scope of EU law. In the *Johnston* case,[95] decided the same year as *Les Verts*, the Court considered that an individual must have the possibility to access a court in order to avail herself of effective judicial control of national measures alleged to contravene EU law. In *Johnston*, effective judicial protection was prevented by the rule laid down by UK law, according to which a national minister's certificate created an irrebuttable presumption that a certain decision was taken for the sake of public safety or public order. This eliminated any possibility for the wronged Ms Johnston to access a court which could check the legality of a decision denying her access to employment in, as she claimed, contravention of the EU guarantee of gender equality. The Court considered it contrary to

[90] Case C-50/00 P *Unión de Pequeños Agricultores v Council* (n 73) paras 38 and 39. The same was confirmed in subsequent case law, as demonstrated by, eg, Case C-550/09 *Criminal proceedings against E and F* EU:C:2010:382 para 44; Case C-583/11 P *Inuit and Others v European Parliament and Council* (n 85) para 91; Joined Cases C-584/10 P, C-593/10 P and C-595/10 P *Commission and Others v Kadi* EU:C:2013:518 para 66; and Case C-362/14 *Maximillian Schrems v Data Protection Commissioner* EU:C:2015:650 para 60.

[91] Case C-64/16 *Associação Sindical dos Juízes Portugueses* (n 74) para 36. For earlier case law, see Cases C-72/15 *PJSC Rosneft Oil Company v Her Majesty's Treasury and Others* EU:C:2017:236 para 73; and Case C-362/14 *Maximillian Schrems v Data Protection Commissioner* (n 90) para 95.

[92] Case C-620/16 *Commission v Germany* EU:C:2019:256 para 85; Joined Cases C-715/17, C-718/17 and C-719/17 *Commission v Poland, Hungary and Czech Republic (Temporary mechanism for the relocation of applicants for international protection)* EU:C:2020:257 para 139.

[93] Art 277 TFEU. The existing case law allows pleas of illegality only in respect of regulations, but not directives or decisions.

[94] Case C-335/09 P *Poland v Commission* EU:C:2012:385 paras 48 and 50–51; Case C-336/09 P *Poland v Commission* EU:C:2012:386 paras 36, 38 and 39.

[95] Case 222/84 *Marguerite Johnston v Chief Constable of the Royal Ulster Constabulary* ECLI:EU:C:1986:206.

the principle of effective judicial review.[96] In this, or similar earlier cases,[97] the Court did not expressly invoke the concept of the rule of law but rather referred to Articles 6 and 13 of the European Convention on Human Rights and explained that 'the requirement of judicial control ... reflects a general principle of law which underlies the constitutional traditions common to the Member States'.[98]

In newer cases, the Court of Justice started to explicitly invoke the concept of the rule of law when it insists on the possibility of access to courts for the purpose of reviewing the compatibility of national measures with EU law. Thus, for instance, in *Schrems*, referring to the earlier cases of *Johnston* and *Heylens*, it stated that '[t]he very existence of effective judicial review designed to ensure compliance with provisions of EU law is inherent in the existence of the rule of law'.[99] In *Commission v Slovakia*, a case initiated on the basis of Article 260 TFEU, Slovakia tried to justify its failure to implement the previous infringement decision by claiming that an administrative decision ordering the closing of a landfill was appealed in an administrative court. The Court of Justice confirmed that the availability of judicial review of administrative decisions is indeed a requirement of the rule of law.[100] However, it did not accept that in the circumstances of the case at hand this could justify the delay in Slovakia's fulfilment of its obligations based on EU law.

Similar to cases reviewing EU measures, it seems that the rule of law does not demand access to the most effective procedure of a particular court when national measures are at stake. What is sufficient is that a certain procedure exists which will eventually enable a court to perform judicial review of a domestic measure. Recently, in *Luxembourg v B and others*,[101] the Court of Justice considered, confirming its earlier case law,[102] that Article 47 of the Charter would be violated if an individual had to breach the law to acquire access to court.[103] However, in disagreement with its Advocate General,[104] the Court did not consider that only indirect access to the court,[105] or only action for damages (instead of the possibility to challenge directly the potentially damageable measure)[106] would be contrary to the requirements of effective judicial protection, and therefore also of the rule of law. This and some other cases[107] seem to suggest that the concept of the rule of law, as understood by the Court of Justice, places emphasis on the availability of judicial review rather than on the most effective protection of an individual's claim for such review.

[96] ibid para 20.

[97] eg, Case 222/86 *Unectef v Heylens* EU:C:1987:442 para 14.

[98] Case 222/84 *Marguerite Johnston v Chief Constable of the Royal Ulster Constabulary* (n 95) para 18.

[99] Case C-362/14 *Maximillian Schrems v Data Protection Commissioner* (n 90) para 95.

[100] Case C-626/16 *Commission v Slovakia* EU:C:2018:525 para 80.

[101] Joined Cases C-245/19 and C-246/19 *Luxembourg v B and Others* EU:C:2020:795.

[102] Case C-263/02 P *Commission v Jégo-Quéré* EU:C:2004:210 para 35; Case C-583/11 P *Inuit and Others v European Parliament and Council* (n 85) para 104.

[103] Joined Cases C-245/19 and C-246/19 *Luxembourg v B and Others* (n 101) para 66.

[104] Joined Cases C-245/19 and C-246/19 *Luxembourg v B and Others* EU:C:2020:516, Opinion of AG Kokott.

[105] Joined Cases C-245/19 and C-246/19 *Luxembourg v B and Others* (n 101) para 79.

[106] ibid para 101.

[107] Case C-575/18 P *Czech Republic v Commission* EU:C:2020:530.

Until recently, cases questioning the effectiveness of judicial control arose only in situations in which Member States acted within the scope of EU law. The Court of Justice, therefore, did not need to explicitly mention the concept of the rule of law, given that it could simply apply the general principle of effective judicial protection, today guaranteed in Article 47 of the Charter. For example, in *FMS*,[108] the Court of Justice explicitly relied only on Article 47 of the Charter to demand the availability of a judicial challenge of a refugee's return decision for contravening relevant EU legislation.[109] However, in newer case law the Court of Justice has stretched the reach of the rule of law (such as imposing requirements of judicial review on Member States) even to situations in which Member States do not 'implement EU law' within the meaning of Article 51 of the Charter.[110] The ground-breaking case was *Portuguese Judges*.[111] The Court of Justice explained that the second subparagraph of Article 19(1) TEU, which requires that Member States 'provide remedies sufficient to ensure effective legal protection in the fields covered by Union law' is a concrete expression of the value of the rule of law.[112] The Court further explained that the expression 'in the fields covered by EU law' in that provision has wider reach than the expression 'when implementing EU law' in the Charter.[113] On this basis, it has established its own jurisdiction to control *in abstracto* whether a national judicial system satisfies the requirements of effective judicial protection, especially the independence of the judiciary, even in a case which has not resulted from an alleged misapplication of EU law. This was justified given that courts in a particular State would, at some point, be required to offer judicial protection to rights derived from EU law.[114]

The newly acquired jurisdiction has enabled the Court of Justice to declare regimes which deprive courts of the quality of independence as contrary to EU law. In all cases relating to judicial reforms in Poland, whether brought to the Court

[108] Joined Cases C-924/19 PPU and C-925/19 PPU *FMS and Others v Országos Idegenrendészeti Főigazgatóság Dél-alföldi Regionális Igazgatóság and Országos Idegenrendészeti Főigazgatóság* EU:C:2020:367 paras 140–41.

[109] Directive 2008/115/EC of the European Parliament and of the Council of 16 December 2008 on common standards and procedures in Member States for returning illegally staying third-country nationals [2008] OJ L348/98; Directive 2013/32/EU of the European Parliament and of the Council of 26 June 2013 on common procedures for granting and withdrawing international protection [2013] OJ L180/60.

[110] Art 51 of the Charter envisages that fundamental rights enumerated in that document apply to Member States only when the latter implement EU law. Even if this expression was given wide interpretation in the CJEU's case law, it still left situations which do not specifically come under the scope of EU law, outside the reach of the Charter. *cf* Case C-617/10 *Åkerberg Fransson* EU:C:2013:105.

[111] Case C-64/16 *Associação Sindical dos Juízes Portugueses* (n 74) EU:C:2018:117 para 31. *cf* M Bonelli and M Claes, 'Judicial Serendipity: How Portuguese Judges Came to the Rescue of the Polish Judiciary' (2018) 14 *EurConst* 622.

[112] Case C-64/16 *Associação Sindical dos Juízes Portugueses* (n 74) para 32; also Case C-216/18 PPU *LM – Minister for Justice and Equality (Deficiencies in the system of justice)* EU:C:2018:586 para 50; Case C-619/18 *Commission v Poland (Independence of the Supreme Court)* EU:C:2019:531 para 47; Case C-585/18 *AK (Independence of the Disciplinary Chamber of the Supreme Court)* EU:C:2019:982 para 167.

[113] Case C-64/16 *Associação Sindical dos Juízes Portugueses* (n 74) para 29.

[114] ibid para 40.

of Justice in infringement proceedings as, for example, was the case *Commission v Poland (Independence of the Supreme Court)*,[115] or via a preliminary reference, as in *AK*,[116] the Court of Justice relied on the concept of the rule of law. Since *Portuguese Judges*, the Court of Justice has given legal force to the value of the rule of law through Article 19 TEU.

The described cases allow us to conclude that the main principle stemming from the concept of the rule of law as understood in the Court's case law is the principle of effective judicial review. When applied on the basis of Article 47 of the Charter, this principle has direct effect[117] in the sense that it creates for individuals a right to demand judicial review of the measures of either EU or Member State institutions. Thus, as follows from *FMS*,[118] a national court which, under national law, lacks jurisdiction to hear a case alleging violation of EU law may establish such jurisdiction directly on the basis of the EU principle of effective judicial protection.

In its case law, the Court of Justice therefore relies on the procedural understanding of the rule of law. The rule of law is invoked to justify the necessity of the judicial review of decisions of public bodies, either European or those of Member States. Effective judicial review requires that all subjects of law, whether private or public actors, have access to a court with power to assess whether the institutions of government have used their discretion lawfully. However, effective judicial control does not create a right to the most effective judicial remedy which would enable judicial review, but only to a judicial remedy that is capable of adducing a public measure to the court's control. The rule of law concept focuses, therefore, on the availability of judicial review, rather than on the maximal effectiveness of an individual right to judicial protection.[119] Finally, as the rule of law is about judicial control of the limits of discretion enjoyed by other branches of government, courts must be independent of those institutions.[120] This couples the concept of rule of law with the principle of separation of powers.[121]

[115] Case C-619/18 *Commission v Poland (Independence of the Supreme Court)* (n 112) paras 46 and 58.

[116] Case C-585/18 *AK (Independence of the Disciplinary Chamber of the Supreme Court)* (n 112) para 120.

[117] Case C-556/17 *Torubarov* EU:C:2019:626 para 56; Joined Cases C-924/19 PPU and C-925/19 PPU *FMS and Others v Országos Idegenrendészeti Főigazgatóság Dél-alföldi Regionális Igazgatóság and Országos Idegenrendészeti Főigazgatóság* (n 108) para 140.

[118] Joined Cases C-924/19 PPU and C-925/19 PPU *FMS and Others v Országos Idegenrendészeti Főigazgatóság Dél-alföldi Regionális Igazgatóság and Országos Idegenrendészeti Főigazgatóság* (n 108) para 144.

[119] However, this position is challenged even from within the Court itself. *cf* the Opinion of AG Kokott in Joined Cases C 245/19 and C 246/19 *Luxembourg v B and Others* (n 101) EU:C:2020:516.

[120] The notion of the independence of courts has been elaborated in recent cases and is still developing. In addition to the already quoted Cases C-619/18 *Commission v Poland* and C-585/18 *AK*, see also Case C-354/20 PPU *Openbaar Ministerie (Indépendance de l'autorité judiciaire d'émission)* EU:C:2020:1033; or Case C-824/18 *AB and Others (Nomination des juges à la Cour suprême – Recours)* EU:C:2021:153; Case C-272/19 *Land Hessen* EU:C:2020:535.

[121] Case C-585/18 *AK (Independence of the Disciplinary Chamber of the Supreme Court)* (n 112) para 124; Joined Cases C-924/19 PPU and C-925/19 PPU *FMS and Others v Országos Idegenrendészeti Főigazgatóság Dél-alföldi Regionális Igazgatóság and Országos Idegenrendészeti Főigazgatóság* (n 108) para 136.

Overall, we may conclude that the Court's case law corresponds to the first requirement of the procedural concept of the rule of law requiring access to effective judicial review by an independent judiciary. Let us now consider the second requirement – reasonable justification of judicial choices.

B. Applying Requirements of the Procedural Rule of Law to Adjudication of the Court of Justice

The procedural outlook of the rule of law, as we explained in the second part of this chapter, considers law as an argumentative discipline which requires holding the judiciary accountable to the standards of the reasoned justification of judicial outcomes. Whether we may apply these standards to the particular context of EU law very much depends on whether the adjudication of the Court of Justice corresponds to the concept of law which goes beyond the formalist requirements of determinacy in law. Namely, the standards of the rule of law which we may require depend significantly on the concept of law by which we are guided in a particular legal context.

The Court of Justice is not a classic formalist adjudicator, as it approaches the concept of law as going beyond merely legal rules. The Court recognises the limits of textualism and thus the indeterminacy of black-letter law.[122] Admittedly, the Treaties are drafted in broad terms, while its provisions are commonly drafted to achieve 'objectives of paramount constitutional importance that the EU must attain'.[123] As such, the Treaties are usually considered as providing 'no more than a framework' that the Court of Justice is required to interpret.[124] This also explains the Court's extensive recourse to teleological interpretation of the law.[125] Koen Lenaerts argues how it compels the Court to fill out the incomplete meaning of Treaty provisions and 'take its responsibility for "finding" the law by fashioning general principles of EU law'.[126] Many authors consider that such legal principles, as well as the Court's (meta-)teleological operating mode, favour systemic

[122] This indeterminacy is accentuated in the EU multilingual legal framework. T Ćapeta, 'Multilingual Law and Judicial Interpretation in the EU' (2009) 5 *Croatian Yearbook of European Law & Policy* 1.

[123] K Lenaerts and JA Gutiérrez-Fons, 'To Say What the Law of the EU Is: Methods of Interpretation and the European Court of Justice' (2013) EUI Working Paper AEL 2013/9, 24.

[124] T Tridimas, *The General Principles of EU Law*, 2nd edn (Oxford, Oxford University Press, 2006) 18.

[125] Lenaerts and Gutiérrez-Fons, 'To Say What the Law of the EU Is' (n 123) 13. See also, MP Maduro, 'Interpreting European Law: Judicial Adjudication in a Context of Constitutional Pluralism' (2007) 1(2) *European Journal of Legal Studies* 137, 151; M Dawson, 'How Does the European Court of Justice Reason? A Review Essay on the Legal Reasoning of the European Court of Justice' (2014) 20 *European Law Journal* 423, 424.

[126] K Lenaerts, 'Discovering the Law of the EU: The European Court of Justice and the Comparative Law Method' in S Rodin and T Perišin (eds), *Transformation or Reconstitution of Europe: The Critical Legal Studies Perspective on the Role of Courts in the European Union* (Oxford, Hart Publishing, 2018) 62.

interpretation of the 'law as a whole', seeking to secure both coherence and the integrity of the EU legal order.[127] The most common approach is that 'EU law does not "run out" with black-letters inscribed in the Treaties or secondary legislation, as the general principles come to aid' in guiding the interpretation of the law.[128] This shows how EU scholarship understands the Court's method largely in terms of Dworkin's theory of constructive interpretation.[129]

Admittedly, the Court's judgments are drafted as 'highly magisterial and deductive', being 'univocal and unsigned'.[130] Nonetheless, they still offer 'distinctly visible marks of interpretive openness' that come along with teleological legal reasoning.[131] The Court commonly relies on open-ended legal sources, such as the principles, proportionality or effectiveness of EU law. This demonstrates how the Court of Justice, in fact, does accept the limits of determinacy of black-letter legal provisions, resulting in the far-reaching effects of its jurisprudence in developing EU law.[132] 'Allocating meaning and weight to general principles, and giving precedence to one principle or teleological purpose over the other' in determining legal outcomes is an exercise of judicial discretion.[133] Such an exercise of normative preference demonstrates that adjudication is a law-making endeavour.[134] By choosing between different interpretive options, the Court is creating new law. Applying legal principles as teleological ideals helps the Court to clarify normative vagueness in the law, and necessarily 'entails a more proactive type of adjudication'.[135]

In other words, the specific style of decision-making of the Court of Justice simply exceeds the formalist expectations of the concept of law. Its adjudication is substantive, focused on teleology, legal principles and values, pursuing (more

[127] MP Maduro, 'Interpreting EU Law: On Why and How Law and Policy Meet at the European Court of Justice' in H Koch, K Hagel-Sørensen, U Haltern and JHH Weiler (eds), *Europe – The New Legal Realism: Essays in Honour of Hjalte Rasmussen* (Copenhagen, DJØF, 2010) 460.

[128] Bačić Selanec (n 23) 361.

[129] In this respect, see J Bengoetxea, N MacCormick and L Moral Soriano, 'Integration and Integrity in the Legal Reasoning of the European Court of Justice' in G de Búrca and J Weiler (eds), *The European Court of Justice* (Oxford, Oxford University Press, 2002) 45; MP Maduro, *Interpreting EU Law: On Why and How Law and Policy Meet at the European Court of Justice* in H Koch, K Hagel-Sørensen, U Haltern and JHH Weiler (eds), *Europe – The New Legal Realism: Essays in Honour of Hjalte Rasmussen* (Copenhagen, DJØF, 2010) 460 and 471–72; K Lenaerts and JA Gutiérrez-Fons, 'The Constitutional Allocation of Powers and General Principles of EU Law' (2010) 47 *Common Market Law Review* 1629, 1632; J Komárek, 'Legal Reasoning in EU Law' in A Arnull and D Chalmers (eds), *The Oxford Handbook of European Union Law* (Oxford, Oxford University Press, 2015) 40; T Ćapeta, 'Ideology and Legal Reasoning at the European Court of Justice' in S Rodin and T Perišin (eds), *Transformation or Reconstitution of Europe: The Critical Legal Studies Perspective on the Role of Courts in the European Union* (Oxford, Hart Publishing, 2018) 95.

[130] M Lasser, *Judicial Deliberations: A Comparative Analysis of Judicial Transparency and Legitimacy* (Oxford, Oxford University Press, 2004) 245.

[131] ibid.

[132] Bačić Selanec (n 23) 362.

[133] ibid.

[134] ibid 364–65.

[135] See Lenaerts and Gutiérrez-Fons, 'The Constitutional Allocation of Powers and General Principles of EU Law' (n 129) 1668.

or less effectively) the integrity of EU law in order to uphold the ideals of a liberal democracy and the protection of fundamental rights.[136] The Court of Justice acts as a realist adjudicator.

As such, the Court should itself uphold procedural guarantees of the rule of law and adhere to high standards of argumentative adjudication. These standards include rationalising judicial choices between different possible interpretations of the applicable law. The Court of Justice, however, does so rarely, if ever. The reason for this might be the European legal tradition, in which legitimacy of judicial law-making is 'not openly acknowledged'.[137] In discovering 'what the law is', courts are still required simply to interpret the law 'as it is'. And while legal interpretation is recognised as a method of 'shaping' the law, courts are still not allowed to engage in making *new* law, as this would be seen as overstepping the limits of judicial powers and intruding 'into the political process'.[138] In this sense, EU law 'operates under a perplexing formalist façade, which discourages both the EU judiciary and legal scholarship from admitting openly the inevitable law-making and policy-making dimensions of the Court's adjudication'.[139]

Such a legal heritage requires the Court of Justice to '[present] the developments in [Union] law as a logical consequence of the Treaty rule and not as a result of any choice or exercise of discretion by the Court'.[140] As a result, the Court's judgments simply do not refer to other possible canons of interpretation of the applicable law, nor does the Court tend to elaborate why one option was chosen over the equally 'lawful' alternative.[141] 'Even if other outcomes, or different reasoning ending in the same judgment, were discussed during the procedure before the Court, this is never revealed in the text of the judicial decision'.[142] In this way, the Court of Justice creates the public image of being 'the Hercules of a Dworkinian

[136] See Tridimas, who argues that general principles of EU law as perceived by the Court 'synergize the fundamental constitutional underpinnings of the EU which are grounded in liberal democracy'. T Tridimas, 'Conclusion – The General Principles of Law: Who Needs Them?' (2016) 1 *Cahiers de Droit Européen* (Colloque 10 septembre 2015, Les principes généraux du droit de l'Union européenne) 419, 422. See also K Lenaerts, 'Judicial Dialogue in a Changing World: Preserving Judicial Independence', ch 2 in this volume.

[137] A Arnull, 'Judicial Activism and the European Court of Justice: How Should Academics Respond?' in M Dawson, B de Witte and E Muir (eds), *Judicial Activism at the European Court of Justice* (Cheltenham, Edward Elgar Publishing, 2013) 212. Also, T Ćapeta, 'Courts, Legal Culture and EU Enlargement' (2005) *Croatian Yearbook of European Law & Policy* 23; Z Kühn, 'European Law in the Empires of Mechanical Jurisprudence: The Judicial Application of European Law in Central European Candidate Countries' (2005) *Croatian Yearbook of European Law & Policy* 55.

[138] K Lenaerts, 'The Court's Outer and Inner Selves: Exploring the External and Internal Legitimacy of the European Court of Justice' in M Adams, H de Waele, J Meeusen and G Straetmans (eds), *Judging Europe's Judges: The Legitimacy of the Case Law of the European Court of Justice* (Oxford, Hart Publishing, 2013) 14.

[139] See Bačić Selanec (n 23) 360.

[140] M Poiares Maduro, *We the Court: The European Court of Justice and the European Economic Constitution* (Oxford, Hart Publishing, 1998) 20.

[141] Bačić Selanec (n 23) 48.

[142] Ćapeta, 'Ideology and Legal Reasoning at the European Court of Justice' (n 129) 97.

legal world'.[143] It thus upholds the publicly expected formalist understanding that the right answer indeed exists, and can always be found by the Court.

To uphold the pretence, the Court of Justice in its judgments most commonly ignores the arguments introduced by the parties, the national courts or its own Advocates General,[144] especially if they do not support the Court's choice of legal reasoning to solve the dispute. It almost never argues or explains its position in relation to conflicting arguments. The ways in which the Court circumvents such arguments differ. It might not even mention them in the text of the judgment, or it might simply reproduce them in the descriptive part of the judgment (usually named 'The dispute in the main proceedings and the questions referred for a preliminary ruling'), but then omit any further reference to them in its own analysis.

An example of the latter mode of circumventing conflicting arguments is the *Faccini Dori* case.[145] To argue against admitting the direct horizontal effect of directives, the referring Italian judge claimed that this amounts to penalising an individual for a Member State's failure to transpose a directive.[146] In its description of the case, the Court of Justice did report this argument of the Italian judge, but never revisited it in the later portions of its judgment, by which it confirmed that directives cannot have direct effect in horizontal relations. The Court also failed to answer any of its own Advocate General's arguments for change in its case law on directives.[147]

An example of the former practice – the Court avoiding the contrary arguments altogether – is in *Dominguez*.[148] This preliminary reference was decided as a classical case on the direct versus indirect (interpretive) effect of directives. The Court of Justice discussed which of the two principles is to be applied first and explained rather extensively both concepts by quoting previous case law. However, the opinion of the Advocate General reveals that the important issue in the case, one discussed by her and by the parties, was different.[149] It concerned the effects of general principles of law in horizontal situations and the consequences they have for the judicial applicability of directives, an issue raised by the preceding controversial *Mangold/Kücükdeveci* case law.[150] Nonetheless, there is not a single mention of these concerns in the text of the *Dominguez* judgment.

These mentions serve merely as examples. The Court of Justice commonly avoids confronting arguments which do not uphold its conclusion, presenting

143 ibid 93.

144 T Ćapeta, 'The AG: Bringing Clarity to ECJ Decisions? A Case Study of Mangold and Kücükdeveci' (2011–12) 14 *Cambridge Yearbook of European Legal Studies* 563.

145 Case C-91/92 *Faccini Dori v Recreb* EU:C:1994:292.

146 ibid para 21.

147 *cf* Case C-91/92 *Faccini Dori v Recreb* EU:C:1994:45, Opinion of AG Lenz.

148 Case C-282/10 *Dominguez* EU:C:2012:33. *cf* also the description of this case in Ćapeta, 'Ideology and Legal Reasoning at the European Court of Justice' (n 129) 98–99.

149 Case C-282/10 *Dominguez* EU:C:2011:559, Opinion of AG Trstenjak, paras 26–35.

150 Case C-144/04 *Mangold* EU:C:2005:709 and Case C-555/07 *Kücükdeveci* EU:C:2010:21.

its judgments as the only available solution simply deduced from applicable legal rules and principles. If the Court of Justice is to live up to the expectations imposed on courts by the procedural concept of the rule of law, this aspect of its judicial method must change. Rationalising judicial choices between different possible interpretations of the applicable law is a crucial procedural requisite of the rule of law. If it wants to truly and consistently safeguard the rule of law in the EU, the Court of Justice must be able to 'meet this challenge'.[151]

IV. Conclusion

The title of this volume, 'The Changing European Union', invited discussion of either the ongoing changes in the EU, or the changes that should be, but are not yet, happening. In our contribution, we have tackled the latter issue.

We have argued that the Court of Justice should change the method of elaborating the justifications of its judgments in such a way that it abandons the formalist narrative of 'one correct legal answer' with no mention of the conflicting interpretations of the applicable law, all of which might be equally 'legal' and possible judicial outcomes. To uphold the rule of law, particularly its requirements of a procedural nature, the adjudication of the Court of Justice must be considered as an argumentative process. The judges in Luxembourg should meet high standards of persuasiveness in their legal reasoning and in the elaboration of their judicial choices, adequately addressing the submissions of the parties, the new developments of the law or departures from previous case law.

As a possible barrier to such a change in method, we have identified the European legal culture which, as a heritage of the long tradition of legal formalism, has created the expectation that courts do not create law. However, in a reality where incontestable determinacy of the law is not possible, insisting on an undisputed and previously determined 'correct meaning' of the law amounts to a call for changing reality. However, one cannot change reality by simply claiming that it is different, as formalist theory attempts to do. To draw a parallel with science, observed differences in the behaviour of particles in macro and micro worlds would not disappear if we insisted that either the theory of relativity or quantum mechanics are good theories for both worlds.[152] This is precisely why scientists are

[151] Inspired by K Lenaerts, 'Constitutionalism and the Many Faces of Federalism' (1990) 38 *American Journal of Comparative Law* 205, 263: 'the [federal] balance [in EU law] must and can be kept through mechanisms of judicial umpiring under the rule of law which governs the common legal order … [The Court of Justice] … will not fail to meet the challenge'.

[152] For other comparisons of law with science, *cf* T Ćapeta, 'Do Judicial Decision-Making and Quantum Mechanics Have Anything in Common? A Contribution to Realist Theories of Adjudication at the CJEU' in M Belov (ed), *The Role of Courts in Contemporary Legal Orders* (The Hague, Eleven, 2019) (also available at: papers.ssrn.com/sol3/papers.cfm?abstract_id=3370280).

attempting to elaborate a new theory to explain both worlds. They are not trying to change one of the two worlds so that it fits one of the two theories.

If this is transposed to the legal world, we may conclude that formalism does not describe the reality of judicial adjudication. Judges cannot avoid making choices, as the law simply cannot carry a predetermined solution for all cases. Formalists insist that judges should not make choices. The narrative effort made by courts to present their decisions as the only available legal truth, made in response to such a formalist vision, cannot, however, change the fact that the law is indeterminate more often than is recognised. As we cannot change the strange behaviour of small particles, we can also not change the reality of adjudication. What has to change instead is the theory. Theories need to describe reality, and not vice versa.

The procedural concept of the rule of law is such a theory. It accepts that the reality of adjudication consists of judicial choices. Once such choice-making activity is recognised, the requirements which the rule of law imposes on judges also change. If judges openly admit and confront different possible interpretations of the law, this does not make their decisions illegitimate. Quite the contrary. Their choice becomes legitimate because they explain it. From the perspective of the procedural rule of law theory, such an explanation is precisely what pays respect to individual freedom, as a tenet of the liberal conception of a democratic society. It is therefore time for the Court of Justice to start paying more attention to the arguments of the parties and other participants of the adjudication process by offering reasons for accepting or rejecting their arguments.

4

Pragmatism, Innovation and Prophecy: Conjectures Concerning the Grounds of Belief in an Inventive Court

ALEXANDER SOMEK*

I. The Enigma

In an article offering a reconstruction of how the European Union (EU) legislature has grown into an agent of the European Court of Justice (ECJ; the Court), my esteemed colleague Gareth Davies states the following:

> The tragedy of the EU … is … not just that it has rushed towards a system in which power is concentrated in judicial hands to a degree unprecedented in any state or legal order to date, but that it has done so without many of its scholars, and even its Member States, seeming to be fully aware of that fact.[1]

There is much to this observation. It actually sums up many decades of EU legal scholarship by alerting us to the fact that there must have been something that has led us to set aside our usual rule of law sensibilities when we turn to EU law. Just as national law is to be set aside in the case of conflict, we, or at least many of us, were ready to set aside our ordinary expectation concerning the legality of expositions of law when it comes to pathbreaking decisions by the ECJ – cases such as *Francovich*,[2] *Centros*,[3] *Mangold*,[4] *Ruiz Zambrano*[5] or *Pringle*,[6] to name but a few. We may have done this inadvertently and automatically; and, it is submitted here,

* I would like to thank Jakob Rendl for his help in preparing this chapter for publication.

[1] G Davies, 'The European Union Legislature as an Agent of the European Court of Justice' (2016) 54 *Journal of Common Market Studies* 846, 858.

[2] Joined Cases C-6/90 and C-9/90 *Francovich* EU:C:1991:428.

[3] Case C-212/97 Centros *Ltd v Erhvervs- og Selskabsstyrelsen* EU:C:1999:126.

[4] Case C-144/04 *Mangold v Helm* EU:C:2005:709.

[5] Case C-34/09 *Ruiz Zambrano v Office national de l'emploi* EU:C:2011:124.

[6] Case C-370/12 *Pringle v Government of Ireland* EU:C:2012:756 (Full Court).

we have not yet reconstructed what it is that has taken their place. In other words, we do not yet understand what 'law' would have to be like in order for the practice of the ECJ to pass as adjudication.

By now, it is of course widely recognised that the jurisprudence of the ECJ is innovative.[7] It is well known that this is not always the case and that innovations may take some time to come to pass and to 'sink in'; but there seems to be a general understanding that, unlike any other court, the Court is particularly heavily engaged in what is called, in German, *Rechtsfortbildung* – that is, amending the law in the process of its interpretation.[8]

The political scientist Martin Höpner has attempted to distinguish between and among six different types and degrees of innovation.[9] It pays to recount them briefly.

First, the filling of gaps in the sense of overcoming clearly unplanned incompleteness of the law.[10]

Second, the interpretation of secondary legislation in a manner that expands on, or which may be even contrary to, its original meaning (*Barber*[11] und *Grzelczyk*[12]). I mention, in passing, that according to Joseph Weiler this type of innovation upsets the equilibrium in the relation between the Council and the Court.[13] While the Court, by virtue of the 'constitutionalisation' of the Treaty, foreclosed selective exit for the Member States, this closure is only tolerable so long as the Member States are also given a voice in the legislative process. If the Court occupies their place, one should not be surprised to see various attempts at selective exit recur.[14]

Third, declaring that something is within the power of the European legislature to regulate, even though this has not been seen like this before.[15]

[7] For accounts, see G Beck, *The Legal Reasoning of the Court of Justice of the EU* (Oxford, Hart Publishing, 2012) and, from a normatively critical angle, G Conway, *The Limits of Legal Reasoning and the European Court of Justice* (Cambridge, Cambridge University Press, 2012). For discussion, see J Bengoetxea, 'Text and Telos in the European Court of Justice' (2015) 11 *European Constitutional Law Review* 184; M Dawson, 'How Does the European Court of Justice Reason? A Review Essay on the Legal Reasoning of the European Court of Justice' (2014) 20 *European Law Journal* 423; J Komárek, 'Judical Lawmaking and Precedent in Supreme Courts' (2011) LSE Law, Society and Economy Working Papers No 4.

[8] See M Potacs, 'Auslegung und Rationalität in der europäischen Rechtsprechung' in G Herzig et al (eds), *Europarecht und Rechtstheorie* (Vienna, Verlag Österreich, 2017) 83. See also F Wasserfallen, 'The Judiciary as Legislator? How the European Court of Justice Shapes Policy-making in the European Union' (2010) 17 *Journal of European Public Policy* 1128.

[9] See M Höpner, 'Von der Lückenfüllung zur Vertragsumdeutung: Ein Vorschlag zur Unterscheidung von Stufen der Rechtsfortbildung durch den Europäischen Gerichtshof' (2010) 3 *der moderne staat* 165.

[10] ibid 170–71.

[11] Case C-262/88 *Barber v Guardian Royal Exchange Assurance Group* EU:C:1990:209.

[12] See Case C-184/99 *Rudy Grzelczyk v CPAS* EU:C:2001:458.

[13] See JHH Weiler, *The Constitution of Europe: 'Do the New Clothes Have an Emperor?' and Other Essays on European Integration* (Cambridge, Cambridge University Press, 1999) 35.

[14] One should also be surprised if they do not. See SK Schmidt, *The European Court of Justice and the Policy Process* (Oxford, Oxford University Press, 2018).

[15] See A Somek, *Individualism: An Essay on the Authority of the European Union* (Oxford, Oxford University Press, 2008).

Fourth, transforming subject matters into matters of EU law and lending them a new substantive reading. *Golden Shares* is an instructive example of this,[16] for these decisions not only absorbed competence from the Member States, they also imposed a certain model of corporate governance that more or less de-privileged all special rights that had been reserved for state actors.

Fifth, interpretations of primary law in a manner that is tantamount to a revision of the Treaty. Many believe that *Dassonville*[17] and *Cassis de Dijon*[18] provide examples of that. Judges present such moves as the 'discovery' of new dimensions of fundamental freedoms, and such a 'discovery' works like a general competence to affect a number of competences simultaneously.

Finally, Höpner singles out those judicial reinterpretations of fundamental principles that are unamendable even if there was unanimous consensus among the Member States.[19] This concerns, for example, the interpretation of unwritten principles, such as the attribution of common constitutional traditions of the Member States.[20] It is difficult to imagine how a repeal via Treaty revision might work. Certainly unamendable is the Court's view of the authority of Union law, namely of its autonomy.[21]

Scholarship has struggled to account for these innovations and to determine their precise extent, not least because detecting innovations is a matter of interpretation, and reasonable people are likely to disagree. In this context, two disciplines – sometimes interacting with one another – have devoted themselves to two different tasks, namely causal explanation, on the one hand, and normative critique, on the other.

Political science attempts to arrive at explanations of the case law, thereby identifying factors such as personal ambition, serving the interest of the institution, Member State interests, party affiliation or, most intriguingly, the internal ethos of the court.[22] Court decisions are thereby rendered as choices made by rational agents in pursuit of their interests or the interests of their institution.

[16] See the references and Höpner, 'Von der Lückenfüllung zur Vertragsumdeutung' (n 9) 173. See also B Werner, 'Why is the Court of Justice of the European Union Not More Contested? Three Mechanisms of Opposition Abatement' (2016) 54 *Journal of Common Market Studies* 1449.

[17] See Case 8/74 *Procureur du Roi v Benoît and Gustave Dassonville* EU:C:1974:82.

[18] Case 120/78 *Rewe-Zentrale v Bundesmonopolverwaltung für Brandwein (Cassis de Dijon)* EU:C:1979:42.

[19] On the difficulties confronting legislative override, see G Davies, 'Legislative Control of the European Court of Justice' (2014) 51 *Common Market Law Review* 1579; see also FW Scharpf, 'Towards a More Democratic Europe: De-constitutionalization and Majority Rule' (2017) 15 *Journal for Comparative Government and European Policy* 84; FW Scharpf, 'Perpetual Momentum: Directed and Unconstrained?' (2012) 19 *European Journal of Public Policy* 127.

[20] See Case C-144/04 *Mangold v Helm* (n 4).

[21] See Höpner, 'Von der Lückenfüllung zur Vertragsumdeutung' (n 9) 176.

[22] See, however with partly conflicting causal explanations, K Alter, 'Who Are the "Masters of the Treaty"? European Governments and the European Court of Justice' (1998) 52 *International Organization* 121; M Blauberger and SK Schmidt, 'The European Court of Justice and Its Political Impact' (2017) 40 *West European Politics* 907; Schmidt (n 14); CJ Carruba, M Gabel and C Hankla, 'Understanding the Role of the European Court of Justice in European Integration' (2012) 106

Legal scholarship, by contrast, has variously attempted to assess the legitimacy of law-making by the judiciary and, from that angle, imagined possible justifications, partly on the ground of recasting the case law in the mould of conventional judicial reasoning techniques.[23] The emphasis rests, then, not only on causes, but on the integrity of judicial expositions of law. Over the last decades, however, the legal literature has grown increasingly sceptical and critical.[24] And even where it has not, and continues to cheer the Court by waving the placard of teleological interpretation, it is committed to some unreconstructed default-positivism; and if it is not a positivism of rules, it is a positivism of values.

Both approaches to the study of the Court's case law have much merit. At the same time, however, they are incomplete, for they filter out what, in the spirit of Max Weber, one might call the *irrational element* of adjudication.[25] Admittedly, the notorious examples of typically irrational legal dispute resolution, such as ordeals, have no place in EU law. But it can scarcely be denied that the apodictic tone in which the law is sometimes announced by the Court is not by accident reminiscent of historical practices where the law was divined by a group of honourable persons or those vested with religious authority.[26] For example, without identifying an explicit and unequivocal anchor in the Treaty, the Court posits that 'Union citizenship is destined to be the fundamental status of nationals of the Member States, enabling those who find themselves in the same situation to enjoy the same treatment in law irrespective of their nationality, subject to such exceptions as are expressly provided for';[27] or that 'the right of individuals to rely on the directly effective provisions of the Treaty before national courts is only a minimum guarantee'.[28] All of a sudden, a judicial finding concludes by saying that 'interpreted in this way the provision [at stake, AS] contains nothing capable of prejudicing the fundamental human rights enshrined in the general principles of Community

American Political Science Review 214. For nuanced criticism of rational choice explanations, see M Höpner, 'Der Europäische Gerichtshof als Motor der Integration: Eine akteursbezogene Erklärung' (2011) 21 *Berlin Journal of Sociology* 203; M Höpner, 'Warum betreibt der EuGH Rechtsfortbildung? Die Politisierungshypothese' (2010) 59 *Sozialer Fortschritt* 141.

[23] See, more recently, A Grimmel, 'Der Kontext als Schlüssel für ein angemessenes Verständnis der Integration durch Recht in Europa – am Beispiel der aktuellen Grundrechtsrechtsprechung des EuGH' (2013) 2 *Europarecht* 146. The most sophisticated and elaborate justification of the case law is offered by Koen Lenaerts: K Lenaerts 'The Court's Outer and Inner Selves: Exploring the External and Internal Legitimacy of the European Court of Justice' in M Adams, H de Waele, J Meeusen and G Straetmans (eds), *Judging Europe's Judges: The Legitimacy of the Case Law of the European Court of Justice* (Oxford, Hart Publishing, 2013).

[24] For a reply to Lenaerts, see JHH Weiler, 'Epilogue: Judging the Judges – Apology and Critique' in M Adams, H de Waele, J Meeusen and G Straetmans (eds), *Judging Europe's Judges: The Legitimacy of the Case Law of the European Court of Justice* (Oxford, Hart Publishing, 2013).

[25] See M Weber, *Economy and Society: Outline of Interpretive Sociology* (eds G Roth and C Wittich, trans E Fischoff et al) (Berkeley, CA, University of California Press, 1978) vol 1, 26 (on the irrationality of commitments to values).

[26] See Weber, *Economy and Society* (n 25) vol 2, 760.

[27] Case C-184/99 *Rudy Grzelczyk v CPAS* (n 12) para 31.

[28] Case 168/85 *Commission v Italy* EU:C:1986:381 para 11.

law and protected by the Court',[29] which is subsequently followed by 'in fact, respect for fundamental rights forms an integral part of the general principles of Community law protected by the Court of Justice'[30] and that 'the Court has already stated, fundamental rights form an integral part of the general principles of law, the observance of which it ensures'.[31] Earlier in the case law we are confronted with the rather surprising statement that 'all trading rules enacted by Member States which are capable of hindering, directly or indirectly, actually or potentially, intra-community trade are to be considered as measures having an effect equivalent to quantitative restrictions'.[32]

Legal scholarship usually ignores the irrational element in the administration of justice, for its chief interest is to examine whether the Court's rulings actually withstand scrutiny from the perspective of the standards of sound legal reasoning and not in pinning down the reason why they may not; likewise, political science is reluctant to take more elusive influences into account as long as there are traces of manifest personal or national interests the pursuit of which can be attributed to judges.

In order to fill the gap in the literature, the following pages would like to offer a few ideas on how the innovative drive of the case law might be accounted for from an angle that accords judicial self-confidence a certain place. The ideas are offered, however, not to replace existing approaches but rather to complement them. The irrational element that is to be captured has its roots in the paradoxical shape of a case law that takes innovation and pushing the envelope as a chief means of being faithful to the law of European integration.[33] Fidelity to the law by moving beyond existing law is, unless we are confronted with real gaps, a decidedly irrational commitment, at any rate from the perspective of the values and maxims of traditional legal scholarship. Accounting for it holds the promise of providing us with a fuller and possibly clearer perspective on the law of European integration.

The sketch that follows is tentative, nonetheless. It is for this reason that this contribution offers three concurring perspectives on this hitherto unexplored element of the Court's case law. It thereby also attempts to catch a glimpse of what law might be like if expositions of it are expected to rewrite it. For this is the question stated at the outset. What would law have to be like for the expositions of Union law by the Court to pass as its adjudication or interpretation?

[29] Case 29/69 *Stauder v City of Ulm* EU:C:1969:57 para 7.

[30] Case 11/70 *Internationale Handelsgesellschaft v Einfuhr- und Vorratsstelle für Getreide und Futtermittel* EU:C:1970:114.

[31] Case 4/73 *Nold v Commission* EU:C:1974:51 para 13.

[32] Case 8/74 *Procureur du Roi v Benoît and Gustave Dassonville* (n 17). Why this statement is surprising is beautifully explained by JHH Weiler, 'The Constitution of the Common Market Place: Text and Context in the Evolution of the Free Movement of Goods' in PP Craig and G de Búrca (eds), *The Evolution of EU Law* (Oxford, Oxford University Press, 1999).

[33] See P Pescatore, *The Law of Integration: Emergence of a New Phenomenon in International Relations, Based on the Experience of the European Communities* (Leiden, Sijthoff, 1974); see most recently, V Fritz, 'Activism On and Off the Bench: Pierre Pescatore and the Law of Integration' (2020) 57 *Common Market Law Review* 475.

The three relevant perspectives are what Ronald Dworkin called 'pragmatism', the idea of 'judicial entrepreneurship' and the recognition of the fact that European Union law, at any rate, whenever the preliminary reference procedure is chosen, is known by means of a decision. This final point will permit us to put a political-theological twist on the matter and raise the deeper question of what it means to view Europe as a project that is rooted in the Christian religious tradition. Hence, yes, the chapter has to conclude with a brief discussion of Weiler's work.

II. Pragmatism

In our context, the term 'pragmatism' is used in the same manner in which Dworkin used it to capture the essence of American legal realism.[34] I think, indeed, that a strong case can be made that a more radical form of such pragmatism explains the most salient instances of the practice of the ECJ.

From the perspective of pragmatism, legal decision-making ought to be based on forward-looking considerations. At first glance, therefore, pragmatism clearly formulates an antithesis to legality, which requires that legal acts be adopted pursuant to standards that have been laid down in advance. But pragmatism can accommodate the demand made by legality. It can treat legal rules and other results of prior decisions as valuable – or 'valid' – inasmuch as they either render government action predictable or serve another value, such as equal treatment. It may make a great deal of sense, for example, for courts to respect acts of the legislature if these acts represent aggregate voter preferences or incorporate social research that courts are notoriously unable to provide. But respect for the legislature is clearly dependent on the good consequences of legislation. When there is reason to believe that the legislature was prey to interest-group capture – or that the political process has not made enough progress – courts should feel free to ignore legislation. The value of predictability is not absolute. It can be overridden by other forward-looking considerations of public policy, in particular when modified rules promise to serve an objective better than the rules that are already in place.

As an approach to adjudication and regulation, pragmatism is defensible on its own terms as long as the social engineering agency, be it a commission or a court, pursues good objectives with rational means. Since pragmatism does not espouse faith in formal values, such as the pedigree of legal enactments, its claim to legitimacy depends entirely on the *substance* of its policies. And it is not entirely unpredictable either. In spite of all its twists and turns, the

[34] See R Dworkin, *Law's Empire* (Cambridge, MA, Harvard University Press, 1986) 151–64. The following text summarises the observations that I made in an earlier article. See A Somek, 'The Emancipation of Legal Dissonance' in H Koch (ed), *Europe: The New Legal Realism* (Copenhagen, DJØF Publishing, 2011).

consequentialist jurisprudence of the ECJ is somewhat patterned. It is possible to anticipate on which side the innovation is going to fall. The Court is predictable with regard to the overall centralising and neoliberal drift of its jurisprudence. When it comes to establishing Community competence, the Court appears to be disposed to construe the power contained in Article 114 of the Treaty on the Functioning of the European Union Treaty (ex Article 95 TEC Treaty) broadly.[35] The Community legislature is thus brought into a position to legislate even where competence seems to be explicitly withheld by the Treaty. The ECJ is also not likely to respect state sovereignty unless the cases affect their inner core, such as the organisation of military forces.[36] The Court continues to be disposed to attribute direct effect where there has been none – possibly even to the opening Articles where this helps to boost daring interpretations of other provisions – and to expand the application of the horizontal effect of fundamental freedoms.[37] The Court may ever more frequently supplant the lack of direct effect of Directives with directly effective Treaty law. The Court appears to be also favourably inclined to transmute fundamental freedoms into guarantees of economic substantive due process.[38] It may take anti-discrimination law very seriously, for it represents the Community's most cherished vintage social legislation.[39] It is also likely to do its utmost to use Union citizenship as a substitute for the Union's lack of a social welfare system in order to provide access for Union citizens to the respective systems of the Member States where citizens choose to reside.[40]

A pragmatist jurisprudence is, however, not without its problems. Two such problems should be highlighted here.

First, consequentialism is an unreliable guide. Instead of vesting authority in consequences, it vests this authority in the speculations of courts as to what these consequences might be. Puzzlingly, upon closer inspection, consequentialism turns out to be a formal criterion. Niklas Luhmann has been right about this. If it turns out that the Court was mistaken about consequences, the decision is nonetheless treated as valid. This creates a situation in which courts can only win: 'Courts … have the power to bestow upon their conjectures legal validity. From the perspective of empirical social research, legal consequentialism is nothing but imagination with the force of law'.[41]

[35] See Somek, *Individualism* (n 15).

[36] Case 285/98 *Tanja Kreil v Bundesrepublik Deutschland* EU:C:2000:2.

[37] Case C-281/98 *Roman Angonese v Cassa di Risparmio di Bolzano SpA* EU:C:2000:296.

[38] See A Somek, 'Idealization, De-Politicization and Economic Due Process: System Transition in the European Union' in B Iancu (ed), *The Law/Politics Distinction in Contemporary Public Law Adjudication* (Utrecht, Eleven International Publishing, 2009).

[39] This, at any rate, is the observation that I have made in A Somek, *Engineering Equality: An Essay on European Anti-discrimination Law* (Oxford, Oxford University Press, 2011).

[40] See, however, for the Court's recent retreat from its expansive approach to Union citizenship, M Blauberger, 'ECJ Judges Read the Morning Papers: Explaining the Turnaround of European Citizenship Jurisprudence (2018) 25 *Journal of European Public Policy* 1422.

[41] N Luhmann, *Das Recht der Gesellschaft* (Frankfurt am Main, Suhrkamp, 2003) 382 (my translation).

Second, even though a theory of good consequences would no doubt mitigate the conflict with legality, no such theory is available, at any rate not in the case of European integration. Admittedly, normative law and economics may have come to play the role of such a theory in certain fields of law, but in these uses it represents clearly the most recent resuscitation of natural law.[42]

III. Entrepreneurship

An alternative account of the irrational element of adjudication reconstructs the authority of the ECJ and acquiescence in its jurisprudence – however porous it might have become – with an eye to sociologically reconstructed *de facto* legitimacy. In this respect, one can follow Weber who distinguished between three forms of legitimate rule: legal, traditional and charismatic.[43]

Arguably, for those asking no further questions, belief in legality is all there is. As long as things are done legally, the result is to be accepted. But legal rule, according to Weber, requires strict adherence to principles of legality, such as respect for clear language and strict construction.[44] This type of legitimacy, therefore, does not appear to be particularly promising when it comes to accounting for the jurisprudential mindset of the ECJ. Traditionalism is also a non-starter. Conceivably, the type of legitimacy that we are interested in must be cognate to what Weber imagined to be 'charismatic' authority.

Obviously, the interpretation of EU law is characterised by a negative element, namely the lack of fit with regard to the standards of modest legal reasoning. But interpretations are not just an array of sloppy judicial doctrines. There is also a positive element, which is the entrepreneurial ethos underwriting the relevant decisions. It is submitted that this might be the key to understanding the irrational allure of EU law.

Entrepreneurship, in the sense relevant here, is best understood as a mode of emancipating oneself from the constraints tying the more faint-hearted to an existing situation. In the context relevant to an economic actor, such as a businessperson, the constraints concern supply and demand.

Generally, emancipation from the shackles of the market can take three different forms. The first form of emancipation is epitomised by the early bourgeois ascent to the independent status of a gentleman.[45] Men of this type are wealthy enough not to have to work for a living. The second form, which is diametrically

[42] See M Kelman, *A Guide to Critical Legal Studies* (Cambridge, MA, Harvard University Press, 1988).

[43] See Weber, *Economy and Society* (n 25) vol 1, 212–40. See also (in German) M Weber, *Staatssoziologie: Soziologie der rationalen Staatsanstalt und der modernen politischen Parteien und Parlamente* (ed J Winckelmann) 2nd edn (Berlin, Duncker & Humblot, 1966) 99–110.

[44] See Weber, *Economy and Society* (n 25) vol 1, 789–92.

[45] See GS Wood, *The Radicalism of the American Revolution* (New York, Vintage Books, 1991).

opposed to the first, concerns the overcoming of individual competition through the cooperative planning of economic production. The third form of emancipation is that which has had the most enduring impact on how we conceive of being successfully human. Entrepreneurship is a mark of emancipation because true entrepreneurs no longer produce and deal in ordinary commodities. Those offering the n-th energy drink are likely to be what neoclassical economics calls 'price-takers'. If anything, cost-effectiveness is their path to success. People of this type can count as entrepreneurs only in the exceptional case that they are so innovative at cost-cutting that everyone else begins to look. The members of the family that operate the Walmart chain may well be a case in point, but they do not represent the archetypical case. Ordinarily, we admire as entrepreneurs those who succeed in making what they produce nearly irresistible for consumers. Consumers believe that they have to have it. Once they do, entrepreneurs overcome constraints because they are no longer price-takers. They can set the price at a level that suits their objectives.

Entrepreneurship is a wellspring of legitimacy. Not only are consumers ready to allow their taste to be dictated by the creators of great things, people rest content with having them enjoy the fruits of their success. The wealth amassed by Bill Gates or Mark Zuckerberg is scarcely ever a topic of political contestation. On the contrary, most people are awestruck when they realise what people of this type are able to accomplish through charitable foundations.

In a market society, entrepreneurs are what the aristocracy used to be in an ancient polity. They count as people who are superior to others because they are better at being human than the commoners belonging to the many.

It is not outlandish, then, by any stretch of the imagination, to treat entrepreneurship as a source of legitimacy in a Weberian sense. In Weber's understanding, legitimacy is the *de facto* readiness to accept authority. Entrepreneurship may well be a self-standing type, even though it clearly shares with charisma the strong element of representing that which is out of the ordinary.

Entrepreneurship may indeed be the key to understanding the allure of what might be called the 'progressive attitude' in international law, which in turn has left its mark in the ethos of the ECJ.[46]

This ethos is poised against sovereignty and encompasses the belief that the principles and elementary structures of international law give us the condition for a well-ordered society. Notably, progressive international law views the nation state not as the ultimate locus for the realisation of liberty, but as a scourge. Progressive international law is decidedly liberal in that it embraces the protection of individual rights and international economic relations. It posits that the fundamental

[46] On the following, see M Höpner, 'Der Europäische Gerichtshof als Motor der Integration: Eine akteursbezogene Erklärung' (2011) 21 *Berliner Journal für Soziologie* 203. See also M Koskenniemi, *The Politics of International Law* (Oxford, Hart Publishing, 2011) 273–76. On 'policy entrepreneurs' – a category that is well established in political science – see NC Roberts and PJ King, 'Policy Entrepreneurs: Their Activity Structure and Function on the Political Process' (1991) 2 *J-PART* 147.

principles of international law are amenable to insight, and that those possessing the relevant insight pass as reasonable people. By its very design, it embraces the elitist spirit of the enlightenment. Not surprisingly, it comes with a strong emphasis on output legitimacy.

Those committing themselves to the progress of public international law are not concerned with democracy, at any rate not in the first place, but with the right results and take it for granted that international adjudication is most likely the path to attain them. Realising good international order, however, requires active engagement on the part of legal scholars since good international order is still in the process of evolution. This is the most paradoxical feature of progressive public international law. Legal scholars have to bring about what they are supposed to apply. They need to be counterfactually asserting that there is already law in order to bring into existence the law that the project commits them to follow. This concerns, in particular, assertions of 'customary law' that thereby attains the quality of a self-fulfilling prophecy. Never mind the dirty little secret that it is safe to say that there is customary international law once the International Court has recognised its existence. Hence, the entrepreneurial spirit needs to nest in an institution that has the power to decide.

IV. Decisionism and Prophecy

Article 19 of the EU Treaty says that the Court of Justice shall ensure that in the interpretation and application of the Treaties the law is observed. Yet, the preliminary reference procedure implies that EU law 'is not just out there' – or, as Oliver Wendell Holmes once put it, 'a brooding omnipresence in the sky'[47] – but that it is to be known in the form of decisions.

The virtues of the preliminary reference procedure are well established. It helps to clarify what would otherwise remain opaque and vulnerable to multifarious expositions. In its judgments, the Court lays down rules governing future cases.[48] Precedents provide guidance and unify. Clarification and unification serve the ends of legality. The ECJ renders as clear what would otherwise remain shrouded in mystery. As a result of repeated clarifications, the preliminary reference procedure enhances the predictability of law. In contrast to having the law determined by a highest appellate court, it is less intrusive of Member State sovereignty, while at the same time more focused on the general clarification of laws. This sets the procedure apart from proceedings in which a court is charged with deciding cases.

Despite these widely recognised virtues, it is important to recognise what the existence of a preliminary reference procedure says about the law of which it is

[47] *Southern Pac Co v Jensen*, 244 US 205, 222 (1917) (J Holmes, dissenting).

[48] See Case 283/81 *Srl CILFIT and Lanificio di Gavardo SpA v Ministry of Health* EU:C:1982335 para 14.

to serve as a wellspring of insight. Its existence suggests that were it not for this procedure the law could not be known at all. It posits that divinations on the part of the ECJ are *essential* to knowing EU law.

The difference to an appellate system should be duly noted. A supreme court is instrumental in clarifying and consolidating the law. It is, however, in principle, only a *primus inter pares*, for there is no single court in which the legal system entrusts the *prerogative* of knowing the law with authority for all others. A supreme court is, when it comes to this task, merely the last in a sequence of contenders. In other words, it is not the one institution to which the legal system confers pre-emptive cognitive authority.[49]

In principle, the technique of knowing the law by virtue of decisions is not tied to the type of law that EU law represents. This technique could be attached to any other type of law. Even if one imagined a legal system that contained only the prohibition of murder and added to it a procedure enabling references concerning its meaning, people may feel encouraged to inquire what this prohibition *might* mean on top of what it is ordinarily taken to mean (eg, 'does it mean that government has to provide food as long as it is in a position to do so?'). The presence of a provision that promises clarification can easily create an incentive for pushing the envelope, even in the face of the risk that the institution providing the answer might say 'no'.

This incentive effect will take hold, however, only if the institution answering these questions is disposed to perform innovative moves. If preliminary references ended up on the desks of traditional legalists, their effect would likely remain unspectacular. In the eyes of traditionalists, the legal system does not act. It merely *reacts*. It is not, in particular, an agent of innovation and change. If properly activated, the law reacts appropriately, that is, in the manner in which it has been programmed to act. The programme is to be found in laws (and what results from the application of laws is 'legality' in the Franco-German sense).[50]

The whole process of question and answer promises to be lively and rewarding, however, if it is based on the premise that the programme triggering answers is not yet fully developed or perhaps not yet in place. In such a case, the legal system

[49] Granted, there are high courts everywhere, but their dispensation of clarification is the by-product of deciding final appeals. The basic supposition is that the law can be known, even though this may be difficult and tricky in singular cases. By contrast, the preliminary reference procedure, by conferring on the judiciary specifically the task of clarifying the law not only *à propos* the decision of disputes and by permitting references from all courts, represents a decisive break with the ordinary self-idealisation according to which the law can be known once it has been adopted and promulgated. For a related observation concerning a 'null proposition' according to which legal norms 'impose no meaningful *substantive* constraints' in the exercise of a court's review authority, see A Stone Sweet, 'The Juridical *Coup d'État* and the Problem of Authority: *CILFIT* and *Foto-Frost*' in M Poiares Maduro and L Azoulai (eds), *The Past and Future of EU Law: The Classics of EU Law Revisited on the 50th Anniversary of the Rome Treaty* (Oxford, Hart Publishing, 2010) 208.

[50] See L Besselink, F Pennings and S Prechal, 'Introduction: Legality in Multiple Legal Orders' in L Besselink, F Pennings and S Prechal (eds), *The Eclipse of the Legality Principle in the European Union* (Leiden, Wolters Kluwer, 2011).

will behave not reactively but proactively. It will begin to churn out new rules and thereby perform the task of a regulatory body.

It takes the entrepreneurial spirit of progressive public international law to make this happen. And those animated by this spirit made it happen because they were convinced that faithfulness to the mission of integration requires rewriting its laws.[51] After the failure of the European Defence Community in the French Assembly in 1954, the EEC Treaty was officially supposed to amount to far less than the blueprint of a federal system. Actually, from the perspective of the contracting parties, it just looked like another conventional international agreement and not at all like 'a new legal order of international law for the benefit of which the states have limited their sovereign rights'.[52] Nevertheless, committed European jurists, in particular working in the so-called *Groupe de redaction*, were able to build into the Treaty a number of elements that had the potential to unfold a more federalising dynamic.[53] The preliminary reference procedure was among those elements. While the Treaty was concluded in a far more muted spirit and emphasised the role of an intergovernmental Council, the juridical elite favouring a federal Europe was able to put in something bolder. Quite remarkably, therefore, the addition of the preliminary reference procedure *contributed* to the ambiguities that it had been designed to resolve. Its presence helped to constitute an indeterminacy that it was allowed to address.

Initially, the Member State governments perceived actions against Member States brought by the Commission or another Member State (then Articles 169 and 170) as major mechanisms for dealing with violations of treaties. Article 177 must originally not have seemed to be capable of giving direct effect to Community law vis-a-vis conflicting national law as part of a 'dual vigilance' system.[54] This explains, however, why initially objections were frequently made to preliminary references that indirectly concerned conflicting Member State laws, for no small part of the governments took it for granted that the procedures of Articles 169 and 170 offered the appropriate avenues for dealing with compliance matters.[55]

[51] On the following, see the very helpful hints to be found in M Rasmussen, 'From *Costa v Enel* to the Treaties of Rome: A Brief History of a Legal Revolution' in M Poiares Maduro and L Azoulai (eds), *The Past and Future of EU Law: The Classics of EU Law Revisited on the 50th Anniversary of the Rome Treaty* (Oxford, Hart Publishing, 2010) 81–83.

[52] See Case 26/62 *NV Algemene Transporten Expeditie Onderneming van Gend en Loos v Nederlandse Administratie der Belastingen* EU:C:1963:1.

[53] See A Boerger-De Smedt, 'Negotiating the Foundations of European Law, 1950–57: The Legal History of the Treaties of Paris and Rome' (2012) 21 *Contemporary European History* 339, 351.

[54] See Cases 28/62 to 30/62 *Da Costa en Schaake NV, Jacob Meijer VN and Hoescht-Holland NV v Nederlandse Belastingadministratie* EU:C:1963:6. For a wonderful introduction, see S Weatherill, *Law and Integration in the European Union* (Oxford, Oxford University Press, 1995). De Witte quite perceptively observes that the innovation brought about by the ECJ in the *Van Gend* case was that the question whether the Treaty was self-executing was decided by the supranational court and not by national courts pursuant to their respective constitutional traditions. See B de Witte, 'The Continuous Significance of Van Gend en Loos' in M Poiares Maduro and L Azoulai (eds), *The Past and Future of EU Law: The Classics of EU Law Revisited on the 50th Anniversary of the Rome Treaty* (Oxford, Hart Publishing, 2010) 10.

[55] See Rasmussen (n 51) 82.

From that angle, Article 177 was to be used in order to elucidate the meaning of regulations but not to resolve a conflict concerning sovereign powers. At the same time, it must have appeared also plausible to use Article 177 to that end, too. The ambiguity to which Article 177 gave rise, in particular with regard to direct effect and its own status in the treaty system, was not least resolved on the basis of this very same Article. But this proves, of course, the point that from the outset Union law was constituted in such a way as to require clarification by means of decisions.

It was no doubt ingenious on the part of the Court to realise that it is in the position of a real chooser.[56] It self-consciously occupied the spot from which the perceived imperfection could be addressed and inform the dynamics of European integration. The judges can act like prophets.

What, however, is remarkable about European decisionism is precisely its particular quasi-religious outlook. It is to this final point that our observations now turn.

V. Political-Theological Coda

There can be little doubt that, if anyone, Joseph Weiler has earned himself the reputation of being the principal political theologian of European integration. He deserves recognition in this capacity with regard to both the Jewish and the Christian religious traditions. From the perspective of Jewish religious history and theology, he views European integration as fuelled with messianic expectations.[57] The process is supposed to end an age-old division and bring harmony and abundance to an aggrieved continent. As Jakob Rendl and I tried to explain, however, there are reasons to doubt the accuracy of this view.[58] This question need not detain us here. At the same time, Weiler has also championed the idea that European integration is a decidedly Christian project.[59] Puzzlingly, Weiler identifies the Christian element of European integration in how the late Pope John Paul II characterised the open-minded and charitable attitude that Roman Catholic Christians ought to adopt towards strangers. Weiler establishes the connection to Christianity by claiming that this very same attitude is inherent in the normative ethos of integration. This is a rather far-fetched idea. One can easily imagine more plausible candidates for what would make contemporary

[56] It was, in a sense, a 'choice for Europe' to paraphrase the title of Moravcsik's famous book. A Moravcsik, *The Choice for Europe: Social Purpose and State Power from Messina to Maastricht* (London, UCL Press, 1998).

[57] See JHH Weiler, 'The Transformation of Europe Revisited: The Things that Do Not Transform' in M Poiares Maduro and M Wind (eds), *The Transformation of Europe: Twenty-Five Years On* (Cambridge, Cambridge University Press, 2017).

[58] See A Somek and J Rendl, 'Messianism, Exodus, and the Empty Signifier of European Integration' (2019) iCourts Working Paper Series No 175.

[59] See JHH Weiler, *Ein christliches Europa* (trans F Reimer, Salzburg, Anton Pustet, 2004).

Europe 'Christian', ranging from the tradition of the *respublica Christiana*[60] to the relevance of Christian democracy in post-war Western Europe.[61]

While neither of Weiler's ideas are ultimately convincing, it may well be the case that the truth lies, nonetheless, in between. Perhaps the attitude towards law and time that is characteristic of the Court's innovative jurisprudence matches how Christianity adapted messianism in order to fit it to a situation in which the coming of the Messiah did not complete the task of redemption. The community lives on, with redemption being limited to the soul of the believer,[62] in the expectation that there will (soon) be a second coming.

What does such a rather enigmatic situation, however, entail for the authority of the received moral and legal traditions (which are Jewish in the case of Christianity)? Taking one's cue from Agamben's interpretation of the letters of Paul the Apostle,[63] it can be said that the old laws are still valid but no longer have any application. While this may help to explain what happens to national law in the face of EU law,[64] the idea can be applied to the Treaties themselves. They are law, but they do not possess any real authority in the face of the upending of a community of nation states. Actually, being faithful to the process of integration requires moving beyond its current state, for otherwise one would scarcely ever arrive at the final destination. The interpretation of law that is faithful to the promise of redemption needs to become a law unto itself.

Suspending the force of existing law in the course of its exposition is undoubtedly a risky process. There is no guarantee outside their faith that the faithful will not go astray. They have to have faith that their faith will guide them through the troubled waters of history. The voice of the judge that thereby becomes a prophet is the voice of faith and confidence in European integration.

Is not this exactly what we have encountered time and again in the apodictic judicial pronouncements of the Court?

[60] See W Grewe, *Epochen der Völkerrechtsgeschichte* (Baden-Baden, Nomos Verlagsgesellschaft, 1984) 77.

[61] See T Judt, *Postwar: A History of Europe Since 1945* (New York, Penguin Press, 2005) 80, 484.

[62] See G Scholem, *The Messianic Idea in Judaism and Other Essays in Jewish Spirituality* (New York, Schocken Books, 1971) 1.

[63] See G Agamben, *The Time that Remains: A Commentary on the Letter to the Romans* (trans P Dailey, Stanford, CA, Stanford University Press, 2005) 95–97.

[64] Jakob Rendl would emphasise this aspect.

5

Analytics and European Union Courts: The Case of Trademark Disputes

SAMUEL DAHAN,* ROHAN BHAMBHORIA,** SIMON TOWNSEND*** AND XIAODAN ZHU****

I. Introduction

As the novel coronavirus has spread and courts around the world have closed in response to the pandemic, a technological transformation has taken place. Courts everywhere, including the Court of Justice of the European Union (CJEU; the Court), adopted new methods of communication, such as Zoom hearings. While the resilience and adaptability shown by courts should be applauded, this chapter contends that 'dropping hearings into Zoom'[1] does not constitute a paradigmatic shift. Grafting technology onto processes that are already broken is a temporary solution that will likely not address the long-standing access-to-justice problem in Europe.

The Covid-19 pandemic has only exacerbated the problem of access to justice. The number of people forced to represent themselves has ballooned over the last 20 years, including in the European Union (EU). As argued by a recent Organisation for Economic Co-operation and Development (OECD) study, more than four billion people live beyond the protection of lawyers, the law and courts.[2] This is further exacerbated in the EU context by the fact that 'access to justice' has

* Assistant Professor of Law, Queen's Law, Cornell Law, Director of the Conflict Analytics Lab, Canada; former Referendaire at the Court of Justice of the European Union.
** PhD Candidate at Queen's Electrical and Computer Engineering.
*** Former JD student at Queen's Law, Canada.
**** Associate Professor, Queen's Electrical and Computer Engineering; Vector Institute, Ingenuity Lab, Canada.

[1] Richard Susskind, 'Covid-19 Shutdown Shows Virtual Courts Work Better' *Financial Times* (7 May 2020), available at: www.ft.com/content/fb955fb0-8f79-11ea-bc44-dbf6756c871a.

[2] This is how Richard Susskind, a leading thinker on the intersection of access to justice and technology, ends his latest book. See R Susskind, *Online Courts and the Future of Justice* (Oxford, Oxford University Press, 2019) 299. See also Susskind, 'Covid-19 Shutdown Shows Virtual Courts Work Better' (n 1).

often been understood narrowly as having the right to access courts. As argued in the literature, the Treaties and pertinent CJEU case law define the concept of 'access to justice' primarily as the access of individuals or legal persons to the EU judicial system.[3]

We argue that this phenomenon should be understood in broader terms. Effective access to justice requires more that promoting access to courts and lawyers.[4] The true challenge for claimants is not merely finding a lawyer or standing directly before the CJEU. Often, the problem is that claimants have limited access to legal help and are sometimes unaware of EU rights violations or the existence of remedies. Accordingly, the challenge is to develop customised solutions that change how the justice system operates, not to digitise broken practices.[5] We believe technology may constitute one avenue for improving effective access to justice and especially legal help. A new generation of direct-to-public (DTP) artificial intelligence (AI) tools can improve access to justice by providing the minimal level of legal help necessary for meeting basic legal needs. Open AI technology has the potential to determine whether someone has a legitimate legal claim, to help lawyers and judges increase the efficiency of their service delivery, and to help litigants for whom litigation is otherwise out of reach.

This chapter goes on to explore the technological transformation triggered by Covid-19 (section II). Next, it discusses the access-to-justice crisis in Europe and shows that the technological transformation triggered by the pandemic is a temporary solution (section III). In the fourth, we focus on accessible AI-powered legal help and how such technology operates in practice. We have chosen trademark disputes as a test case given the recent innovations and implementation in this field. Specifically, we review how a combination of online dispute resolution (ODR) and predictive analytics employing machine learning and deep learning can positively affect EU trademark dispute resolution. The system operates as a legal aid tool for small- to medium-sized enterprises (SMEs) to determine potential Intellectual Property Rights violations. We then discuss empirical evidence concerning the feasibility and performance of the system, especially relating to image retrieval, services and goods classification, verbal comparison, and the predictability of trademark disputes, especially likelihood of confusion (section IV). Finally, we discuss how legal aid technology could affect court processes, with specific focus on how adjudicators may use AI technology adjudicators to make better and more consistent decisions (section V). Conclusions are presented at the end (section VI).

[3] M Pinedo, 'Access to Justice as Hope in the Dark: In Search for a New Concept in European Law' (2011) 1 *International Journal of Humanities and Social Science* 9.

[4] See K Roach and L Sossin, 'Access to Justice and Beyond' (2010) 60) *University of Toronto Law Journal* 373; TCW Farrow, 'What Is Access to Justice?' (2014) 51 *Osgoode Hall Law Journal* 957.

[5] See Susskind, 'Covid-19 Shutdown Shows Virtual Courts Work Better' (n 1).

II. Covid Technological Transformation

In March 2020, in response to the rapid spread of a newly identified coronavirus, SARS-CoV-2, court buildings around the world began to close. To ensure ongoing access to justice, governments and judiciaries rapidly introduced various forms of 'remote court': audio hearings (largely by telephone), video hearings (eg, via Skype and Zoom) and paper hearings (decisions delivered on the basis of written submissions only).[6] According to Courts Worldwide – a website designed to help the global community of justice workers to share their experiences of 'remote' alternatives to traditional court hearings – more than 50 countries adopted a digital response to the pandemic.[7] While many lawyers expressed reluctance about the prospect of virtual hearings, they quickly adapted, and some of them were converted overnight to the benefits of remote court.[8]

The EU justice system has not been spared Covid disruption. The Court had to demonstrate an exemplary crisis management response driven by adaptability and resilience.[9] The Court was forced to assess its working methods and accelerate transformations – not only relating to the judicial processes, but equally, to issues affecting its managerial aspects. In addition to remote working, a recent study published by a Court administrator suggests that the staff demonstrated an innovative and inventive spirit and the capacity to implement homemade solutions in the service of their respective objectives.

There is no doubt this transformation should be applauded. However, a question remains: does the digitalisation or 'Zoomification' of court operations constitute a radical paradigm shift that will address the crisis of access to justice in the EU?

The short answer is, probably not. Covid-19 may have triggered or accelerated a digital transformation in the justice system, but shifting hearings onto the Zoom platform will not solve the access-to-justice crisis. The 2016 OECD report suggests that more than four billion people live outside the protection of lawyers, courts and the law.[10] In some countries, the backlog is staggering: some 80 million cases in Brazil, for instance and 30 million in India. Even in advanced legal systems such as the EU, the process is often understandable only to lawyers and is too expensive for most people, and civil cases take far too long.[11]

[6] See generally 'Remote Courts', *Remote Courts Worldwide*, available at: www.remotecourts.org/.

[7] R Susskind, 'The Future of Courts' (2020) 6 *The Practice* 54. As of today, Remote Courts Worldwide report over 150 countries with remote hearing processes. See also 'Remote Courts' (n 6).

[8] S Dahan and D Liang, 'The Case for AI-Powered Legal Aid' (2021) 46 *Queen's Law Journal* 415.

[9] C Popotas, 'COVID-19 and the Courts. The Case of the Court of Justice of the European Union (CJEU)' (2021) 12 *International Journal for Court Administration* 22.

[10] See Organisation for Economic Co-operation and Development & Open Society Foundations, 'Leveraging the SDGs for Inclusive Growth: Delivering Access to Justice for All' (2016), available at: www.oecd.org/gov/delivering-access-to-justice-for-all.pdf.

[11] Susskind, 'Covid-19 Shutdown Shows Virtual Courts Work Better' (n 1).

Recent evidence suggests that Covid-19 has only exacerbated the crisis. In fact, disadvantaged groups are likely to experience increased legal need, and this is true for both individuals and SMEs. Accordingly, it is difficult to believe that the recent digitalisation of the CJEU and other European courts will suffice to address the problem. Richard Susskind notes that the Covid-19 shutdown constitutes a huge unscheduled pilot – a great experiment in the use of a variety of technologies in our courts. However, we are only at the foothills of the transformation.[12] The Covid-19 virus intervened and generated a sense of urgency that triggered superficial innovation under constraints.

We argue that there is a much more significant role for technology. However, before investigating any technological solutions, it is necessary to assess the EU access-to-justice problem itself.

III. Effective Access to EU Justice

A. The Legal Basis for Access to Justice

Effective access to justice is a fundamental right, as well as a general principle of EU law,[13] but it is not an absolute right, at least not in practice. In fact, the right of access to justice used to be understood in a restrictive manner, mainly as 'the aggrieved individual's formal right to litigate or defend a claim'.[14] The 'access to justice' within the meaning of the Treaty of Lisbon and the pertinent CJEU jurisprudence is primarily seen as access to the EU judicial system, ie to the EU Member States' national courts applying EU law or/and the CJEU.[15] The concept has, however, evolved from a mere formal right of access to a more comprehensive right, incorporating greater enforcement aspects and the right to legal aid which is the main focus of this study.[16]

In practical terms, effective access to courts requires that litigants be able to institute proceedings before a dispute resolution body. Article 47 of the EU Charter and Article 6(1) of the European Convention on Human Rights (ECHR) embodies the 'right of access to a court' while providing that everyone is entitled to a fair and

[12] See Susskind, 'The Future of Courts' (n 7) 4.

[13] G Cuniberti, 'The Recognition of Foreign Judgments Lacking Reasons in Europe: Access to Justice, Foreign Court Avoidance, and Efficiency' (2008) 1 *International & Comparative Law Quarterly* 25.

[14] Nathy Rass-Masson and Virginie Rouas, 'Effective Access to Justice' (European Parliament, DG Internal Policies, 2017), available at: www.europarl.europa.eu/RegData/etudes/STUD/2017/596818/IPOL_STU(2017)596818_EN.pdf.

[15] N Daminova, '"Access to Justice" and the Development of the Van Gend En Loos Doctrine: The Role of Courts and of the Individual in EU Law', available at: www.vdu.lt/cris/handle/20.500.12259/35949.

[16] M Cappelletti, J Weisner and M Seccombe (eds), *Access to Justice and the Welfare State* (Publications of the European University Institute, Alphen aan den Rijn, Sijthoff, 1981), available at: cadmus.eui.eu//handle/1814/18560.

public hearing within a reasonable time by an independent and impartial tribunal established by law.[17] More importantly, according to the case law of the European Court of Human Rights (ECtHR), the right of access to a court must be practical and effective, which means that litigants must have a clear and practical opportunity to challenge an act that interferes with their rights.[18]

The EU Treaties, however, refer to 'access to justice' without defining it. Article 67(4) of the Treaty on the Functioning of the European Union (TFEU) provides that 'the Union shall facilitate access to justice, notably through the principle of mutual recognition of judicial and extrajudicial decisions in civil matters'. Article 81(2)(e) of the TFEU states that the EU shall adopt measures, particularly when necessary, for the proper functioning of the internal market, to ensure effective access to justice in the field of civil justice. Article 47 of the EU Charter provides for the right to an effective remedy and to a fair trial. It states that if the legal protections of those whose rights and freedoms are guaranteed by EU law are violated, those people are entitled to an effective remedy before a tribunal. Articles 6 and 13 of the ECHR also recognise the right to a fair trial and the right to an effective remedy, respectively.

European courts have also played a significant role in the development of the concept. According to the CJEU, access to justice is one of the constitutive elements of a Union based on the rule of law,[19] and individuals must be able to obtain reparation when their rights are infringed by a breach of Union law for which a Member State can be held responsible.[20] The ECtHR has also developed the right of access to justice in the context of Article 6, enlarging the scope of the notion of 'civil rights' such that considerable parts of administrative law are now also safeguarded by this provision.[21]

[17] See *Golder v the United Kingdom* App no 4451/70 para 36. See also the Guide on Article 6 of the European Convention on Human Rights, available at: 16 www.echr.coe.int/Documents/Guide_Art_6_ENG.pdf.

[18] See ECtHR case *Bellet v France*, Series A no 333-B paras 36–38; see Communication from the Commission to the European Parliament, the Council, the European Central Bank, the European Economic and Social Committee and the Committee of the Regions COM(2018) 364 final EU Intellectual Property Office (EUIPO), Intellectual Property (IP) SME Scoreboard 2016.

[19] European Union Agency for Fundamental Rights, *Access to Justice in Europe: An Overview of Challenges and Opportunities* (European Union Agency for Fundamental Rights, FRA, 2011) 17. It is argued that this can be seen in the CJEU's reasoning for establishing the principles of direct effect (Case 26-62 *Van Gend en Loos* EU:C:1963:1) and supremacy (Case 6/64 *Costa v ENEL* EU:C:1964:66), as well as the concept of state liability (Case C-6/90 and C-9/90 *Francovich and Bonifaci v Italy* EU:C:1991:428) and the requirement that national remedies for breaches of rights derived from Community law comply with the principles of equivalence and effectiveness (Case C-78/98 *Preston v Wolverhampton Healthcare NHS Trust* EU:C:2000:247).

[20] European Union Agency for Fundamental Rights (n 19) 18–19.

[21] European Union Agency for Fundamental Rights and European Union Council of Europe, *Handbook on European Law Relating to Access to Justice* (Publications Office of the European Union 2016) 16.

B. The EU Access to Justice Problem

The direct standing criteria of individual applicants ('any natural or legal persons') include 'one of the most contentious issues' for the EU access to justice debate.[22] In fact, the literature has argued that the Treaties and pertinent CJEU case law define the concept of 'access to justice' primarily as the access of individuals or legal persons (*Van Gend en Loos*) to the EU judicial system.[23] Accordingly, the CJEU has been much criticised over the years for its narrow interpretation of direct standing rules of individual applicants.[24]

However, we argue that access to justice should be understood in broader terms. For instance, recent studies have shed light on a new judicial approach, whereby EU courts act according to judicial subsidiarity: that is, by reducing CJEU intervention and enabling judicial matters to be resolved closer to the citizen.[25] What this means is that private applicants are left to seek judicial protection via national jurisdictional venues or EU agencies, as opposed to challenging legislative proceedings directly at the international level. Viewing this evolution through the prism of judicial subsidiarity serves to accentuate the important role of national courts in promoting access to EU law and the need to appreciate these, alongside the CJEU, as the 'guardians' of the EU legal order.[26]

While this evolution may be applauded, it poses additional hurdles for individual applicants and EU courts. Access to courts, at both the national and EU level, without legal help and representation is an incomplete solution that may reinforce the already severe access-to-justice problem.

Recent evidence shows that lack of legal representation is a growing problem.[27] The number of people forced to represent themselves has ballooned over the last 20 years, and the Covid-19 pandemic has only exacerbated the access-to-justice problem. Chief among the causes of this phenomenon are the high cost of litigation and the complexification of legal issues and court processes. This does not affect only low-income Europeans and SMEs: many people with average incomes are also priced out of the justice system. Hiring a lawyer for low-cost disputes makes little financial sense in most cases, as the legal fees are often higher than the value of the disputes.

Another problem deserving of attention is the consistency of case law at both the national and EU level. In fact, there are many instances where national courts

[22] Case C-583/11P *Inuit Tapiriit Kanatami and Others* EU:C:2013:625; Case C-583/11P *Inuit Tapiriit Kanatami and Others* EU:C:2013:21, Opinion of AG Kokott.

[23] Pinedo (n 3).

[24] S Bogojević, 'Judicial Protection of Individual Applicants Revisited: Access to Justice through the Prism of Judicial Subsidiarity' (2015) 34 *Yearbook of European Law* 5.

[25] ibid.

[26] Opinion of the Court (Full Court) of 8 March 201 pursuant to Article 218(11) TFEU – Draft agreement – Creation of a unified patent litigation system – European and Community Patents Court – Compatibility of the draft agreement with the Treaties ECLI:EU:C:2011:123.

[27] Rass-Masson and Rouas (n 14) 61–78.

have expressed an unwillingness to apply EU law, including the preliminary ruling procedure, when exercising this discretion.[28] Examples include cases where national courts have challenged the supremacy of EU law without further referring the case to the CJEU for interpretation,[29] and records of individual applicants attempting to challenge the implementation of EU law but being rejected of the national courts' own accord.[30]

In addition to intentional divergences, there are many instances where national and EU courts have adopted judgments that are inconsistent with previous case law, thus creating uncertainty for the applicants. So far, the consistency requirement has not emerged as an independent legal principle at either level. However, it is a guarantee of the rule of law and has been described as a standard for rational public administration.[31]

IV. AI-Powered Legal Tools in the EU Justice System

Effective access to justice requires more than enhancing access to courts and lawyers.[32] The challenges for claimants are not limited to finding lawyers or standing before the CJEU. Often, the problem is that claimants do not have access to legal assistance and may not even be aware of their EU rights or the existence of remedies. They need a coherent and accessible system of remedies. We believe technology may help to achieve that goal.

Although recent data suggest that the Covid technology response has been welcomed by court users, there is a much more significant role that technology can play.[33] The pandemic should be seen as an opportunity to encourage a genuine policy-learning process whereby policymakers and courts develop new judicial tools.

One solution is to extend the role of the courts beyond their primary function of delivering authoritative binding adjudications. This is what Susskind calls the 'extended court'.[34] The idea is that technology can provide a service with a

[28] B Smulders and K Eisele, 'Reflections on the Institutional Balance, the Community Method and the Interplay between Jurisdictions after Lisbon' (2012) 31 *Yearbook of European Law* 112, 123.

[29] ibid 112, 123. Recently, BVerfG, Judgment of the Second Senate of 5 May 2020 – 2 BvR 859/15 – paras 1-237, available at: www.bverfg.de/e/rs20200505_2bvr085915en.html.

[30] See for instance, *R (HS2 Action Alliance Ltd) v The Secretary of State for Transport* [2014] UKSC 3 paras 155–56. See case law analysis, D Edwards, 'HS2: The First Spike' (2014) 26 *Journal of Environmental Law* 319, 319; V Heyvaert, J Thornton and R Drabble, 'With Reference to the Environment: The Preliminary Reference Procedure, Environmental Decisions and the Domestic Judiciary' (2014) 130 *Law Quarterly Review* 413, 413.

[31] J Langer and W Sauter, 'The Consistency Requirement in EU Law' (2017) 24 *Columbia Journal of European Law* 39.

[32] See Roach and Sossin (n 4); Farrow (n 4).

[33] Dahan and Liang (n 8).

[34] 'Remote Courts' (n 6).

much wider remit than a traditional court. This includes, but is not limited to, improving access to legal representation and legal help. This section focuses on direct-to-public legal assistance technology, which includes decision trees; diagnostic systems that can help court users understand their entitlements and identify the options for resolution; tools that can help non-lawyers organise evidence and formulate arguments; and mediation and other dispute resolution services.

A. AI-Based Legal Help

Machine learning and deep learning, which fall under the general category of 'artificial intelligence', have progressed significantly in recent years. They have reached a point at which judgments, including those of EU courts, can be used not only for the lawyer to understand the application of legal principles, but also for computers to apply that reasoning to create a computerised prediction for new fact patterns.[35]

Statistical machine learning has shown great promise for the development of predictive tools capable of evaluating the odds of winning cases or estimating damages. The application of AI to law has the potential to shed new light on how legal decisions are made, illuminating the evolution of case law and the consistency (and predictability) of judicial decisions. It is important to note that machine learning is not applicable to every sub-field of law and is unable to contend with large amounts of data. These techniques are generally intended to be used with highly processed data. The most promising areas of application concern legal questions in which the court's determination lends itself to identifying a discrete set of factors, and for which sufficient historical data exist which can be manually annotated.

In addition, providing access to efficient AI systems could create invaluable AI-powered legal aid tools for improving access to justice, currently a prominent issue in Europe and North America. AI-based legal assistance tools are a direct-to-public technology that can help members of the public locate and identify legal information, as well as provide assistance with routine questions, legal system navigation, contract analysis, legal document generation and outcome prediction.

[35] S Dahan, 'AI-Powered Trademark Dispute Resolution' (European Union Intellectual Property Office (EUIPO), 2020) Expert Opinion; S Dahan and Others, 'Predicting Employment Notice Period with Machine Learning: Promises and Limitations' (2020) 65 *McGill Law Journal* 711; B Alarie, A Niblett and A Yoon, 'Using Machine Learning to Predict Outcomes in Tax Law' (Social Science Research Network 2017) SSRN Scholarly Paper ID 2855977, available at: papers.ssrn.com/abstract=2855977; Daniel L Chen and Jess Eagel, 'Can Machine Learning Help Predict the Outcome of Asylum Adjudications?' *Proceedings of the 16th Edition of the International Conference on Artificial Intelligence and Law* (ACM, 2017), available at: doi.acm.org/10.1145/3086512.3086538; S Dahan, M Cohen and C Rule, 'Conflict Analytics: When Data Science Meets Dispute Resolution' [2020] *Management Business Review*; R Copus, R Hubert and H Laqueur, 'Credible Prediction: Big Data, Machine Learning and the Credibility Revolution' in M Livermore and D Rockmore (eds), *Law as Data: Computation and the Future of Legal Analysis* (Santa Fe, NM, SFI Press, 2019), available at: papers.ssrn.com/abstract=3156795.

Self-help tools are not new. The first experiments – rule-based expert systems – date back to the 1980s.[36] Since then, several courts around the world have developed legal help tools. For example, the Solution Explorer of the Civil Resolution Tribunal in British Columbia provides a guided pathway through the law, integrated with an online negotiation facility that allows users to reach informal agreements themselves.[37] If the negotiation does not work, a case manager helps facilitate an agreement. Then, if a settlement has still not been achieved, an adjudicator can render a formal decision, akin to a court order.

The authors argue that legal help tools should ideally be part of the public court service and not outsourced to the private sector. The main reason is that the current combination of available legal websites and tools – mostly private initiatives – can confuse lay people. In addition, it is also difficult for non-lawyers to determine whether the materials are accurate or up to date. That being said, it is unlikely that in the near future courts will find the resources to invest in such costly and time-consuming developments.

As a result, most leading AI legal initiatives remain the result of private sector initiatives for the benefit of the legal profession. For instance, legal technology companies, including Lex Machina, Blue J Legal, and Ross, have used analytics to develop predictive tools capable of determining how courts will rule on a specific legal issue, as well as the odds of winning a case.[38] Leading research institutions, such as CodeX at Stanford Law, Cyberjustice at the University of Montreal, SMART Law at HEC Paris, and the Conflict Analytics Lab (CAL) at Queen's University, have also engaged in data analytics research. It is important to note that these institutions have mainly focused on using technology to improve access to justice or have undertaken a more theoretical agenda.

For instance, the CAL at Queen's launched an AI-powered legal aid system during the pandemic – MyOpenCourt.org – to help workers and SMEs. The system uses AI to determine the odds of winning a case in the fields of employment law, vaccine injury, personal injury and bankruptcy, and will soon include EU trademark law (which will be the focus of this section). Should the algorithm conclude that a user has a legitimate legal claim, MyOpenCourt offers the option of working with a dispute resolution professional (a lawyer or a mediator) to resolve the disputes online.[39]

[36] Wikipedia, 'Legal Expert System' Wikipedia (2021), available at: en.wikipedia.org/w/index.php?title=Legal_expert_system&oldid=997811220; DH Berman and CD Hafner, 'The Potential of Artificial Intelligence to Help Solve the Crisis in Our Legal System' (1989) 32 *Communications of the ACM* 928.

[37] See generally: 'Civil Resolution Tribunal': civilresolutionbc.ca/.

[38] Dahan, Cohen and Rule (n 35).

[39] To this date, MyOpenCourt has already attracted more than 10,000 users and the researchers are now considering building an assisted negotiation algorithm trained on past negotiation agreements.

B. AI Tools in Practice: The Case of Trademark Disputes

There are various ways in which the application of predictive legal technology can enhance the accessibility of EU justice. We believe that trademark disputes provide a particularly useful test case for the viability of this technology for two reasons. First, there has been remarkable innovation in AI in the field of trademark disputes and registrations in the last few years. Machine learning and deep learning with computer vision have developed to the point where AI can assess the similarity between marks as well as good and services, flagging potential conflicts. Second, commercial search and IP agencies have been at the forefront of technological developments. In 2018, the World Intellectual Property Organization (WIPO) convened a review of the experiences of intellectual property offices that had experimented with AI algorithms to increase efficiency and reduce costs.[40] Several agencies, including the Australian IP office, the European Union Intellectual Property Office (EUIPO) and the WIPO, have also used the commercially available TrademarkVision Image Recognition software for this purpose. The software incorporates a deep learning-based reverse-image search, similar to the facial recognition algorithms of Facebook and Google but applied to figurative marks and logos.[41]

Considering that we do not have access to the algorithms or datasets developed by these companies, we are unable to review in detail how these tools operate. However, the authors have explored new AI approaches to deploy an open-access trademark confusion assessment system.[42] Accordingly, this section draws from the larger algorithmic work of a structured, extensive database of likelihood of confusion cases from both the General Court and the EUIPO.[43] Much of the technology developed in this project relies on the classification of legal text in a database and the use of advanced algorithms to derive predictions from this structured data.

For the purpose of this research, we gathered data relevant to assessing the likelihood of trademark confusion, mostly consisting of case law from the EUIPO and the General Court, but also all the trademarks officially registered. The determination of likelihood of confusion is in principle governed by a set of objective factors established by Article 8(1)(b) of the EUIPO Trademark Guidelines. It reads:

> [I]f because of its identity with, or similarity to, the earlier trade mark and the identity or similarity of the goods or services covered by the trade marks **there exists a**

[40] See generally the Meeting of Intellectual Property Offices (IPOS) on ICT Strategies and Artificial Intelligence (AI) for IP Administration, 23–25 May 2018, Geneva (WIPO/IP/ITAI/GE/18). The responses to a survey relating to AI usage are contained in the WIPO Secretariat, 'Original Replies from IPOs in English, French or Spanish' 29 March 2018 (WIPO/IP/ITAI/GE/18/2 REV).

[41] World Trademark Review (31 October 2018), 'Clarivate Analytics Snaps Up TrademarkVision as New Research Offerings Eyed', available at: www.worldtrademarkreview.com/ip-offices/clarivate analytics-snaps-trademarkvision-new-research-offerings-eyed.

[42] The research was developed by the Conflict Analytics Lab at Queen's University, in collaboration with Professor Zhu from the Vector Institute and the Ingenuity Labs.

[43] The authors have produced an extensive study for EUIPO on the feasibility of predictive analytics in the field of trademarks.

> **likelihood of confusion** on the part of the public in the territory in which the earlier trade mark is protected; the **likelihood of confusion includes the likelihood of association** with the earlier trade mark (emphasis added).[44]

The factors relevant to a court's assessment of likelihood of confusion, derived from Article 8(1)(b), are as follows: comparison of goods and services; relevant public and degree of attention; comparison of signs; distinctiveness of the earlier mark; any other factors; and global assessment of likelihood of confusion. These factors and other aspects of judgments by the General Court or the EUIPO were transcribed into a database. Using that amalgamation of data, a machine-learning algorithm can provide an assessment of likelihood of confusion. In theory, most or all of the reasoning of the General Court and the EUIPO on Article 8(1)(b) can be used to aid users (decision-makers and litigants) seeking to register a trademark in assessing legal risk and/or creating legal certainty.

The research relies on three complementary deep-learning and machine-learning models, which will be weighed together to determine the likelihood of confusion between marks, represented as a percentage. The following sections will thus explore how these models operate to generate a likelihood of confusion assessment.

i. NICE Classification of Goods and Services

Based on a description of goods and services provided by a user, the model determines which class a particular mark belongs to according to the Nice Classification. It can also identify the keywords in the description that led to that classification. In other words, a user would at the outset provide the system with a description of the goods and services, in natural language, without any understanding of the legal implications of their description, and the system would then classify the trademark into the correct Nice Class. This automatic classification system is trained on EUIPO and General Court case law. A mock-up of this design is shown in Figure 1. Early evidence already shows a high level of accuracy on that assessment.

Table 1 shows how the model operates in more technical terms. The classification model was developed using extensive historical data – the case text of the General Court – and successive rounds of machine training. In other words, the model learned how the Court has used the Nice Classification with 'term frequency–inverse document frequency' (TF-IDF) algorithms. The model converts sample text into numerical representations. These numbers are in turn classified by 'Multinomial Naïve Bayes' (MNB) functions that output a corresponding Nice Classification for users.[45]

[44] EUIPO Trademark Guidelines, Section 2 Double identity and Likelihood of Confusion, available at: guidelines.euipo.europa.eu/1803468/1788020/trade-mark-guidelines/section-2-double-identity-and-likelihood-of-confusion.

[45] The development of both the TF-IDF and MNB processes involved the fine-tuning of multiple hyper-parameters designed to optimise our predictive accuracy, while the MNB classifier minimises error via iterative learning.

Figure 1 Mock-up design of NICE Classification of Goods and Services

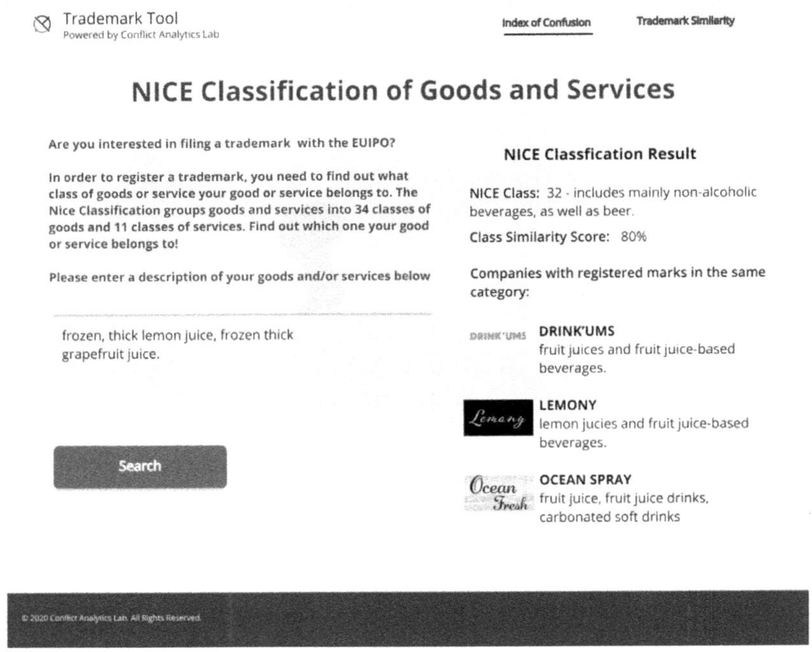

Table 1 Importance of tokens (words) in making predictions where all cases belong to the true Nice Class of '1'

Text with Highlighted Words for Interpretability	Confidence of Prediction	Outcome
Chemical composition material use cosmetic Additives Chemical use binding asphalt Gluten industrial purpose Additives Chemical use repairing asphalt citric acid adhesive industrial purpose Emulsifiers use manufacture cosmetic Gluten industrial use Glucose industrial purpose Fatty acid industrial purpose Gluten food industry Roofing adhesive starch use manufacturing industry Produce stabilizer used preserving food Salts industrial purpose flour industrial purpose Glutamic acid industrial purpose Asphalt release agent Raw salt Amino acid industrial purpose acid pectin industrial purpose chemical used oil drilling Chemicals used industry potassium chloride emulsifier starch industrial purpose polyols Glucose syrup industrial purpose Chemical polymer artificial sweetener Cationic polymer Glucose food industry Chemical product absorbing Starch use industry Adhesives paving Dough	1 1.00 5 0.00 7 0.00 40 0.00 Other 0.00	Correct
We provide chemicals for cosmetics which can be used for cosmetic additives. Some of the chemicals that we provide include glucose, gluten, glutamic acid and glucose syrup.	1 0.84 5 0.11 35 0.04 30 0.01 Other 0.01	Correct

(continued)

Table 1 ***(Continued)***

Text with Highlighted Words for Interpretability	Confidence of Prediction	Outcome
We provide various chemicals which may be useful in the form of additives. Some of the chemicals that we provide include gluten for industrial purposes and stabilizers which can be used to produce food salts.	5: 0.92 1: 0.04 35: 0.03 42: 0.00 Other: 0.01	Wrong

The results indicate that our model exceeds accuracy expectations insofar as the model predicts the correct class with 94 per cent accuracy. Furthermore, the model indicates high reliability across other measures including precision, recall, and f1-score. Our findings also suggest that the TF-IDF model outperforms statistical models insofar as it overcame the 'bias' identified in the EUTM Open Dataset. As shown in Figure 2, some classes are more frequent than others – 9, 35, 41 and 42.

Figure 2 Distribution of classes in EUTM Open Dataset[46]

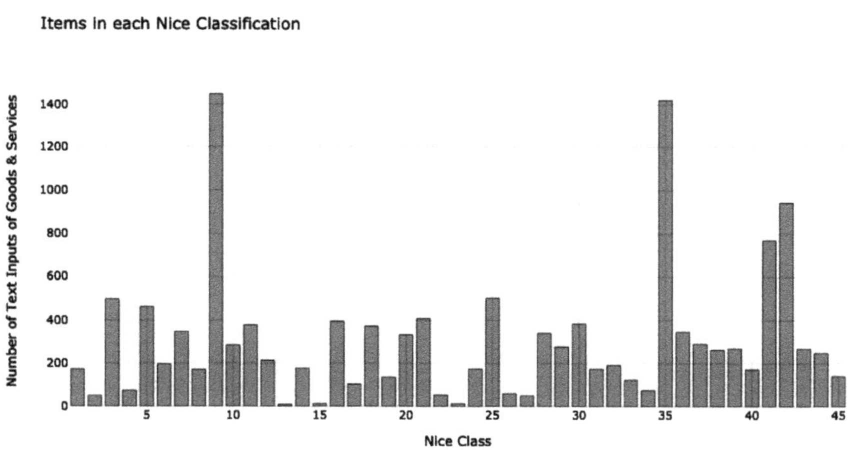

In this context, a basic statistical machine-learning model – unable to capture the actual words – would be biased towards these classes, assuming that they are statistically more likely to occur. That being said, word-frequency models also have limitations as shown in Table 1. The main weakness of this model is its inability to understand natural language, ie readable language. The word frequency was only trained on Nice Classification headings and terms, which are not natural terms that would be employed by a user.

[46] See: euipo.europa.eu/ohimportal/en/open-dat.

Several agencies have used commercially created AI algorithms to automatically recommend classes for goods and services contained in trademark applications.[47] For instance, in order to avoid rejections based on inaccurate terminology or mistaken classifications, the Intellectual Property Office of Singapore (IPOS) has developed an International Classification of Goods and Services (ICGS) Autochecker software tool, which relies on a Natural Language Processing AI system. China, Japan and Germany have also apparently invested in such systems, while WIPO is working on an AI feature that will predict the most relevant Nice Class. (This would be a replica of the model we have presented in this section.)

ii. Visual Analysis of Trademark Images and Logos

Comparing images and logos is a difficulty for the human brain. There is an information processing challenge when it comes to comparing figurative marks. In addition, as argued by Professor Dev Gangjee, there are several, oftentimes subjectively prioritised, parameters according to which similarity might be assessed.[48]

Accordingly, it is not surprising that computer vision innovations were welcomed by IP offices and practitioners. This seems like an enhancement that merely allows users of registries to do what they already do, but better. Trademark registry officials, analysts and lawyers can focus on what is important – analysing relevant results in greater detail – as opposed to spending time on searching for those results through trial and error.[49]

Thanks to advanced computer vision, the system would identify the images 'most similar' to the uploaded trademark and provide a similarity assessment. Both WIPO and the EUIPO offer a similarity search tool (TM View). This new AI-based system innovates 'by using deep machine learning to identify combinations of concepts – such as an apple, an eagle, a tree, a crown, a car, a star – within an image to find similar marks that have previously been registered'.[50] However, it is worth noting that the system's output consists of a list of similar figures that can be filtered by class and jurisdiction. While this initiative should be applauded, it is apparent that there is room for improvement.

Findings suggest that our computational model for the visual analysis of trademark images or logos represents a meaningful improvement on the existing standard, ie TMView (Figure 3).

[47] Dev Saif Gangjee, 'Eye, Robot: Artificial Intelligence and Trade Mark Registers' in N Bruun et al (eds), *Transition and Coherence in Intellectual Property Law* (Cambridge, Cambridge University Press, 2020) 4.

[48] ibid 7.

[49] ibid 8.

[50] WIPO Launches State-of-the-Art Artificial Intelligence-Based Image Search Tool for Brands, 1 April 2019 (PR/2019/831), available at: www.wipo.int/pressroom/en/articles/2019/article_0005.html.

Figure 3 Mock-up design for Content-Based Logo Retrieval (input) – Mock-up design for outcome of Content Based Logo Retrieval. Three key aspects are prominent in this tool: (1) retrieving accurate results; (2) providing feedback in the form of saliency maps; and (3) predicting classification in the form of text or the Vienna Code

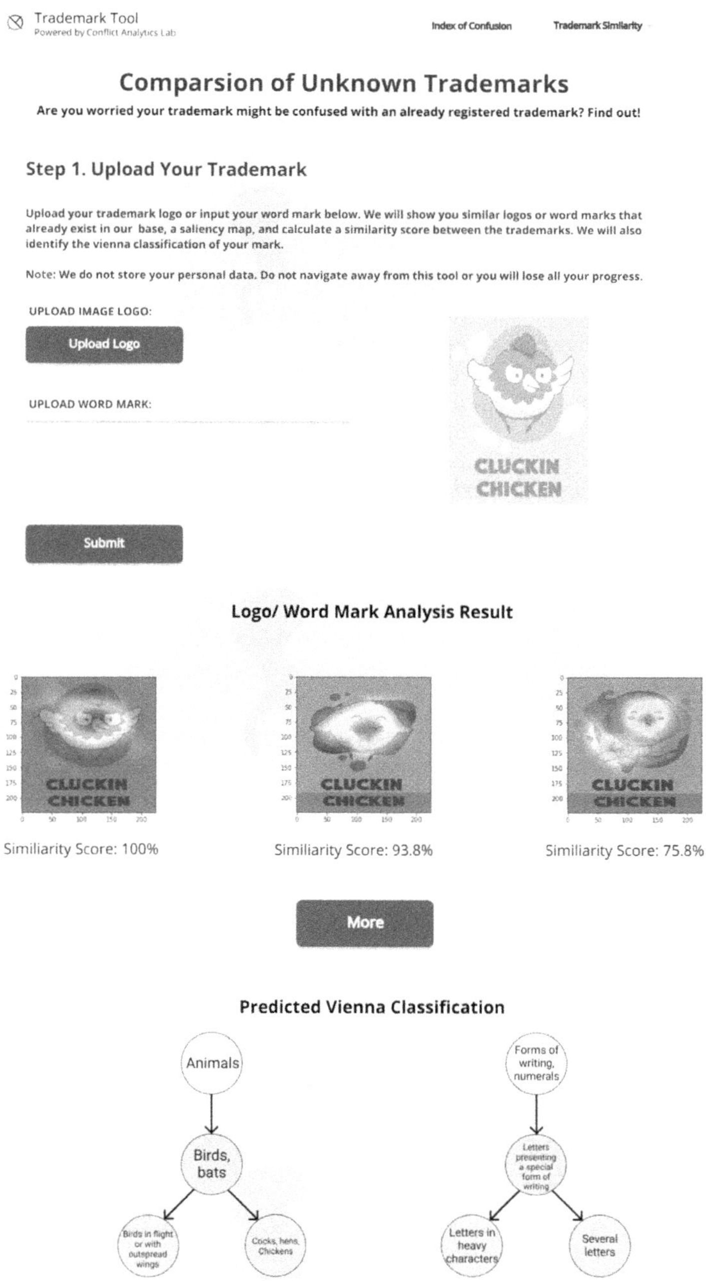

Current deep-learning models fail to attend to the most appropriate or relevant visual cues within sample images. It can be argued that the classic models underperform mainly because of the underlying pre-training, which would have been sourced from natural images,[51] and notably exclude two-dimensional, abstract images that are hand-drawn.

As a result, we believe there is a functional gap between the pre-training and fine-tuning processes in current image models. To bridge the gap, we propose furthering the process of training on large, weakly supervised datasets[52] that are available for trademark logos, and to further take into consideration fine-grained visual cues via object localisation.[53] The purported model will perform more accurately on various tasks such as image retrieval, and potentially even more important tasks such as automated Vienna classification of unseen images.

It is also worth exploring a revised model that can combine different measures of similarity – such as the words and images in the two complex marks being compared – to achieve an integrative assessment. The idea is to mimic the assessment of a human examiner who combines visual, aural and conceptual similarities to reach an overall conclusion.

iii. Assessment of the Verbal Elements

Verbal models can also compare trademarks' verbal elements (or verbal trademarks).[54] Users provide their sample text, which are in turn cross-compared with existing marks, generating quantitative similarity scores for every corresponding match. Moreover, the model qualifies sample text contextually to define 'related words' that might be linked to other marks by means of external knowledge bases.[55]

The system would rely on: (a) an external knowledge base (Princeton University's WordNet),[56] which contains relationships between words; and (b) a matrix featuring representations (embeddings) of words in order to identify common characters between the most similar company names (see Figure 4). Drawing upon these models, the system would assess the phonetic similarity from a normative standpoint and translate this assessment into legal terms. For example, any level of verbal similarity above 90 per cent could translate to a 'high'

[51] Jia Deng and Others, 'ImageNet: A Large-Scale Hierarchical Image Database' 2009 IEEE Conference on Computer Vision and Pattern Recognition (2009).

[52] Maxime Oquab and Others, 'Is Object Localization for Free? Weakly-Supervised Learning with Convolutional Neural Networks' *Proceedings of the IEEE Conference on Computer Vision and Pattern Recognition* (2015).

[53] Zhong-Qiu Zhao and Others, 'Object Detection with Deep Learning: A Review' (2019) 30 *IEEE Transactions on Neural Networks and Learning Systems* 3212.

[54] Dahan (n 35).

[55] Ali Muttaleb Hasan, 'A Proposed Method Using the Semantic Similarity of WordNet 3.1 to Handle the Ambiguity to Apply in Social Media Text' in Noorhuzaimi Mohd Noor and Others (eds), *Information Science and Applications* (Singapore, Springer, 2020).

[56] ibid.

level of phonetic similarity based on the following scale: low, average, high, or identical.[57]

Figure 4 Comparison of Verbal Elements of the Marks

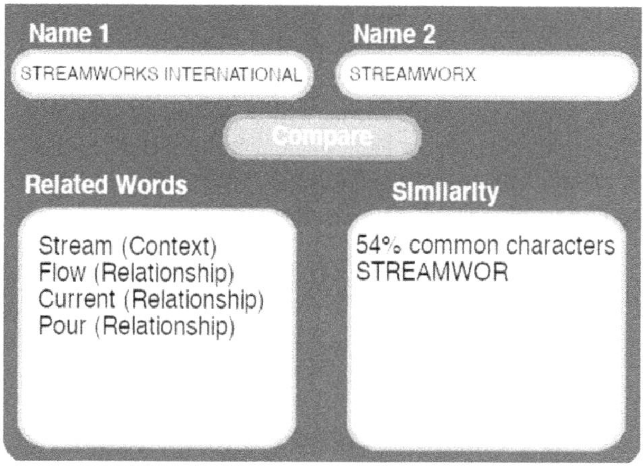

iv. Interpretable Outcome

This component of the confusion assessment relies on a highly supervised machine-learning system trained on the case law of the General Court of the EU. Unlike end-to-end methods, which can produce results solely from raw text, this technique requires significant effort in the collection, organisation and harmonisation of the legal and non-legal factors relevant to likelihood of confusion. To that end, we have constructed an extensive dataset of likelihood of confusion cases. The database is structured around legally relevant factual predictors – the features that judges take into consideration in determining likelihood of confusion, and that are available prior to the formulation of any judgment.

This model would partially rely on a user questionnaire, in addition to computer-generated scores. For example, a user may be asked: is your product a pharmaceutical product? If the user answers 'yes', we know from Article 8(1)(b) judgments that pharmaceutical products garner a higher degree of attention, which will therefore lead to a higher score under the 'relevant public' factor. The higher score will be translated to a summary of the hypothetical situation, along with the results from other answers in the questionnaire and automatically generated scores. The summary may state, 'The relevant public's attention to the

[57] Note that all scales used in the dataset (discussed below), correspond with the legal descriptions of each category in the applicable EUIPO guidelines. If the guidelines indicate that the scale on a particular factor applied by judges of the EUIPO or General Court can range from weak, minimal, normal, above average, to high (as with the distinctiveness of a common aspect), then that is the scale used to collect factors on the judgments.

marks is high; the phonetic similarity between the signs is low; the visual similarity between the signs is high', and so on. The block of text will be compared with all EUIPO raw text decisions to determine whether there is a likelihood of confusion.

In other words, the output generated by the questionnaire is a unique fact pattern that will be compared with previous cases in the database to find similar cases and determine whether there is confusion (see Figure 5). This is only possible because previous cases will have been labelled as resulting in 'confusion' or 'no confusion', so that the programme will be tooled to compare the summary with thousands of previous decisions;[58] and when the system identifies a matching fact pattern, it would claim that the EUIPO or General Court would likely make a similar decision (assuming the Court decides to follow its own case law).

Figure 5 Mock-up design of a subjective tool for a user to introduce their own bias based on results provided to them in previous stages

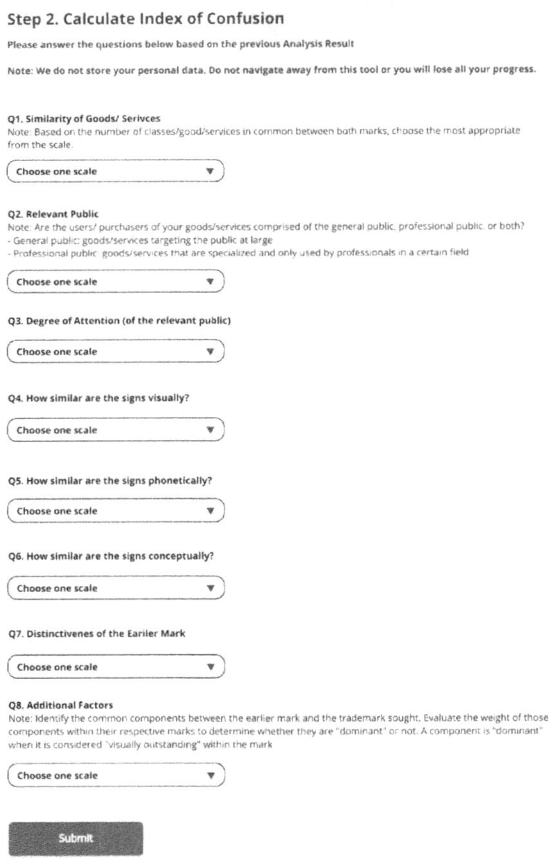

[58] Note that the text output may be generated automatically without the use of a questionnaire, and be based on the computer's assessment of the facts inputted by a user and the corresponding images as they relate to already-registered images.

Figure 6 Mock-up design of results obtained from subjective inputs. Results contain the following: (1) Outcome; (2) Confidence of outcome; and (3) Relevant text from cases corresponding to inputs by user

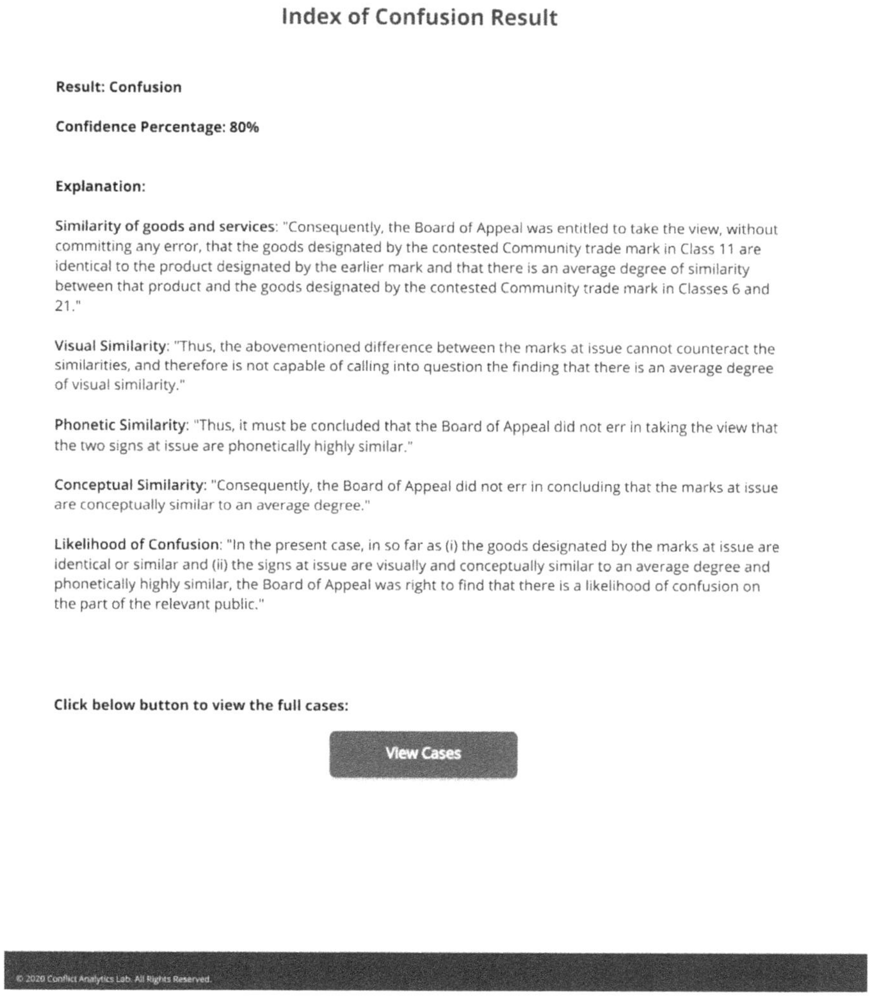

V. Implications for Courts/AI and Court Processes

AI legal tools can take many forms and can be used at various stages of the judicial process by many actors. Some AI tools can serve as part of direct-to-public legal help systems, while others can be used as decision-making support for the adjudication process. However, no matter when or how these tools are used we argue that such technology should ideally be an integral component of the 'extended court' described earlier.[59] Specifically, we propose an AI-powered ODR system with an integrated legal-help tool aimed at guiding users and judges in assessing the validity of a claim, thanks to a text-analytics system assessing data from past cases. We discuss below the potential implications of such a proposal for the judicial process.

A. Assisting with Adjudication and Case Management

AI tools may help both litigants and adjudicators to assess crucial aspects of a dispute. As discussed earlier, trademark tools can help to assess the similarity of goods and services as well as signs, the probative weight of evidence submitted in the context of reputation or proof of use of a trademark, and putting forward a prognosis (see section IV.B above). Such a forum may be established by a European institution such as the EUIPO, although it could also work as a stand-alone tool similar to the legal aid system developed by the Conflict Analytics Lab (MyOpenCourt.org).[60]

An open-access prognosis tool would help SMEs at both the pre-registration and pre-claim stages to assess their cases before registering a trademark and/or filing a claim.[61] It would especially help SMEs with searches of most similar trademarks and the corresponding risk index on the likelihood of confusion with existing and registered trademarks at the EU level, as well as drafting appropriate goods and services descriptions based on the Nice Classification system. Arguably, this knowledge would bolster the EUIPO mediation process by helping the parties to develop a more informed negotiation strategy.

These techniques are already assisting several registries with examinations, including the Japanese Patent Office as well as IP Australia.[62] This speeds up the process for checking whether the correct product classes have been indicated in the application, as well as the field of prior marks with which to compare the new application. IP Australia has already launched Trade Mark Assist, an online tool that assists users wishing to check whether their chosen sign is a good candidate for registration.[63]

While it is difficult to predict how litigants would respond to such IP tools, one can expect to see several immediate results for the EU IP system. First, it

[59] Susskind, 'The Future of Courts' (n 7).

[60] Note that the Trademark Confusion tool was launched in August 2021. See: www.MyOpenCourt.org.

[61] Note that this tool may be integrated into the EUIPO dispute resolution process, but it may also be developed as a stand-alone system.

[62] The Japanese Patent Office uses an AI-assisted goods and services similarity assessment tool so that its examiners can identify the closest match between a new application and previously registered (approved) terms to describe goods and services. IP Australia has been developing a 'Smart Assessment Toolkit' for examiners, using machine-learning models to flag up potential issues. This includes identifying prior similar word marks for similar goods or services to prioritise conflicting marks. It also incorporates a form of distinctiveness assessment. For more detail, see Gangjee (n 47) 10.

[63] See: assist.ipaustralia.gov.au/trademarks/welcome.

would constitute a triage system that could help the EUIPO to filter inadmissible complaints. Second, AI tools can assist adjudicators when making recommendations. As argued by Professor Gangjee, AI algorithms can augment human judgement – by effectively sifting through ever-increasing volumes of registration data – but not replacing it. Machine learning technology can filter the growing number of trademark applications and registrations, displaying the most relevant list of results for human experts to assess.[64]

We acknowledge that these tools raise several issues as to their legality and trustworthiness, especially when it comes to the accuracy of the tool. For instance, what would happen if the system indicated there is confusion, but the EUIPO found that there is no confusion? Are there remedies for inaccurate predictions? And who would be responsible?

While these questions fall beyond the scope of this chapter, it is worth noting that direct-to-public and adjudication-support tools highlight regulatory tensions between public protection risks and access-to-justice opportunities. These tensions and their attendant complexities are worthy of further exploration. The risks are especially challenging for tools that are aimed at the legal consumer, as the technology could fall well short of the standards required by people seeking assistance with legal issues.

Another issue that should be explored relates to the bias effect these tools may exert on judges. Machine learning can help to assess behavioural anomalies and inter-judge disparities in judicial decision-making (see section V.C), but excessive reliance on analytics by adjudicators may create additional biases in the form of an anchoring effect, which could give rise to a culture of judicial conformity and inertia. As pointed out by Dean Roquilly, consistency is not conformity. An overly strong focus on rigid analytics could lead to a diminishment of justice. Rather, non-conformist views should exist, and perhaps even be encouraged, when backed up by solid argument.

Besides predictive analytics, several courts have already leveraged AI tools, including automated docketing, legal information and assistance, and optical character recognition. These tools can significantly reduce overall workload and increase staff effectiveness. In particular, such technologies can eliminate or streamline many manual processes, allowing the same number of staff to better serve more members of the public. For instance, Palm Beach County's bots are now docketing about 12,000 filings a week. Through attrition, the county has eliminated many entry-level positions, freeing up budget resources for better-paying, more skilled positions and giving greater emphasis to human interaction in more complex matters.[65]

[64] Gangjee (n 47) 11.
[65] Joint Technology Committee, 'Introduction to AI for Courts' (JCT, 2020) 8.

B. Encouraging Data-Driven Dispute Resolution

We argue that AI has the potential to disrupt long-standing intuitive legal reasoning and may encourage a more data-driven approach to dispute resolution. In fact, predictive legal analytics may change the nature of the dispute resolution process by turning it into a data-driven undertaking, provided users are willing to engage in principled negotiation – which may not happen if users are driven by vindictive motivations. For instance, objective data on the existence of likelihood of confusion can become a reliable bargaining chip for litigants and mediators. In other words, the machine can help litigants to determine their best alternative to a negotiated agreement (BATNA)[66] at an early stage.

Considering that many trademark disputes are resolved through mediation, we believe that analytics tools can facilitate party-to-party negotiations through synchronous or asynchronous communications, either with or without the assistance of a neutral third party. In particular, the negotiation and mediation phases represent a crucial aspect of a successful ODR for three main reasons: first, people place greater value on things they build themselves – the so-called 'IKEA effect'. People are more likely to be satisfied with a consensual agreement, and they are also more likely to adhere to it.[67] In addition, should ODR be provided by or through the court system – for example the EUIPO – it would carry the authority of the court, giving parties greater confidence in the process and the outcome.

C. Exposing Inconsistencies and Judicial Biases

Beside predictions, AI research has helped to shed new light on how judges make decisions, revealing whether non-legal biases drive judicial decision-making, as well as exposing inconsistencies in CJEU judgments.[68] For instance, one court used AI statistical modelling to analyse all traffic tickets issued over the last 15 years. The models revealed that women were less likely than men to be cited for the same infraction and, when cited, were more likely to be offered a plea deal.[69]

Evidence from our trademark study suggests that the subjective and factual nature of trademark cases, as well as the high volume of cases, may have encouraged divergence, especially when it comes to comparing trademarks. Whether these divergences are intentional or driven by non-legally relevant biases, it can be argued that excessive inconsistency may be damaging to the perception of legal certainty and eventually undermine the legitimacy of the EUTM system.

[66] The BATNA is the best solution a negotiator can achieve away from the negotiation table; R Fisher, WL Ury and B Patton, *Getting to Yes: Negotiating Agreement Without Giving In* (New York, Penguin, 2011).

[67] See D Shestowsky, 'The Psychology of Procedural Preference: How Litigants Evaluate Legal Procedures Ex Ante' (2013) 99 *Iowa Law Review* 637.

[68] Dahan and Others (n 35).

[69] Joint Technology Committee (n 65) 8.

It may also be argued that the consistency of case law is a prerequisite for legal certainty, a central component of the concept of rule of law. Legal certainty is an essential aspect of many legal systems[70] insofar as it contributes to public confidence in the courts. Conflicting court decisions, especially those of appellate courts, can trigger breaches of the due process requirement. As observed by the ECtHR, 'justice must not degenerate into a lottery'.[71] Thus, not only can this research be used to assess likelihood of confusion, it can also be used to identify inconsistencies in the case law, or help decision-makers make better and more consistent decisions.

This raises an important question: how does one assess whether judges or agencies are consistent? One technique involves examining the algorithm's accuracy, or, put differently, examining the 'outliers', the case outcomes that the algorithm predicted incorrectly. Recent research suggests that low predictive accuracy may signal cases of judicial 'indifference' – essentially, conditions in which judges are unmoved by legally relevant circumstances.[72] For instance, it is possible that circumstances such as the outcome of a football game[73] or the time of day[74] can substantially affect legal decisions.[75] In other words, we argue that algorithms are not inherently biased: humans are. Algorithms simply learn and reflect biases by reproducing similar patterns.

i. Accuracy of the Algorithm

We used this technique to assess the accuracy of our trademark algorithm, as well as, incidentally, inconsistencies in the case law. While we have only a partial dataset (398 annotated cases), our trademark tool is 76.25 per cent accurate when we do not consider the presence of figurative trademarks, and 78.75 per cent accurate when we do. Note that we have only used the cases of the CJEU to train this model. This range will be increased as additional models are trained with the full text of EUIPO cases. Arguably, it is remarkable that likelihood of confusion can be predicted with this degree of accuracy and precision using only half of the General Court's case law and a simple machine-learning algorithm.

[70] The principle of legal certainty is implicit in all the Articles of the European Convention on Human Rights and constitutes one of the basic elements of the rule of law; see *Beian v Romania (No 1)* App no 30658/05, judgment of 6 December 2007, para 39.

[71] *Şahin and Şahin v Turkey* App no 13279/05, judgment of 20 October 2011, Joint Dissenting Opinion para 17.

[72] DL Chen, 'Machine Learning and the Rule of Law' in M Livermore and D Rockmore (eds), *Law as Data: Computation and the Future of Legal Analysis* (Santa Fe, SFI Press, 2019), available at: papers.ssrn.com/sol3/papers.cfm?abstract_id=3302507>; Copus, Hubert and Laqueur (n 35).

[73] Chen (n 72); Dahan and Others (n 35).

[74] S Danziger, J Levav and L Avnaim-Pesso, 'Extraneous Factors in Judicial Decisions' (2011) 108 *Proceedings of the National Academy of Sciences* 6889.

[75] Dahan, Cohen and Rule (n 35); Dahan and others (n 35).

While there are some inconsistencies, this signals strong general consistency across the case law. It also confirms a common intuition that has been acknowledged by most trademark lawyers, namely that a global assessment of likelihood of confusion is intuitive for a trained legal mind. That said, while there may be consistency in outcomes, further research should investigate whether there is consistency when it comes to legal analysis, that is, whether judges use the same legal reasoning and whether they follow the same precedent.

ii. Revealing Judicial Patterns and Biases

Another approach consists of examining judicial patterns by running a feature-importance analysis (Figure 7). This helps to assess the factors and potential biases (legal and non-legal) that drive the decision-making process.

Figure 7 Feature Importance Analysis (F score)

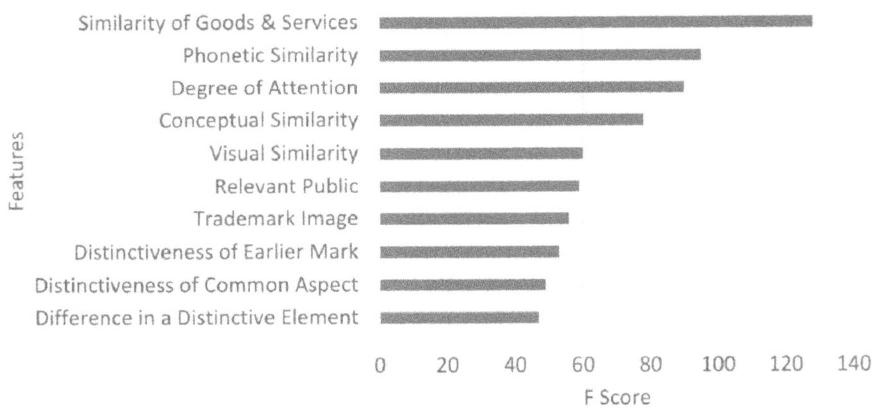

TRADEMARK IMAGE (TRADEMARK SOUGHT) TM is a feature indicating the presence of a figurative trademark for trademark sought. Similarly, TRADEMARK IMAGE (TRADEMARK SOUGHT) noTM indicates a trademark with no figurative element

In this regard, a preliminary analysis of the case law of the General Court shows that the factor correlating most strongly with likelihood of confusion is 'Similarity of Goods & Services' (127), highlighting the importance of identity or similarity of goods and services for the determination of likelihood of confusion. As argued in the Trademark Guidelines, if all goods and services are found to be dissimilar, one of the conditions contained in Article 8 of the European Union Trade Mark Regulation (EUTMR) is not fulfilled, and the opposition must be rejected without addressing the remaining sections of the decision.[76] The 'Degree

[76] EUIPO Guidelines, Part C Opposition, Section 2, Chapter 2 Comparison of goods and services, 1.1 Relevance, available at: guidelines.euipo.europa.eu/1803468/1787444/trade-mark-guidelines/1-introduction.

of Attention' follows in terms of importance (with a score of 112), which is not surprising considering the decisive role of this factor in the assessment of both the EUIPO and the courts.[77] It is clear from the case law of the Court that likelihood of confusion exists if there is a risk that the public might believe that the goods or services in question come from the same undertaking or from economically linked undertakings.[78]

Phonetic, conceptual and visual similarity follow in terms of importance. Again, this confirms the analysis of the Court, reiterated in the Trademark Guidelines as follows: 'similarity (or identity) of signs is a necessary condition for it to be found that there is a likelihood of confusion for the purposes of Article 8(1)(b) EUTMR'.[79] That said, further analysis should investigate how each factor correlates with the others, and especially the importance of visual similarity in figurative marks relative to non-figurative marks. This should shed new light on the EUIPO and the CJEU decision-making processes, considering that whether likelihood of confusion exists depends on an assessment of several interdependent factors (including the aforementioned factors). Finally, 'distinctiveness of earlier mark' is the least important factor, probably due to the limited number of cases concerning 'earlier distinctive marks'.

Again, this analysis suggests a high level of consistency across the case law of the CJEU, one that is not driven by extrajudicial variables such as the location of a company. However, while it is beyond the remit of this chapter, this research signals – at least in theory – the existence of a gap between the likelihood of confusion test for relative grounds (EUIPO decisions) and infringement (CJEU cases). As argued by Gangjee,[80] conflict analysis for registry clearance purposes is a thinner, more formalistic version of the multifactor likelihood of confusion test for infringement.[81] Accordingly, further research – such as a feature-importance analysis – should be conducted to assess discrepancies between EUIPO decisions and CJEU cases.

VI. Conclusion

In March 2020, the Covid-19 crisis paralysed many courts around the world. With the onset of the pandemic, many courts, including EU courts, swiftly responded by shifting their operations online. This would have been considered unthinkable a few years ago, but Covid converted many sceptics overnight. This chapter argues

[77] See Case C-251/95 *Sabèl* EU:C:1997:528 para 23; Case C-342/97 *Lloyd Schufabrik* EU:C:1999:323 para 25.

[78] Case C-39/97 *Canon* EU:C:1998:442 para 29.

[79] EUIPO Guidelines, Part C Opposition, Section 2, Chapter 4 Comparison of Signs, 1.1 Overview, available at: guidelines.euipo.europa.eu/1803468/1787444/trade-mark-guidelines/1-introduction.

[80] Gangjee (n 47) 12.

[81] As recognised in Case C-533/06 *O2 Holdings Ltd v Hutchison 3G Ltd* EU:C:2008:339 para 66. See also *Specsavers International Healthcare Ltd v Asda Stores Ltd* [2012] EWCA Civ 24 [78]–[88] (Kitchin LJ).

that the technological transformation that consists of 'dropping hearings into Zoom' does not constitute a full-blown paradigmatic shift. While commendable, these changes are too modest to address the root causes of the access-to-justice crisis in the EU. As argued by the OECD, more than half of the world's population has no access to legal services. This phenomenon is not the result of the pandemic: Covid has only exacerbated the problem. We argue that technology may constitute a valid solution, but serious efforts must be made to develop customised solutions that change how the justice system operates. It is not sufficient to shift broken practices online.

However, the development of analytics tools for EU courts will very much depend on whether there is sufficient political will, as well as acceptance and trust of AI applications. Another limitation relates to the legal implications, including legality and the ethical issues associated with the predictive tools. This too should be explored in further detail. In particular, it would be worth exploring whether there is a legal basis in the treaties and in case law to support a right to legal information and legal aid for SMEs.

That said, there are a growing number of industry and academic projects involving the use of AI, including AI applications supporting case management and decision-making in the field of EU law. As technologies improve, AI tools may become a useful resource to augment human expertise. Trademark law offers an interesting case study, but there are further possible avenues of research that could ultimately change how EU courts operate. For instance, it may be worth exploring an analytics system for general EU law questions such as a pan-European screening system for preliminary references. Such a tool would help the Research and Documentation Directorate at the CJEU to assist judges in assessing the validity of preliminary rulings.

We anticipate a new wave of transformation involving AI-powered tools for legal help. It is our hope to see EU courts engaging with both academia and industry to explore innovations that go beyond grafting technology onto old ways.

PART II

Substantive Areas Triggering Structural Change in EU Law

6

The Beauty and the Beast: Is European Union Internal Market Law 'Over-Constitutionalised'?

STEPHEN WEATHERILL*

I. Introduction

My concern in this chapter is to show the vertical and horizontal implications of the approach of the Court of Justice of the European Union (the Court; the Court of Justice) to the interpretation of the Treaty provisions on free movement. Vertical implications concern the grip exerted by the European Union (EU) rules on Member State autonomy; horizontal implications concern the relationship between the EU's judicial institutions and its political/legislative institutions. I want to interrogate the strength of the criticism that the Court is guilty of having deepened existing anxieties that EU law is 'over constitutionalised' – that is, that too much lies within the grip of primary law, which is extremely hard to amend, so that EU law channels regulatory options within a narrow range rigidly fixed by the Treaty on the Functioning of the European Union (TFEU; the Treaty) to the detriment of the vitality of political contestation at both national and EU level.

I argue in this chapter that there is some truth in this argument, and I consider how it could and should be addressed, but I argue too that it is important not to exaggerate the scale of the problem. Much of the Court's admittedly ambitious interpretative activity concerning free movement law operates benevolently to put anachronistic or calculatedly protectionist national practices to the sword. This is the beauty of free movement law. And, where more sensitive issues are put to the test, the Court is usually attentive to the need to place limits on the EU's authority as a basis for review of national policy choices. Moreover, where EU law does claim authority, the Court usually loads in awareness of the importance of non-economic values and interests in the application of the free movement rules and, in assessing

* Somerville College and Faculty of Law, University of Oxford.

justification, it grants a margin of appreciation to national political and judicial decision-makers. This sensitivity is constitutionally mandated by the several provisions of the TFEU and the Charter of Fundamental Rights (the Charter) which direct that matters such as consumer and environmental protection shall inform the definition and implementation of all other EU policies, including the internal market.

The Court takes this constitutionally mandated sensitivity seriously. Internal market law is normally applied with careful respect for the legitimate claims of the Member States to regulate beyond its reach in matters of purely local concern and, when within its reach, to promote social welfare policies even where they conflict with trade integration. But on occasion the Court takes a false step, and neglects the balancing of values which is mandated by primary EU law with the result that deregulation is driven too fiercely. This is the beast of free movement law.

So how dangerous is the Court? I argue that the Court is normally wedded to beauty, so the problem – the beast – is not as large or ugly as is sometimes alleged. Consequently the solution needs to be carefully and cautiously shaped for fear that not only the beast but also the beauty is caged. The argument of this chapter in short is that most of the time free movement law is safe in the hands of the Court of Justice and that the more radical proposals for addressing over-constitutionalisation risk causing more sickness than they will cure. The beauty should rescue the beast – the beast must not be allowed to corrupt the beauty.

II. The Beauty

Every student knows the famous *Cassis de Dijon* case – more properly, *Rewe-Zentrale AG* v *Bundesmonopolverwaltung für Branntwein*.[1] And rightly so. *Cassis* was the landmark case in which the Court of Justice elaborated its plan to transform what is today Article 34 TFEU from a norm forbidding discrimination to one that instead, and much more broadly and ambitiously, addresses more subtle forms of protectionism. True, the Court had a few years previously in *Dassonville*[2] opened a window on a test rooted in the *effects* of a national measure, rather than any discriminatory taint, and moreover in the field of services it had in *Van Binsbergen*[3] already adopted the shape of the approach that would be embraced subsequently in *Cassis*. But *Cassis*, though not an unforeseeable novelty when judged against the Court's evolving case law, pronounced a fresh formula of enduring significance in EU free movement law. Most of all, the ruling asserts the

[1] Case 120/78 *Rewe-Zentrale AG v Bundesmonopolverwaltung für Branntwein* EU:C:1979:42.
[2] Case 8/74 *Dassonville* EU:C:1974:82.
[3] Case 33/74 *Van Binsbergen* EU:C:1974:131.

review of national technical standards which, though in law equal in their application to all products and all producers, nonetheless operate in fact in favour of local products and producers, which naturally tend to comply with local standards, and to the disadvantage of imported products and producers, which typically do not. Make no mistake: *Cassis de Dijon* is a ruling that deserves its iconic status.

A. The Taste of *Cassis de Dijon*

The facts of the case, though certainly well known, merit repetition in order to emphasise, first, how simple was the problem and, second, how elegant was the Court's solution. Cassis de Dijon was a blackcurrant fruit liqueur which was made in France with an alcohol content of between 15 and 20 per cent. It could not be sold in Germany because it did not comply with German law, which by contrast required that such products should have a minimum alcohol content of 25 per cent. The key point is that the German rules were not targeted at imports. They applied to all products, wherever they were made and whoever made them, and they acted as a threshold condition which had to be met in order to secure an entitlement to be marketed in Germany. The problem was the *effect* of the rule, not its form. In practice, German-made goods would typically comply with the German rules. French-made goods would not – French-made goods would typically comply with French law. The heart of the problem was simply that German standards governing the composition of blackcurrant liqueur were *different* from French standards. The consequence of that regulatory diversity between France and Germany was an obstacle to the free movement of goods and the fragmentation of the internal market along national lines. French-made goods could not be sold in Germany.

The Court's approach finds its most elegant expression in paragraph 8 of the ruling in *Cassis*. This is a thing of beauty, a judicial work of art. The Court correctly identifies that it is dealing with obstacles to movement between Member States 'resulting from disparities between the national laws relating to the marketing of the products in question'. It asserts that those obstacles 'must be accepted' – which suggests that it is willing to defer to Germany's regulatory autonomy and to accept blockages within the EU's internal market – but it immediately subverts that impression by adding that the acceptance of obstacles caused by national rules is conditional on their recognition 'as being necessary in order to satisfy mandatory requirements relating in particular to the effectiveness of fiscal supervision, the protection of public health, the fairness of commercial transactions and the defence of the consumer'. Put better still, advancing to paragraph 14 of the Court's ruling in *Cassis*, the question is whether the obstructive rules 'serve a purpose which is in the general interest and such as to take precedence over the requirements' of free movement. In this way EU free movement law insists on the review of the application of national technical standards where they operate to restrict inter-State trade, but it leaves space to the regulating authority to show a good reason – a justification – for maintaining those standards.

This is not mutual recognition of technical standards. Germany is not obliged to defer to the different French choice. But equally Germany may not simply demand compliance with the German rulebook. It must *justify* that demand. The vital structural point is that the Court's interpretation identifies Article 34 TFEU as a provision laying down a *conditional* or *non-absolute* rule of 'mutual recognition' of the adequacy of technical standards set by the Member States. The free movement provisions of the Treaty serve as instruments for the allocation of regulatory competence.

Accordingly and logically, the ruling in *Cassis de Dijon* proceeds to consider whether Germany possessed a good reason for standing firm and insisting that all goods marketed on its territory, including imports, must cross the relatively high threshold of minimum alcohol content. This did not detain the Court for long. Germany's arguments in support of its rules were spectacularly and memorably weak. In particular, EU law teachers down the decades have been grateful to Germany for the light relief supplied in classes and lectures by the bizarre claim that Germany needed to suppress weak, but not strong, alcoholic drinks on its territory in order to prevent drinkers being lured down a slippery slope of toleration of alcohol and excessive consumption by the ready availability of dangerously weak alcoholic drinks. As a measure of public policy, this made no sense at all and the Court, though open in principle to Germany's competence to justify its trade-restrictive rule, found the arguments presented wholly unconvincing.

The Court's approach is consistent with the Treaty. Articles 34 and 56 TFEU prohibit barriers to inter-State trade in goods and services. Articles 36 and 62/52 TFEU soften the prohibition by allowing the regulating State to show justification for its choices where they impede inter-State trade. The pattern established by the Treaty is therefore one of conditional mutual recognition or non-absolute home State control – which is the same as that developed by the Court in *Cassis*. *Cassis* looms large in any account of EU free movement law because it offers a more elegant and sophisticated explanation of the legal treatment of trade-restrictive State measures under EU law than is found in the Treaty superstructure, but it does not depart from the model established by primary law.

B. *Cassis* Applied: Goods and Services

The variety of national technical standards that have been attacked before the Court is immense, which reveals how deeply rooted are such obstacles to trade. They are, after all, often the product of centuries of regulatory diversity accumulated as a result of the jurisdictional kaleidoscope of a fragmented Europe. There is in truth a strong stench of regulatory absurdity. One can readily imagine how the judges in Luxembourg were first puzzled and then frustrated as their time was taken up with attempts to argue that consumers need to be protected by rules which required margarine to be packed only in a cube,[4] that Edam cheese be regulated according to

[4] Case 261/81 *Walter Rau* EU:C:1982:382.

strict minimum fat rules,[5] that bleach must cross a defined threshold of strength,[6] that a 'shallot' must be reproduced directly from bulbs not from seedlings,[7] and that advertising medical and surgical treatments be banned on national television networks when they are permitted on local television networks.[8]

The Court commonly uses the 'reasonably circumspect' consumer as a benchmark in these cases. This entails that national measures which it regards as unnecessary to protect such a consumer are normally not justified. So, for example, in *Verein gegen Unwesen in Handel und Gewerbe Köln eV v Mars GmbH*, the Court decided that such a consumer would not be deceived by a marketing practice which had been prohibited in Germany (but not elsewhere), and so the German intervention was ruled incompatible with free movement law.[9] The consumer is used instrumentally in such circumstances: he or she becomes a lever to prise open national regulatory choices in order to liberalise cross-border trade and to expand a distinct vision of consumer interest, that of choice in the internal market enjoyed by circumspect consumers. This, in fact, is central to understanding the purpose of the free movement rules. The point of the application of free movement law in *Cassis* was not that German consumers would be *required* to drink weak alcoholic drinks of the type favoured in France. The point was instead that German consumers should have the *choice* to do so, and the blockage on their choice imposed by the technical standards policed by German public authorities should be lifted. This is the intended nature of the EU's internal market! So, in the famous 'Beer Purity' case, *Commission v Germany*, Germany was not prevented from confining use of the word 'Bier' to products brewed in Germany using only malted barley, hops, yeast and water, but it could not extend this rigid rule governing composition to brewers based in other Member States using different recipes and traditions.[10] They had to be allowed access to the German market for 'Bier' – their success on that market would depend not on the rigidities introduced by the centuries-old *Reinheitsgebot*, but rather on the preferences of the German consumer. The Court's attachment to the versatile and alert consumer as a model and as a lever in the internal market is emphasised by its acceptance in the judgment that even if the arrival on the German market of new and unfamiliar beers might surprise buyers, this could not justify the rigid application of composition standards in such a way as to keep differently brewed beers off the market altogether. The problem could be addressed adequately and less restrictively by informing the consumer about the product's composition by requiring that the product be labelled, if necessary on beer taps.

This same model of informed consumer choice is visible in cases arising in the services sector. *Commission v France*, the so-called 'Tourist Guides' case, is a

[5] Case 286/86 *Deserbais* EU:C:1988:434.
[6] Case C-358/01 *Commission v Spain* EU:C:2003:599.
[7] Case C-147/04 *de Groot* EU:C:2006:7.
[8] Case C-500/06 *Corporación Dermoestética SA* EU:C:2008:421.
[9] Case C-470/93 *Verein gegen Unwesen in Handel und Gewerbe Köln v Mars GmbH* EU:C:1995:224.
[10] Case 178/84 *Commission v Germany* EU:C:1987:126.

typical example, and in many respects it applies to services the same logic which informs the *Cassis de Dijon* approach to goods.[11] France required tourist guides to hold a local qualification as a precondition of offering their services on French territory. The qualification was available to any guide, irrespective of nationality, but entirely unsurprisingly it was in practice typically held by a French-based guide, but not by a guide based in and qualified according to the rules of another Member State. The problem, just as in *Cassis*, was therefore divergence between national rules governing entry to the market. This was an obstacle to inter-State trade on which the French authorities could rely only provided they could show a good justification for insisting on the need for the local qualification. And, as in *Cassis*, no such justification was demonstrated. The ruling is of particular illustrative value because the Court goes out of its way to explain that the intervention in the market is unnecessary to protect the consumer of guiding services. The Court stated that competition between tour operators would ensure the hiring of competent guides and that accordingly a State licensing regime governing access to the profession could not be justified. *Choice* was explicitly at the centre of the Court's analysis. The French rule 'prevents tourists taking part in such organized tours from availing themselves at will of the services in question'.[12] The market would take care of consumers: 'the profitable operation of such group tours depends on the commercial reputation of the operator, who faces competitive pressure from other tour companies' and 'the need to maintain that reputation and the competitive pressure themselves compel companies to be selective in employing tourist guides and exercise some control over the quality of their services'.[13] For goods as for services, the animating concern in the application of the free movement rules is not that consumers are *required* to buy or use unfamiliar imports, but rather that they are provided with the opportunity to do so. The 'Tourist Guides' case is no one-off: the Court has treated its *Cassis* approach as applicable across the several Treaty provisions on free movement.[14]

C. The Vertical Implications of the Court's Choice

The Court's approach cuts deep into the regulatory autonomy of the Member States. This is the vertical implication of the Court's case law. It is in the nature of the internal market as a project and as a concept that the Member States have surrendered their unconditional right to regulate and have instead accepted subjection to the discipline of free movement law and the authority of the Court of Justice.

[11] Case C-154/89 *Commission v France* EU:C:1991:76.
[12] para 13.
[13] para 20.
[14] Case C-55/94 *Gebhard* EU:C:1995:411 was particularly important for the development of a generally applicable formula.

One should be wary of exaggerating the impact of *Cassis*. The Commission's landmark 1985 White Paper on 'Completing the Internal Market' placed great faith in transformative strategies inspired by the ruling in *Cassis*,[15] but latterly it has been more circumspect in its assertions about the depth of change in commercial and administrative practice. So, for example, in 2005 it noted that 'neither producers nor market surveillance authorities are sure to what extent products from one Member State can enter another Member State's market without modification' and added that according to the European Business Test Panel, 53 per cent of businesses are not even familiar with the principle of (conditional) mutual recognition.[16] In any event, litigation is a relatively slow and costly means of improving the functioning of the internal market and so the Commission has wisely invested energy in promoting models that, it hopes, will dig deeper into national administrative practice in order to address problems before they erupt in litigation. This trend covers advance notification to the Commission of draft technical standards,[17] procedures to be followed where restrictions are placed on products lawfully marketed in another Member State,[18] identification of designated contact points within the Member States,[19] legislative obligations to evaluate existing standards,[20] and the SOLVIT mechanism.[21] But, although strategies for managing the internal market properly reach *beyond* litigation, they do not eliminate the value of litigation as a means to tackle obstructions within the internal market. And the Court's case law in the vein initiated by *Cassis* is plentiful. The consequence of these cases where Member States restrict inter-State trade without demonstrated good reason is deregulation – the national rules must be disapplied in so far as they collide with the impetus to inter-State trade. In this way the regulatory detritus of centuries is commonly exposed as inappropriate to an integrating EU internal market. EU law, driven by interested litigants, provokes such renovation. EU internal market law draws legitimating force from its transformative impact on Member State regulatory practices. The very fact that Member States troubled to send their lawyers to Luxembourg to defend protectionist absurdities and anachronisms of the type encountered above is concrete proof that leaving the matter to be resolved through national political processes would have been fruitless. In truth, such rules, defended as measures of consumer protection,

[15] COM (85) 310, especially paras 13, 65, 77, available at: aei.pitt.edu/1113/1/internal_market_wp_COM_85_310.pdf.

[16] Commission, Second Implementation Report of the Internal Market Strategy 2003–2006, COM (2005) 11, 8.

[17] Originally mandated by Directive 83/189, now Directive 2015/1535 [2015] OJ L241/1.

[18] Regulation 764/2008 [2008] OJ L218/21.

[19] Reg 764/2008 (n 18) Arts 9–11; also visible in sector-specific measures, eg, the 'Services Directive', Directive 2006/123 [2006] OJ L376/36 Art 6.

[20] eg Directive 2006/123 (n 19) Art 39.

[21] See: ec.europa.eu/solvit/. See E Kokolia, 'Strengthening the Single Market through Informal Dispute Resolution Mechanisms in the EU: The Case of SOLVIT' (2018) 25 *Maastricht Journal of European and Comparative Law* 108.

were simply measures of protection to the benefit of local producers. EU law, as a correcting force rescues not only consumers and out-of-State traders, but local political actors trapped by vested interests.[22]

D. Conditional Deregulation and the Role of Justification

This is vibrant deregulation. But it is not unconditional deregulation. The point is to place an obligation on the regulating State to justify its choices where they impede cross-border trade: only in the absence of a rational explanation does the deregulatory impact of EU law bite. The track record is admittedly of routine failure to justify national rules, but this is predominantly attributable to the poverty of the arguments advanced by regulating Member States rather than any entrenched deregulatory bias antagonistic to genuine and targeted measures of social protection. On occasion, the Court has been persuaded that the protection of the economic interests of consumers justifies the application of measures that cause obstruction to inter-State in goods or services.

A-Punkt Schmuckhandels GmbH v Claudia Schmidt concerned the prohibition of home jewellery parties in Austria.[23] If this was found to be a barrier to inter-State trade, which was a matter to be determined by the national court, then the Court of Justice was open to the possibility of finding it to be justified despite its restrictive effect on commercial freedom. The Court noted that the rule reflected the potentially higher risk of the consumer being cheated due to a lack of information when buying in the home, and noted too the impossibility of comparing prices and the greater psychological pressure to buy where the sale is organised in a private setting.[24] This was the protection of consumers who may be vulnerable in a particular setting (at home). It was not the untargeted overregulation of the type which the Court was asked to examine in *Cassis de Dijon* and myriad other cases. Where the national regulator has identified a particular need for protection and crafted a law that is appropriately nuanced and specific, the Court responds by judging its justifiability with respect for that nuance. This is *conditional* deregulation: the legitimate regulatory aspirations of the Member States are given room to breathe through the window of justification.

[22] I acknowledge here, without interrogating further, a rich literature which connects the scope of legitimate authority to put national regulatory autonomy to the test to deficiencies of representation of interests detectable in the shaping of the national rules in question: see M Poiares Maduro, *We the Court: The European Court of Justice and the European Economic Constitution* (Oxford, Hart Publishing, 1998); A Somek, 'Argument from Transnational Effects' Part I Representing Outsiders through Freedom of Movement, Part II Establishing Transnational Democracy (2010) 16 *European Law Journal* 315 and 375.

[23] Case C-441/04 *A-Punkt Schmuckhandels GmbH v Claudia Schmidt* EU:C:2006:141.

[24] ibid para 29.

Citroën Belux reveals the same sensitivity to national regulatory concerns in the context of the free movement of services.[25] Citroën offered six months of free insurance on the purchase of a Citroën vehicle. This was treated in Belgium as a prohibited 'combined offer' of services. But could the prohibition be justified as a means to protect the economic interests of consumers, given its restrictive effect on the cross-border provision of services? It could. The Court accepted that 'financial services are, by nature, complex and entail specific risks with regard to which the consumer is not always sufficiently well informed'.[26] It added that a combined offer of which one component is a financial service tends to lack transparency as regards the conditions, the price and the exact content of that service. This persuaded the Court that such an offer may mislead consumers as to the true content and actual characteristics of the combination offered and, at the same time, deprive them of the opportunity of comparing the price and quality of that offer with other corresponding services from other economic operators. The point is that the Court is prepared to accept that consumer choice released by the suppression of national measures that obstruct cross-border trade in goods and services is not *inevitably* beneficial. The consumer may be exposed to harm. This is part of the Court's assessment of the justification of national measures. Since the entry into force of the Treaty of Lisbon in 2009, Article 12 TFEU and Article 38 of the Charter of Fundamental Rights have commanded a commitment to the protection of the consumer in the context of the application of (inter alia) the rules of the internal market. But such openness to justification of national measures as means to protect the consumer even where they impede trade integration has always been written into the Court's supple interpretation of free movement law. What matters is the *quality* of the arguments advanced by regulating States seeking to justify their trade-restrictive rules.

E. The Horizontal Implications of the Court's Choice

Cassis, the first case to deal directly with inter-State divergence in non-discriminatory technical standards as a barrier to trade in goods, addresses the vertical distribution of competences in the EU. EU law controls State choices: national measures which restrict inter-State trade must be set aside unless justified. But *Cassis* is also highly significant for its impact on the horizontal distribution of powers in the EU. It is easy to forget with the advantage of distant hindsight that the Court was faced with a fundamental choice in *Cassis de Dijon*. It could feasibly have refused to bring technical standards within the scope of free movement law on the basis that the free movement rules touch only physical barriers to trade and overtly discriminatory practices. That would have left in place the relevant

[25] Case C-265/12 *Citroën Belux NV* EU:C:2013:498.
[26] ibid para 39.

German rules as obstacles to the marketing in Germany of French-made Cassis, but the Treaty envisaged and envisages a means to address that problem, namely legislative harmonisation. So the Court could have adopted a restrained view of its own role and assumed instead the responsibility of the legislative process to deepen the process of market integration. And it certainly knew this. Precisely this argument was advanced by the Bundesmonopolverwaltung in *Cassis* and discussed in the Opinion of Advocate General Capotorti in the case. What the Court in fact did in *Cassis de Dijon*, in rejecting this line, was to choose an approach that enhanced the significance of free movement law as means to cleanse the internal market of the trade-restrictive rules of the type encountered in the case, at the expense of the need to introduce common harmonised EU standards. This is institutionally significant. By enhancing the role of the Court and its national judicial allies in policing national technical standards that obstruct inter-State, it reduced the weight of the load which is undertaken by the political institutions in adopting legislation to tackle obstructions to inter-State trade. Their intervention is now required only where national rules survive examination pursuant to the free movement rules because they are shown to be justified. The Commission published a Notice in 1980 which embraced exactly this consequence of *Cassis*[27] and moreover it located this thematic readiness to reduce the intensity of the programme of legislative harmonisation and instead to place heavier reliance on judge-driven free movement law at the heart of the agenda set by the 1985 White Paper on 'Completing of the Internal Market'.[28] This, then, is the horizontal implication of the ruling in *Cassis*.

This is not only institutionally significant. It matters, too, to the type of internal market that is being created. Had the Court in *Cassis* declined to employ Article 34 TFEU in the case of diverse but non-discriminatory technical standards, then a vast amount of harmonisation would have been required to tackle such market-fragmenting regulatory diversity. This would have led to centralisation and homogeneity. This, as the Commission put it in 1985, would have been 'over-regulatory … inflexible and could stifle innovation'.[29] The Court protects the EU's internal market from this outcome by its willingness to let directly effective free movement law bite even where legislative intervention has not.[30]

F. The Chosen Internal Market

The Court, faced in *Cassis* with an ambiguity about the reach of free movement law and its relationship with legislative harmonisation, made a choice that

[27] Case C 256/2 OJ [1980].

[28] White Paper (n 15).

[29] ibid para 64.

[30] This theme is openly stated not only in *Cassis* but also in other landmark rulings on the scope of application of free movement rules such as Case 2/74 *Reyners* EU:C:1974:68 and Case C-212/97 *Centros* EU:C:1999:126.

privileged the former over the latter which in turn promoted a model of consumer choice and regulatory plurality in the market over a vision of legislatively defined harmonised 'Europroducts'. At stake is both the vertical distribution of competences and the horizontal distribution of powers in the EU.[31] This is not simply an abstract remark. The point that internal markets take different shapes all over the world is made with force by comparing the EU experience with that of Canada,[32] Australia[33] and the United States.[34] Arrangements vary according to the extent to which constituent units are permitted to pursue different regulatory policies; they vary according to the scope of law-making competence and powers allocated to the central authority; they vary according to the governing institutional (judicial and political) arrangements. There is no single concept of an internal market.[35] *Cassis de Dijon* was of the highest significance in shaping the EU's own particular version of an internal market.

III. The Beast

Such beauty! The beauty of *Cassis de Dijon* visible in the vertical distribution of competences is that EU law is employed to put national measures that restrict inter-State trade to the test while remaining open to compensating justifications, and in the horizontal distribution of powers whereby the judicial role and the legislative role combine to preserve a healthy degree of diversity in the market backed up by harmonisation of laws only where necessary to supplement the axe of free movement law.

But this is not to assert that the Court's approach to the EU's free movement rules is always respectful of the sensitive assessment that is required when Member States abandon the fatuous arguments advanced in cases such as *Cassis* itself and instead present coherent and sincere accounts of the motivations for local regulatory choices which happen also to impede cross-border trade. Any claim that

[31] See, eg, P Caro de Sousa, *The European Fundamental Freedoms: A Contextual Approach* (Oxford, Oxford University Press, 2015); A Saydé, 'One Law, Two Competitions: An Inquiry into the Contradictions of Free Movement Law' (2010–11) 13 *Cambridge Yearbook of European Legal Studies* 365; J Snell, 'The Internal Market and the Philosophies of Market Integration' in C Barnard and S Peers (eds), *European Union Law*, 2nd edn (Oxford, Oxford University Press, 2017); W Kerber and R Van Den Bergh, 'Mutual Recognition Revisited: Misunderstandings, Inconsistencies, and a Suggested Reinterpretation' (2008) 61 *Kyklos* 447.

[32] eg A Hinarejos, 'Free Movement, Federalism and Institutional Choice: A Canada/ EU Comparison' (2012) 71 *Cambridge Law Journal* 537.

[33] eg C Staker, 'Free Movement of Goods in the EEC and Australia: A Comparative Study' (1990) 10 *Yearbook of European Law* 209.

[34] eg E Knook, 'Guns and Tobacco: The Effect of Interstate Trade Case Law on the Vertical Division of Powers' (2004) 11 *Maastricht Journal of European and Comparative Law* 347; JA Gutiérrez Fons, 'Transatlantic Adjudication Techniques: The Commerce Clause and the EU's Internal Market Harmonization Clause in Perspective' in E Fahey and D Curtin (eds), *A Transatlantic Community of Law* (Cambridge, Cambridge University Press, 2014).

[35] See S Weatherill, *The Internal Market as a Legal Concept* (Oxford, Oxford University Press, 2017).

the Court is not locked into a diabolically deregulatory tendency to prioritise economic freedom over social and political protections must reckon with the December 2007 rulings of the Grand Chamber of the Court of Justice in *Viking Line* and *Laval*.[36] These are decisions that are as famous as *Cassis*, but for quite different reasons.

A. *Viking Line* as an Expression of Internal Market Orthodoxy

The two cases had their factual and contextual twists, but, stripped down to the core, they both involved a collision between EU free movement law and the exercise of collective labour rights. They asked whether EU free movement law protected firms wishing to evade the relatively high costs of establishment in the Nordic countries by taking advantage of the lower wage and regulatory costs prevailing in the Baltic states. In *Viking Line* the planned movement was by a Finnish company to Estonia, in *Laval* the planned movement was by a Latvian company and its workers to Sweden. The challenged barrier to inter-State mobility was collective action taken or threatened by labour unions in the Nordic countries aimed at deterring this corporate exploitation of EU free movement law.

The problem in *Laval* was that the stated objective, the protection of workers from the undercutting of standards by cross-border providers of services, was tainted by the absence in Sweden of provisions which were sufficiently precise and accessible to enable the provider to determine the applicable obligations. This created a risk of arbitrary or discriminatory conduct.[37] *Viking Line* was more awkward, because in *Viking Line* the Finnish rules and the collective action taken by the unions in their name, though restrictive of cross-border trade, were not contaminated by any such risk. The clash of values and interests was in sharper focus. So I now focus on *Viking Line*, and leave *Laval* to one side.

In *Viking Line* the Court found a restriction on the company's freedom of establishment. The unions were entities governed by private law, but the relevant Treaty provisions which protect the free movement of natural and legal persons have long been interpreted to apply not only to the actions of public authorities, but also to rules of any other nature aimed at regulating employment in a collective manner. The Court was also faced by the contention that the Treaty – then Article 137(5) EC, today Article 153(5) TFEU – places the right of association and the right to strike beyond the EU's reach. But the Court treated that exclusion as limited to the particular Title in which it is located, Title X of Part Three of the TFEU concerning legislative competence in the field of Social Policy. It did not operate also to limit

[36] Case C-438/05 *International Transport Workers' Federation v Viking Line ABP* EU:C:2007:772; Case C-341/05 *Laval un Partneri* EU:C:2007:809.

[37] para 110. See A Ericsson, 'The Many (Mis)readings of the *Laval* Case' (2016) 19 *Europarättslig Tidskrift* 113.

the reach of the Treaty rules on free movement, found in Title II of Part Three. In a similar vein, the plea that the right to strike constitutes a fundamental right which, as such, falls outside the scope of the Treaty provisions on free movement failed to impress the Court. The fundamental nature of the right to take collective action did not take the matter outside the scope of free movement law, although it did inform the examination conducted in order to determine whether the action was justified. And this is thematically central to the Court's judgment in this case. One may object that the Court is here revealing its unwillingness to place operationally significant limitations on the jurisdictional reach of EU free movement law and that accordingly, by loading the weight onto assessment of whether the measures are justified, it is placing itself at the very centre of the process. True. But nothing new: this approach in general, and the *Viking Line* judgment in particular, are fully in line with the Court's orthodoxy.[38]

That is not to claim that the prevailing orthodoxy is inevitably correct. In particular the Court's view that the free movement rules extend much further than the Treaty-conferred grant of legislative competence even where those legislative provisions, of which Article 153(5) is a prime example, have been explicitly and carefully written to include limits is not in any sense *wrong* – and the Member States could after all have written the restriction more widely, also explicitly to apply to free movement law as well, had they so chosen – but it is also not the only possible interpretation either. Reading the restriction on the scope of legislative competence also to determine the reach of the free movement rules was at least possible as an interpretative choice. In truth, the Court's explanation of its choice feels disingenuous. Holding that the rules of free movement apply even in areas where the EU's legislative reach is surpassed, the Court notes that in such areas 'the Member States are still free, in principle, to lay down the conditions governing the existence and exercise of the rights in question'.[39] True, they are – but the grip of free movement law may exert radical transformative effects by ruling out national choices that would conflict with EU free movement law, even if the EU is denied a legislative competence to re-shape the organisation of such matters. But, once more, it is not *Viking Line* that is the problem here, it is the Court's consistent case law. As paragraph 40 of *Viking Line* mentions, the same formula has been employed in relation to social security and direct taxation (and other examples exist too),[40] so here too the Court was simply following its own orthodox approach.

[38] See, eg, N Nic Shuibhne, 'Settling Dust? Reflections on the Judgments in Viking and Laval' (2010) 21 *European Business Law Review* 683, highlighting that structurally the ruling is not out of line with the Court's orthodox approach to free movement law. See also S Reynolds, 'Explaining the Constitutional Drivers behind a Perceived Judicial Preference for Free Movement over Fundamental Rights' (2016) 53 *Common Market Law Review* 643.

[39] Case C-438/05 (n 36) para 40.

[40] eg, education, Case C-73/08 *Nicolas Bressol, Céline Chaverot* EU:C:2010:181; healthcare, Case C-372/04 *ex parte Watts* EU:C:2006:325; and sport, Case C-415/93 *Bosman* EU:C:1995:463.

B. The Unorthodox Twist in *Viking Line*: The Matter of Justification

The reach of internal market law is broad. This is nothing new. The Court's interpretation of justification is the most operationally significant place to mediate the tensions between deregulation and nationally mandated social protection. This too is nothing new. What is new in *Viking Line* – or at least what is abnormal in *Viking Line* – is the Court's unsympathetic treatment of justification.

Let it first be understood that the Court's task was awkward. Once it had concluded that collective action which restricts inter-State trade may be taken only on condition that it meets standards recognised by EU law, it had to give shape to those standards. But in shaping those standards of justification the Court had no mandate set out in the Treaty. Worse, the Treaty actively distances EU legislative action from any association with this awkward matter of policy in consequence on the explicit exclusion of the right to strike found now in Article 153(5) TFEU. So the Court, rejecting the exclusion's significance for the purposes of free movement law, had no EU policy directions on which to draw. So the Court was in uncharted terrain. All the more reason for caution and deference. But that is what the judgment lacks.

The Court began by accepting in principle that the right to take collective action to protect workers is a legitimate interest which justifies a restriction of economic freedoms guaranteed by the Treaty. It added that the Community, which is now the Union, has 'not only an economic but also a social purpose'.[41] This is vivid rhetoric and plainly directed at advertising the limits of EU law's deregulatory bite, for in the particular context of free movement law it is only national measures, not EU measures, that are apt to deliver social objectives. Here the Court seems careful to shun any priority *in principle* of economic rights and freedoms over other rights and interests. What matters are the particular circumstances. And this is where the judgment becomes more controversial.

The Court cautioned that justification should not be found by the national court 'if it were established that the jobs or conditions of employment at issue were not jeopardised or under serious threat'.[42] And even if the jobs or conditions of employment of the union members liable to be adversely affected by the reflagging of the ship were in fact jeopardised or under serious threat, 'it would then have to ascertain whether the collective action initiated by FSU is suitable for ensuring the achievement of the objective pursued and does not go beyond what is necessary to attain that objective'.[43]

A test that entails that it must be checked *in the particular circumstances of this case* whether the collective action is apt to achieve its stated ends of protecting

[41] Case C-438/05 (n 36) para 79.
[42] ibid para 81.
[43] ibid para 84.

workers' jobs and employment conditions demands a difficult and unpredictable assessment of whether the action goes beyond what is necessary to attain its objective. If the ruling is interpreted even more broadly to mean that *only* action aimed at protecting the jobs of union members is ever recognised as capable of being justified under EU law, then the Court has excluded the possibility of more long-term strategic action taken by unions and even the 'political strike' in so far as it impedes cross-border economic activity. That would constitute a dramatic incursion into the internationally recognised permitted scope of collective labour rights.

The judgment was greeted with outrage.[44] And it remains the principal target and case study for more recent critiques lamenting a perceived neoliberal turn in EU free movement law.[45] It subordinates one type of fundamental right (to take industrial action) to another (cross-border trading freedom). The Court's understanding of permissible justification, the orthodox safety valve designed to prevent free movement law acting as a deregulatory force insensitive to social values pursued by national rules, is cramped and thin.

C. The Horizontal Implications

All this occurs in circumstances where there is no serious possibility to readdress the balances at stake through the political process at EU level. In the wake of the judgment the Commission hopefully pleaded that 'Political forces have to engage in a search for a solution, in line with the Treaty objective of a social market economy'.[46] It published a Proposal for a Regulation on the exercise of the right to take collective action within the context of the freedom of establishment and the freedom to provide services,[47] the so-called 'Monti II' text which was designed to achieve a modest clarification of the law in this area. It could not be advanced under Article 153 TFEU, because of Article 153(5)'s above-mentioned exclusion of application to the right to strike – the very exclusion which the Court

[44] *cf*, eg, L Azoulai, 'The Court of Justice and the Social Market Economy: The Emergence of an Ideal and the Conditions for Its Realisation' (2008) 45 *Common Market Law Review* 1335; A Davies, 'One Step Forward, Two Steps Back? The Viking and Laval Cases in the ECJ' (2008) 37 *Industrial Law Journal* 126; C Joerges and F Rödl, 'Informal Politics, Formalised Law and the "Social Deficit" of European Integration: Reflections after the Judgments of the ECJ in *Viking* and *Laval*' (2009) 15 *European Law Journal* 1.

[45] *cf*, eg, D Ashiagbor, 'Unravelling the Liberal Bargain: Labour and Social Welfare Law in the Context of EU Market Integration' (2013) 19 *European Law Journal* 303; D Nicol, 'Europe's Lochner Moment' [2011] *Public Law* 308; A McCann, 'The CJEU on Trial: Economic Mobility and Social Justice' (2014) 22 *European Review of Private Law* 729; L Niglia, 'Eclipse of the Constitution' (2016) 22 *European Law Journal* 132; S Giubboni, 'Freedom to Conduct a Business and EU Labour Law' (2018) 14 *European Constitutional Law Review* 172.

[46] *A New Strategy for the Single Market: At the Service of Europe's Economy and Society*, the 'Monti Report' of May 2010, 68–69, available at: ec.europa.eu/internal_market/strategy/index_en.htm.

[47] COM (2012) 130, 21 March 2012.

had treated as ineffective to curtail the application of the free movement rules. So instead, Article 352 TFEU was the envisaged legal base, which dauntingly requires unanimity in Council. This was never feasible. The proposal, although far from radical in its substance, generated sufficiently fierce political resistance among some Member States, national parliaments and the European Parliament for the Commission to feel the need to withdraw it.[48]

D. Assessing the Vertical and Horizontal Implications

Free movement law interpreted by the Court digs deep into the autonomy of regulation of collective labour action – the vertical implication of free movement law – and the adjustments made in the shadow of free movement law are not open to change through the legislative process – the horizontal implication. Politics are disabled. Free movement law reigns, and it is a free movement law which is insensitive to the vocation of labour law as a means to do more than simply accept the market as the dominant organising force.

The criticism has not been universal. Damjan Kukovec has insisted that assessment should extend beyond the collision between the interests of workers in the Nordic states and mobile corporate entities. The aspirations of workers in the Baltic states who are 'struggling to improve their livelihood, dignity as well as fair and just working conditions' should also be addressed.[49] Perspective matters: where are the claims of the workers in the Baltic states in the critical literature? There is an answer of sorts, which is that their interests are served in the short term by corporate mobility but not in the long term in so far as the European social model may come to be degraded, but that is a debate I do not want or need to pursue here. I want only to make the point that in *Viking Line* the Court produced winners (the companies, Baltic workers in the short term) and it produced losers (Nordic workers, arguably Baltic workers in the long term). The adjudication undertaken by the Court in *Viking Line* was intensely politically controversial. This is nothing like *Cassis de Dijon*! The Court in *Cassis*, finding that national measures which restricted inter-State trade were unlawful and not justified, created only deserving winners (out-of-State producers, sellers, local consumers) and deserving losers (local producers previously sheltered from competition). But in *Viking Line* the losers were not deserving losers in the way that German producers in *Cassis* were deserving losers. This was politically contested terrain. The Court in *Viking Line* has radically destabilised existing and hard-won political settlements within the Member States: EU free movement law makes a sharp vertical intrusion into local

[48] For the Commission's explanation, see Annual Report 2012 on Subsidiarity and Proportionality, COM (2013) 566, 6–8; also The Adoptive Parents, 'The Life of a Death Foretold: The Proposal for a Monti II Regulation', ch 5 in M Freedland and J Prassl (eds), *EU Law in the Member States: Viking, Laval and Beyond* (Oxford, Hart Publishing, 2014).

[49] D Kukovec, 'Law and the Periphery' (2015) 21 *European Law Journal* 406, 415.

practices and in circumstances where the EU political process – the horizontal implication – is disabled from introducing correction.

Viking Line is a beast of a judgment.

IV. Over-Constitutionalisation

I want first to explain the 'over-constitutionalisation' critique. Then I want to set out proposals for reform that it has generated. But then, in the section that follows, I want to argue that the critique is exaggerated and that therefore so too are the proposed reforms. In particular I want to argue that normally – though admittedly not in *Viking Line* – the Court is attentive to the proper limits of review conducted in the name of the internal market and to the need to load into assessment of rules that it does review due respect for local autonomy and social welfare. Then I want to assess proposals for reform, which, given my generally favourable assessment of the Court, are less inclined to the radical ideas advocated by those who doubt the Court's worth. In that sense I want to argue that *Viking Line* is an aberration, not a congenital defect, in internal market law. So I want solutions to be appropriately modest.

A. Over-Constitutionalisation

The relevant literature is rich and sophisticated, and there is peril in attempting to distil it to its essence, for fear of imposing a superficial narrative on matters that are anything but superficial. However, running that risk with eyes wide open, the over-constitutionalisation critique holds that EU law contains a structural imbalance which favours deregulation over (re-)regulation, which, translated into constitutional terms, comprises a superiority for primary rules that force open markets and are justiciable before national courts over secondary rules of mitigating (re-)regulation which are dependent on political constellations falling into place and which, even when they do, commonly produce rules that are not, or not readily, translated into directly enforceable legal rights but rather are manifest as collective programmes which are hard to enforce. Primary rules therefore become constitutional norms promoting deregulation: they are dominant and they are very hard to alter. This is, in short, over-constitutionalisation. The EU suffers from this far more than typical states, because a great many issues which are locked into the grip of primary law in the EU are at State level open to political contestation and legislative adaptation over time under the influence of the representative democratic process. So whereas almost all political systems choose to place certain matters beyond alteration by everyday majoritarian whim, the anxiety is that the EU goes too far in entrenching certain (deregulatory) choices. And the Court deepens the problem by its extravagant reading of the Treaty rules' deregulatory strength, driven both by its broad reading of the scope of free movement and its narrow reading of available justifications. Primacy and direct effect ensure these are not simply abstract norms, nor norms the enforcement of which is at the discretion of the Commission in the allocation of its scarce resources: they are directly enforceable as individual rights before national courts.

Viking Line pours salt into these open and festering wounds. It takes a deregulatory model which favours market opening over social protection, and it both deepens it and entrenches it. Locally determined political choices are undermined by the deregulatory aggression of free movement law. And, worse, the Court shows itself inattentive to the absence of compensatory action capable of being taken at EU level. For reasons of constitutional competence, political feasibility, institutional resources and budgetary capacity the EU simply cannot aspire to intervene to achieve the balance between market deregulation and socially motivated market re-regulation which in States has been pieced together over decades of political struggle. *Viking Line* tilts the balance between markets and social solidarity at national level, and that balance cannot be tilted back at EU level. The Court in general and the Court in *Viking Line* in particular, so the criticism runs, accentuates a neoliberal bias that already infects EU internal market law. The Court over-constitutionalises what is already over-constitutionalised.

The problem has attracted wonderfully vivid criticism – Turkuler Isiksel laments the locking away of the matter of defining the scope of freedoms in the EU market in 'the forbidding crypt of constitutional entrenchment',[50] while for Damian Chalmers the EU is guilty of 'over-responsibilisation', and the Court is part of this centralising malaise.[51] On this account the understanding of EU law as a means to tame States' capacity to harm each other has led to States being tamed by the EU *too much*. This is what is dangerous in 'the totalization of the process of integration'.[52] The vertical implications of free movement law constrain national political choices, the horizontal implications constrain EU political choices.

B. Correcting Over-Constitutionalisation

If one believes the Court is generally antagonistic to values other than those of the market, then one is tempted to propose a power of correction on the Court by the legislative process and/or, more radical still, structural changes to the Treaty superstructure to relieve the Court of jurisdiction to rule in this invasive way. In the former vein it is sensible to draw a distinction between rulings of the Court

[50] T Isiksel, *Europe's Functional Constitution* (Oxford, Oxford University Press, 2016) 103.

[51] D Chalmers, 'The Unconfined Power of European Union Law' (2016) *European Papers*, available at: www.europeanpapers.eu/en/e-journal/unconfined-power-european-union-law.

[52] L Azoulai, 'The "Retained Powers" Formula in the Case Law of the European Court of Justice: EU Law as Total Law?' (2011) 4 *European Journal of Legal Studies* 192. See also G Davies, 'The European Union Legislature as an Agent of the European Court of Justice' (2016) 54 *Journal of Common Market Studies* 846.

which interpret primary law and those which deal with the interpretation of secondary legislation. The latter are capable of adjustment by the EU legislative institutions, which, though not easy, is easier than effecting change to rulings dealing with primary law, which requires Treaty revision. This occurs only periodically and only with the support of all the Member States, and it is no surprise that, given such blockages, Court rulings which interpret primary law have almost never been overturned through the treaty-making process. This, then, is the place of principal anxiety for the 'over-constitutionalisation' critique. One could therefore be tempted to champion an easier means to change Court rulings even where they interpret primary law, for example through an adapted version of the ordinary legislative procedure. The prize would be the release of a more vibrant political culture. The problem is that it would surely be rare to find judgments which attract such a high level of antipathy that the sanction could be applied. *Viking Line*, largely welcomed by Central and Eastern European Member States, would not have been vulnerable. Few, if any judgments, ever would be – it would be strange to find the Court regularly (or at all) deciding cases in a way that that runs dramatically contrary to the interests of the majority of the Member States.[53] But allowing for the possibility of reversal outside the process of Treaty revision at least opens up space for democratic contestation.

More ambitious remedies, reaching beyond legislative override of judicial decisions, would promote reform of the Treaty provisions themselves. Several possible models could be envisaged, such as curtailing the breadth of the notion of a barrier to inter-State trade, limiting the personal scope of the free movement provisions to public authorities and providing that the defence of non-economic values is not compressed through the mill of justification but instead is ring-fenced as a protected expression of national autonomy. Several of the interpretative choices which have expanded the reach of the relevant Treaty provisions are choices made by the Court and in theory they could be reversed by the Court.[54] But for good reasons associated with legal certainty and consistency the Court has only rarely and on an ad hoc basis adjusted its conventionally expansive approach. So, to achieve a thorough reform, revision of the Treaties would be required.

C. De-Constitutionalisation

The boldest suggestion on the menu of reforms is to 'deconstitutionalise' EU law. The aim would be to convert the Treaty into a set of principles not rules, and to leave much more space for legislative choices (at both Member State and EU

[53] I compress here several issues. Member States' governments often protest ex ante but are happy with judgments ex post, not least because they may allow the circumvention of powerful domestic interest groups; the Court is also generally attuned to the risk of rejection of its rulings, although it is probably national courts, not political elites, to which it is most sensitive.

[54] There are inviting comparisons to be made with experience in the United States during Roosevelt's 'New Deal', but I do not pursue them here.

level). Fritz Scharpf is in the forefront of this critical literature. He is radical, he is critical; he is thoughtful, he is constructive. His analysis and prescriptions deserve the most careful and respectful attention. There is, he has noted, a 'legitimate diversity' of socio-economic institutions and policies across the Member States, 'shaped by intense political conflicts and historical compromises'.[55] They are highly politically contested and 'they need to be defended in public debates by governments facing the sanctions of political accountability. Instead the supremacy of European law allows for judicial interventions that may short-circuit these political processes. The title of a recent essay captures what he wants to achieve: 'De-constitutionalisation of European Law: The Re-empowerment of Democratic Political Choice'.[56] It repays close attention.

He diagnoses multiple crises – he lists Brexit, the euro crisis, the refugee crisis as well as the crises in Europe's relations with its eastern and southern 'near abroad' – which are generating anxiety about the EU's capacity to address them effectively, harming its output legitimacy. But input legitimacy is undermined too, in so far as those institutions in which citizens invest trust that they will shape the legal, economic and social conditions of our collective existence lack the necessary capacity. The essay focuses on what he calls the excessive 'constitutionalisation' of the EU's Treaties as a factor in this constraining of democratic processes. He argues that the EU Treaties go far beyond typical State constitutions because they regulate in detail a wide range of matters that would be allocated to political contestation and the legislative process at State level. Most of all, the Treaties amount to an economic constitution which place rules and policy beyond political determination, whether at EU level or at national level. And he fingers the Court as having made important choices, most prominently the push beyond a mere anti-discrimination norm, which minimised the need for legislative elaboration of the EU's market-making mission and instead cemented the rules on free movement as individual rights enforced directly against Member State governments by virtue of the constitutional character of EU law. It was, he remarks, 'a revolutionary act of judicial self-empowerment',[57] with a horizontal and vertical constraining impact.

He does not pretend to offer a comprehensive overview of the case law, but of the few decisions he does mention *Viking Line* is of course prominent. I fully share the anxiety that in *Viking Line* the Court placed the Treaty commitment to free movement above national rules governing the regulation of labour markets, and that anxiety is accentuated by awareness that the circumscription of national rules is accompanied by blockages to corrective political action at EU level. This generates a deregulatory impact which is felt most keenly in those societies

[55] F Scharpf, 'The asymmetry of European integration, or why the EU cannot be a social market economy' (2010) 8 *Socio-Economic Review* 211, 241.

[56] Ch 17 in S Garben and I Govaere (eds), *The Division of Competences between the EU and the Member States: Reflections on the Past, the Present and the Future* (Oxford, Hart Publishing, 2017).

[57] At 289.

which have chosen a non-liberal model. Scharpf's solutions – drawing also on Dieter Grimm[58] – are 'de-constitutionalisation' of the Treaties, so that most of the rules now found in the TFEU would be downgraded to the status of secondary law. This would have both vertical and horizontal implications in the sense that it would release space for political contestation at both national and EU level about the structuring and regulation of markets and it would reduce the judicial capacity to lock in interpretations that are irreversible short of Treaty amendment.

Scharpf is not engaged in proposing a tweak here, a nudge there. The radical character of his suggestions needs to be appreciated. He does not want to stop 'litigation and infringement proceedings challenging protectionist measures impeding the access of foreign suppliers or consumers to national markets'.[59] This at first glance seems to want to retain *Cassis de Dijon*, for the point about the rules in that case and myriad other similar cases is precisely that the rules were not discriminatory but rather protectionist (in effect if not always in intent). But Scharpf's accompanying footnote explains that this entails

> a return to the Court's case law before the *Dassonville* and *Cassis* decisions had moved from intervening against protectionist discrimination to intervention against all national rules or practices 'that are capable of hindering, directly or indirectly, actually or potentially' the exercise of a Treaty-based liberty: it would be a 'return to non-discrimination'.

So Scharpf means to retain control according to primary law only over measures that are discriminatory on the basis of their origin *on their face*. This would mark a major retreat in the scope of the free movement rules. It would open up space for more political debate at national level about patterns of market regulation unaffected by EU demands flowing from free movement. According to Scharpf, any future (re-)assertion of a wider scope to the freedoms should be decided through the EU political process, and remain open to subsequent change in the same way.[60] Politics as normal, one might think – *more* politics as normal than we have now.

D. But Not So Fast: Questioning De-Constitutionalisation

I have a high level of sympathy for Scharpf's diagnosis of structural imbalance loaded into the EU legal order and for his flaying of *Viking Line* as a subversion

[58] His fn 10 cites: D Grimm, '"The Democratic Costs of Constitutionalization": The European Case' (2015) *European Law Journal* 21 460–73. D Grimm, 'Europe's Legitimacy Problem and the Courts' in D Chalmers, M Jachtenfuchs and C Joerges (eds), *The End of the Eurocrats' Dream: Adjusting to European Diversity* (Cambridge, Cambridge University Press, 2016) 218–40. D Grimm, *Europa ja – aber welches? Zur Verfassung der europäischen Demokratie* (München, CH Beck, 2016).

[59] At 298.

[60] And in a companion paper motivated by the same critical diagnosis he proceeds also to propose (with due caution) loosening the constraints on legislative activity at EU level, eg by removing the Commission's exclusive right of initiative and promoting more scope for majority-based decision making: F Scharpf, 'De-constitutionalisation and Majority Rule: A Democratic Vision for Europe' (2017) 23 *European Law Journal* 315, esp 323 et seq.

too far off national social choices. But I regard that ruling as a corruption of the Court's orthodox approach to free movement law, not as typical of it. I find the problem of over-constitutionalisation to be much less deep rooted than Scharpf, and so I am much less attracted than Scharpf to such a radical reform of the law of the internal market. I fear too that Scharpf's approach would stimulate pernicious protectionism practised by Member States of the type that *Cassis de Dijon* has been so helpful in washing away. In short, I think free movement law works much better than is portrayed in the literature on over-constitutionalisation and so I want to resist this de-constitutionalisation. I am willing to put my trust in the Court's concern not to allow a drift from control over *Cassis*-type protectionism to a general function of review of economic regulation; and, within that sphere of review, to maintain an open-minded approach to justification which takes seriously the several values, not only market opening, which are inscribed in the Treaties and the Charter. But this claim – that free movement law deserves more approval than Scharpf allows – needs fuller explanation. That is the purpose of the next section.

V. How Free Movement Law should be Interpreted and Applied (and Normally is)

The law of free movement must respect the principle located in Article 5 of the Treaty on European Union (TEU) that the EU possesses only the competences conferred on it by its founding Treaties. This is constitutionally fundamental in the sense that it locates ultimate authority in the Member States as masters of the Treaties, and more generally it expresses the value of local regulatory autonomy. Free movement law must also be sensitive to the Treaty commitments, also embedded within the Charter, *not only* to the integration of national markets into a wider EU internal market *but also* to the quality of the regulation practised within that market.[61] This is a law of free movement that will live up to its constitutional mandate.

In this vein there are two questions which structure the investigation into whether a national measure contradicts the demands of EU free movement law. The first asks whether that national measure acts as a restriction on inter-State trade. If it does not, the enquiry ends – the matter is beyond the reach of free movement law. This, then, is a jurisdictional matter. If the measure does cross the threshold and is shown to affect inter-State trade, the second question is asked, which is whether the objectives of the national measure are of sufficient weight

[61] eg, public health (Art 35 Charter, Art 168(1) TFEU); environmental protection (Art 37 Charter, Art 11 TFEU); consumer protection (Art 38 Charter, Art 12 TFEU); respect for national identity (Art 4(2) TEU).

and are sufficiently well targeted by the measure to rank above the interests of free movement and increased competition across borders. In short, this is a qualitative assessment – is the national measure justified?

Both questions, if answered with care, are apt to filter out the danger of over-constitutionalisation. They are screening devices. The first question filters out national measures that do not have any impact on the construction of the EU's internal market. It protects national autonomy in policymaking where that is unconnected to the EU's aims. The second question is substantive. It asserts the reviewing function of EU internal market law, but it filters out, and allows the retention of, national measures that pursue an interest that is more important than trade integration. These devices act as essential firewalls against the contamination of neoliberal deregulation, and, relying on them, the Court is most of the time attentive to concerns about the value of diversity of (in short) social constitutional choices among the Member States.

Both structuring questions require explanation.

A. What is a Restriction on Inter-State Trade?

The critical jurisdictional dividing line lies between national measures which obstruct inter-State trade (where EU free movement law applies) and national measures unconnected to the impetus to promote cross-border trade (where it does not). That test is easily stated – it is not so easily applied.

There is no denying that the Court rarely finds a matter to lack the necessary nexus. *Berlington Hungary* concerned legislative restrictions placed by the Hungarian authorities on Hungarian operators of slot machines, but the Court noted that some of the players were tourists on holiday from other Member States and that it was 'far from inconceivable' that operators established in Member States other than Hungary might be interested in opening amusement arcades in Hungary.[62] That observation, devoid of any supporting empirical evidence, was enough for it to establish that inter-State trade was sufficiently affected by the rules and that therefore the EU's internal market laws were triggered. This approach, used generously by the Court across the several freedoms,[63] ensures that it is frequently easy to rely on EU law even in circumstances which might initially seem to be confined to a single Member State. A similar expansionist story applies to the personal scope of the Treaty freedoms. Although Article 34 TFEU

[62] Case C-98/14 *Berlington Hungary and others* EU:C:2015:386 para 27.

[63] The same phrase, 'far from inconceivable', appears in, eg: Case C-470/11 *Garkalns* EU:C:2012:505 para 21; Case C-367/12 *Susanne Sokoll-Seebacher* EU:C:2014:68 para 10; Case C-327/12 *Ministero dello Sviluppo economic v SOA* EU:C:2013:827 para 48; 'by no means inconceivable' appears in Case C-168/14 *Grupo Itevelesa SL* EU:C:2015:685 para 36; 'it is conceivable' appears in Case C-523/12 *Dirextra Alta Formazione srl* EU:C:2013:831 para 22; Case C-265/12 *Citroën Belux* (n 25) para 33.

controls only the actions of public authorities where goods are affected,[64] the Court has long treated the other freedoms as apt to bind private parties as well as public authorities,[65] and when confronted by the argument that this robbed private parties of the possibility to justify their practices in line with the public interest tests found in the Treaty, the Court breezily retorted that '[t]here is nothing to preclude individuals from relying on justifications on grounds of public policy, public security or public health'.[66]

The consequence is that it is relatively rare for a matter to be placed beyond the Court's review. *Cassis* is part of this narrative: it asserts a readiness to review non-discriminatory but protectionist practices from which the Court has never departed. And so the focus of the analysis conducted in the name of free movement law turns to justification.

But the Court is aware of the need for a limit. It does not use free movement law to examine *all* restrictions on commercial freedom found within the Member States. It was briefly lured down that path, but it has learned from its mistakes.

Thirty years ago the Court committed the sin of extending review of protectionist rules into a more general review of any form of economic regulation even where no impact on cross-border trade patterns could be discerned. Its 'Sunday Trading' cases stand as the most prominent example. In *Torfaen BC v B&Q plc* the Court, asked whether an eccentric bunch of laws restricting retail sales on a Sunday were compatible with free movement law, correctly stated that the rules 'apply to imported and domestic products alike' and that 'the marketing of products imported from other Member States is not therefore made more difficult than the marketing of domestic products'.[67] This, in short, was not like *Cassis de Dijon*, where the technical standard at stake *did* make marketing of products imported from other Member States more difficult than the marketing of domestic products. And so the Court, equipped with that shrewd insight, should have concluded that the Sunday trading rules were untouched by EU free movement law. But it mistakenly required that the rules be justified and even though it subsequently made clear that the rules were indeed justified,[68] it had extended EU free movement law beyond its intended purpose of making an internal market. Its approach was a genuine threat to national regulatory autonomy, as it converts free movement law into a charter for reviewing *any* restriction on commercial freedom in the Member States even in the absence of any demonstrated harm to inter-State trading. The Court quickly appreciated the problem and it recanted. That arrived in *Keck and Mithouard*.[69] *Keck* attracted plenty of deserved criticism

[64] eg Case C-112/00 *Schmidberger v Austria* EU:C:2003:333; Case C-159/00 *Sapod Audic* EU:C:2002:343; Case C-573/12 *Alands Vinkraft AB* EU:C:2014:2037.

[65] Case 36/74 *Walrave and Koch* EU:C:1974:140.

[66] Case C-415/93 *Bosman* (n 40) para 86.

[67] Case 145/88 *Torfaen BC v B&Q plc* EU:C:1989:593 para 11.

[68] Case C-169/91 *Stoke on Trent and Norwich City Councils v B & Q plc* EU:C:1992:519.

[69] Joined Cases C-267/91 and C-268/91 *Keck and Mithouard* EU:C:1993:905.

at the level of detail, and its significance and fate continue to animate academic analysis today.[70] It was, however, motivated by a well-founded concern to confine the reach of what is now Article 34 TFEU to national measures which have a demonstrable impact on cross-border trade, not simply on selling opportunities more generally. This is the jurisdictionally crucial insistence of the Court that Article 34 does *not* apply where national measures apply equally in law and in fact to all traders and to all goods irrespective of origin. The only exception arises where a complete ban, or a restriction on use that is so severe that it is tantamount to a ban,[71] is imposed on a product: such a rule may apply equally in law and in fact but it isolates the regulated national market from the wider EU internal market and so it needs to be checked by free movement law. So over time the Court has refined and confined its understanding of the reach of free movement law. Laws on the opening hours of shops and similar legally and factually equally applicable rules are no concern of EU free movement law – unless there is some demonstrated connection to an obstruction to the internal market, such as discrimination on grounds of origin.[72]

The test involves examination of the effects of a national measure in order to determine whether it truly applies equally in law and in fact. The Court in *Keck* emphatically did not intend to overturn the *Cassis* line of case law. Technical standards governing product composition are not factually equal in application because local products typically comply with them whereas imported products, made according to a different regulatory tradition, do not, and in the immediate aftermath of *Keck* the Court demolished attempts by regulators to shelter such protectionism behind the *Keck* curtain.[73] Moreover, the Court has shrewdly resisted the argument that a complete ban on advertising a product is inevitably legally and factually equal in in its effects. It will not be – if the ban serves to consolidate the existing advantage of a product familiar to local consumers at the expense of a new unfamiliar product.[74] Advertising and other forms of marketing serve as methods for achieving dynamic change in markets, and their suppression at national level may require control in the name of the internal market for fear

[70] eg L Gormley, 'Inconsistencies and Misconceptions in the Free Movement of Goods' (2015) 40 *European Law Review* 925; I Lianos, 'In Memoriam Keck: The Reformation of the EU Law on the Free Movement of Goods' (2015) 40 *European Law Review* 225; R Schütze, 'Of Types and Tests: Towards a Unitary Doctrinal Framework for Article 34 TFEU?' (2016) 41 *European Law Review* 826; J Holst, 'Keine einheitliche Dogmatik des EuGH für die sachgerechte Begrenzung des Anwendungsbereich der Warenkehrsfreiheit – ein Erklärungsversuch' [2018] *Europarecht* 87.

[71] This, I think, is the Court's intent in Case C-142/05 *Åklagaren v Mickelsson, Roos* EU:C:2009:336.

[72] eg Cases C-401 and C-402/92 *Tankstation 't Heukste & JBE Boermans* EU:C:1994:220; Case C-483/12 *Pelckmans Turnhout* EU:C:2014:304.

[73] eg Case C-470/93 *Verein gegen Unwesen in Handel und Gewerbe Köln v Mars GmbH* (n 9); Case C-244/06 *Dynamic Medien* EU:C:2008:85.

[74] See especially Case C-405/98 *Konsumentombudsmannen v Gourmet International Products* EU:C:2001:135.

that the effect of a ban will be to impose a static structure on the market which consolidates factual advantage enjoyed by local producers.[75]

So the identification of when a measure applies equally in law and in fact must take account of effects, not form. This implies a case-by-case examination. And this case-by-case examination, which will not be simple for national courts to conduct, appears to apply to all the freedoms. The Court has never explicitly exported its decision in *Keck*, which concerned goods, to the interpretation of the scope of the other Treaty freedoms, but it has found similar ways to limit their reach to catch only national measures that hamper the functioning of the internal market.

Volker Graf v Filzmoser Maschinenbau concerned Austrian rules which denied a worker entitlement to compensation where he or she chose to terminate a contract of employment, whereas compensation was payable where the contract ended without the termination being at the worker's own initiative.[76] Graf had been offered a job in Germany and complained that the Austrian rule deterred his readiness to take up the offer. Perhaps it did – but equally it would deter his readiness to take up *any* job offer, in Austria or anywhere else. The Austrian rule applied equally in law and in fact to all workers. It exerted no impact on the creation of an internal market as such but rather merely restricted economic freedom. The Court did not explicitly apply its *Keck* solution to the free movement of workers, but it did reach a comparable result which immunised the Austrian rule from review. The Court concluded that the Austrian rules did not deter a worker from ending a contract of employment in order to take a job with another employer, because the entitlement to compensation on termination of employment was dependent on a future and hypothetical event, namely the subsequent termination of his contract without such termination being at his own initiative. This, the Court ruled, was an event 'too uncertain and indirect a possibility for legislation to be capable of being regarded as liable to hinder freedom of movement for workers'.[77]

In *Mobistar* and *Belgacom Mobile*, providers of telecommunications services challenged Belgian taxes imposed on transmission pylons, masts and antennae as violations of their right to provide services across borders.[78] They had no joy. The taxes added to the costs of providing the services in question but they affected the provision of services between Member States and within the taxing Member State in precisely the same way.[79] That placed them outside the reach of the free movement rules. The Court did not mention *Keck*: it surely could have done. In *ANGED*, a case concerning the freedom of establishment rather than the provision of services, the Court reached a similar conclusion in its assessment of a tax

[75] See eg Case C-239/02 *Douwe Egberts* EU:C:2004:445; Case C-441/04 *A-Punkt Schmuckhandels GmbH v Claudia Schmidt* (n 23); Case C-333/14 *Scotch Whisky Association* EU:C:2015:845; Case C-148/15 *Deutsche Parkinson Vereinigung* EU:C:2016:776.

[76] Case C-190/98 *Volker Graf v Filzmoser Maschinenbau* EU:C:2000:49.

[77] para 25.

[78] Joined Cases C-544/03 and C-545/03 *Mobistar* and *Belgacom Mobile* EU:C:2005:518. See similarly Case C-98/14 (n 62).

[79] para 31.

imposed on large retail establishments.[80] It did not mention *Keck* – and it did not mention *Mobistar* either. The Court avoids any explicit embrace of a convergent approach between the freedoms. But the solution seems to run in common and it is the same as that offered in *Keck*. A particular cross-border dimension must be shown before the matter falls within the scope of free movement law. The result is to shelter national tax-raising capacity from disruption caused by the demands of free movement law – on condition that the tax is applied equally on all operators irrespective of their place of establishment. This reveals the Court's sensitivity to the need to protect local regulatory autonomy.

The Court's caution emerged again in *Kornhaas*.[81] This concerned the application of provisions of German insolvency law to the managing director of a debtor company based in the United Kingdom, but with a branch established in Germany. In a manner thematically consistent with the above-mentioned cases, the director tried to rely on free movement law to resist his subjection to German law. But the Court was not willing to help. It made clear that what was at stake was not a rule concerning the formation of a company in a Member State nor one addressing its subsequent establishment in another Member State, but rather a rule applicable to the running of the company once it has been formed. It could have pointed out that the rule applied equally to all those operating in Germany in an equal manner, and it could have invoked *Keck*. It did not. But the consequence was the same. Articles 49 and 54 TFEU did not preclude the application of German insolvency law. Something similar is found in *Konrad Erzberger*, which concerned German rules governing worker representation on company boards.[82] Once again the litigation focused on an optimistic attempt to invoke free movement law, but with a different motivation. Here the claim was that free movement law required that the German rules apply not only to the company established in Germany, but also to subsidiaries of the group located in another Member State. Otherwise, it was argued, German workers, unable to – in effect – export this benefit, would be dissuaded from exercising their right to free movement throughout the territory of the Union. This argument, though ingenious, failed. Free movement law

> cannot guarantee to a worker that moving to a Member State other than his Member State of origin will be neutral in terms of social security, since, given the disparities between the Member States' social security schemes and legislation, such a move may be more or less advantageous for the person concerned in that regard.[83]

Keck was not mentioned and nor was *Graf*, but the underlying idea seems to be the same. The German rules were different from rules applicable elsewhere, but they applied equally in law and in fact in Germany and the Court was not willing to find that they exerted any detrimental impact on the internal market.

[80] Joined Cases C-236/16 and C-237/16 *ANGED* EU:C:2018:291.
[81] Case C-594/14 *Kornhaas* EU:C:2015:806.
[82] Case C-566/15 *Konrad Erzberger* EU:C:2017:562.
[83] para 34.

There is, then, a jurisdictionally vital threshold, but it is hard to locate. In *Konrad Erzberger* the loss of advantages consequent on the differences between the German system and a less generous one prevailing in another Member State could surely be understood as a disincentive to take advantage of free movement. The Court's observation that primary EU law cannot guarantee to a worker that moving to a Member State other than his Member State of origin will be neutral in its impact on available legislative benefits and protection is assertion, rather than explanation. It must be the Court's point that such national rules, applicable according to objective and non-discriminatory criteria, are not *enough* to constitute an impediment to the free movement of workers. They do not close off access to the market of other Member States nor are they tantamount to exerting such an effect. Exactly when they would be *enough* is evaded, and left for case-by-case consideration (usually by a national court). The Court's refusal to permit reliance on free movement law depends on the factual context – of course it does, the test rests on a search for factual (in)equality in application and/or partitioning of national markets. Imagine if, in *Mobistar*,[84] the tax was set at a very high rate, far higher than in any other Member State. Would its application to all traders really place the matter outside the scope of free movement law? Probably not if it has the effect of greatly restricting the supply of the service in Belgium, thereby isolating the Belgian market from the wider EU internal market.

So rules that close off the regulated market are caught, while rules that limit exercise of commercial freedom within it are not. But the margin between 'closing off' access to the market and restricting exercise of commercial freedom within it is not precise, and it is exactly here in defining the borderline that the Court has assembled a whole array of tests. A national measure is caught if it prevents or *greatly* restricts use of a product[85] or if it causes an individual *serious* inconvenience;[86] it is not caught if its effect on inter-State trade is *remote* or *uncertain*[87] or if it causes an obstacle that is *hypothetical*.[88] The Court here is addressing the jurisdictionally fundamental question when EU free movement law applies and where instead national autonomy is conserved, but these are just words: they are not measurable thresholds.[89] In the same vein, what *Keck* does for the conservation of

[84] Joined Cases C-544/03 and C-545/03 (n 78).

[85] Case C-142/05 *Åklagaren v Mickelsson, Roos* (n 71) para 28.

[86] Case C-208/09 *Ilonka Sayn-Wittgenstein v Landeshauptmann von Wien* EU:C:2010:806; Case C-353/06 *Grunkin, Paul* EU:C:2008:559.

[87] Case C-190/98 *Volker Graf v Filzmoser Maschinenbau* (n 76); Case C-69/88 *Krantz v Ontvanger der Directe Belastingen* EU:C:1990:97; Case C-339/89 *Alsthom Atlantique* EU:C:1991:28; Case C-93/92 *CMC Motorradcenter* EU:C:1993:838; Case C-291/09 *Guarnieri* EU:C:2011:217; Case C-602/10 *SC Volksbank Romania* EU:C:2012:443.

[88] Case 180/83 *Hans Moser v Land Baden-Wűrttemberg* EU:C:1984:233; Case C-299/95 *Kremzow* EU:C:1997:254.

[89] S Weatherill, 'The Court's Case Law on the Internal Market: "A Circumloquacious Statement of the Result, Rather than a Reason for Arriving at It"' in M Adams, H De Waele, J Meeusen and G Straetmans (eds), *Judging Europe's Judges: The Legitimacy of the Case Law of the European Court of Justice* (Oxford, Hart Publishing, 2013).

national autonomy from Article 34, *Tobacco Advertising* does for the conservation of national autonomy from Article 114,[90] but here too, and instructively, imprecise words mark the limits of EU competence to intervene where national practices vary.[91] Moreover, the complexity is accentuated by the Court's determined refusal to consider a convergent approach across the freedoms, so that sometimes different tests appear in the same judgment applicable to different freedoms.[92] The Court's multiple tests stand accused of tending to obscure what is at stake rather than to illuminate it.[93] It is well said that 'an obligation to sustain case law coherence stems from the constitutional responsibilities of the Court of Justice'.[94] But the Court's case law pushes a lot of emphasis on case-by-case analysis by national courts asked to apply a bewildering diversity of tests.

These anxieties are well founded. But they should not be exaggerated. The Court paints the big picture correctly: it is visibly concerned not to push the four freedoms to become a truly alarming neoliberal charter. There is no explicitly convergent approach across the several Treaty freedoms, but there is a convergent anxiety, expressed in different ways, to find a limit to EU law's intrusive potential. It is 30 years since it tarnished the legitimacy of free movement law by lurching towards a general review of economic regulation in the 'Sunday Trading' cases: today the Court backs off when asked to allow the exploitation of EU law to attack practices that are a purely local concern.[95] Free movement law is dedicated to achieving the internal market as defined by Article 26 TFEU: it is not intended 'to encourage the unhindered pursuit of commerce in individual Member States'.[96] Although the Court has shied away from stipulating a precise and convergent test, its concern evidently rests in sheltering national rules that apply equally in law and in fact and do not partition the regulated market from the wider EU internal market from review. The Court has chosen to treat the free movement rules as *less* than a charter for general review of Member State economic policy but as *more* than a mere anti-discrimination rule. And by acknowledging the legitimate scope for national regulatory choices – on taxation, on worker representation, on marketing methods – which are untouched by free movement law, the Court is building a wall over which neoliberal deregulation may not slide. The idea is that it

[90] Case C-376/98 *Germany v Parliament and Council* EU:C:2000:544.

[91] eg Case C-58/08 *Vodafone* EU:C:2010:321: Art 114 may be used where disparities between national rules cause 'significant' distortions of competition (para 32) or to prevent the emergence of obstacles to trade resulting from the divergent development of national laws where the emergence is 'likely' (para 33).

[92] eg, Case C-483/12 *Pelckmans Turnhout NV* (n 72) (*Keck* for Art 34, uncertainty for Art 56).

[93] J Snell, 'The Notion of Market Access: A Concept or a Slogan?' (2010) 47 *Common Market Law Review* 437, 470. See also, eg, A Tryfonidou, 'The Notions of "Restriction" and "Discrimination" in the Context of the Free Movement of Persons Provisions: From a Relationship of Interdependence to One of (Almost Complete) Independence' (2014) 33 *Yearbook of European Law* 385.

[94] N Nic Shuibhne, *The Coherence of EU Free Movement Law* (Oxford, Oxford University Press, 2013) 31.

[95] A different, but explicitly exceptional, story may be discerned in application to third-country nationals where the Treaty rules on Citizenship have been interpreted to apply to situations internal to a single Member State, Case C-34/09 *Ruiz Zambrano* EU:C:2011:124.

[96] Case C-292/92 *Hunermund* EU:C:1993:863, Opinion of AG Tesauro para 1.

is possible to establish a true internal market within which there is nevertheless a degree of local heterogeneity in regulatory choices. Access to the regulated market must be unhindered, but that does not mean that treatment on it will mirror that in the trader's home State.

So the Court is conscious of the harm that motivates Scharpf's critique of neoliberalism and over-constitutionalisation. It has responded to it. But Scharpf wants to go much further backwards than *Keck*. He wants to roll back *Cassis*. But that retreat would not simply protect legitimate national regulatory diversity, it would shelter protectionism and harm to local consumers and out-of-State traders from judicial review. I think Scharpf overstates the problem and so offers a dangerously inflated remedy. I will return to this in my Conclusion, in summarising the case against the radical retreat proposed by Scharpf.

B. Justification as a Safety Valve

Where there is a demonstrated obstacle to cross-border trade, space is allowed for recognition of the legitimate concerns motivating national market regulation, for they are mediated through the test of justification. Justification in this sense acts as a necessary safety valve to loosen the pressure exerted by the Court's typically broad understanding of the material and personal scope of EU internal market law. Deregulation occurs only when national measures are *not* underpinned by, as the Court put it in *Cassis de Dijon*, 'a purpose which is in the general interest and such as to take precedence over the requirements of the free movement of goods'.[97] And testing national measures in this way gives room to open up a discussion about the purpose(s) of often long-standing rules and to check their persisting worth in a climate of deepening economic interdependence.

It is perfectly true that many of the Court's decisions concerning free movement take little time to interrogate the justifiability of the national measures at stake. This is not because the Court places a priority on deregulation. It is because the arguments advanced to justify the measures are so frequently at best weak and at times plain daft. *Cassis de Dijon* itself is of this type: the Court can hardly be blamed for swiping aside with polite derision the idea that keeping weak, but not strong, alcoholic drinks off the German market constituted any form of coherent public health policy.

But such absurdity is commonplace. The dismal trickle of cases decided in the wake of *Cassis*, concerning claims that consumers need protection from margarine that is not packed in a cube,[98] that advertising should be banned on national television networks even while it is permitted on local television networks,[99] and so on, were considered above in section II.B. They are regrettably typical. In *Eric Libert*

[97] Case 120/78 *Rewe-Zentrale* AG (n 1) para 14.
[98] Case 261/81 *Walter Rau* (n 4).
[99] Case C-500/06 *Corporación Dermoestética* (n 8).

the Court was asked to accept that Flemish rules restricting the acquisition of property by those without a 'sufficient connection' to the local commune were justified despite their restrictive effect on cross-border movement because they served to hold down costs in order to prevent the exclusion of socially and/or economically disadvantaged locals.[100] The Court accepted this purpose as legitimate in principle, but, on closer inspection, the rules in question attached no significance whatsoever to affluence, so even well-off locals would meet the requirement. This is not the Court using free movement law to undermine locally determined social welfare choices, this is the Court exposing regulatory mendacity.

A good – and profoundly under-researched – question asks why Member States even bother to defend such blatantly unjustified rules which had no conceivable virtuous purpose in an integrating EU-wide market. The best guess is that their sole virtue lay in the protection they afforded to local producers, sheltered from competition, and that those producers had enough political clout to provoke the public authorities to try to defend them, rather than cleanse the statute book of their inhibiting effect. This immediately highlights the value of EU free movement law – it provides a lever to dislodge rules which harm out-of-State producers, local consumers and the general competitive process but which would not have been challenged if left to be addressed exclusively in the domestic context.[101] So EU law promotes deregulation and regulatory renovation which is frequently much needed.

But more sincere justifications sometimes reach Luxembourg, and the Court has carefully interpreted free movement law to be open to their recognition. *A-Punkt* and *Citroen Belux*, in which the Court found particular measures of targeted consumer protection to be justified, were considered above,[102] but the Court's approach is by no means confined to testing economic arguments of this type. In fact the Court's general public interest test shaped in and since *Cassis* means that in principle the Court has long been prepared to admit to the examination of whether a national measure is justified a wide range of interests and values that are left unmentioned in Articles 36, 45, 52 and 62 TFEU themselves. In principle the Court will assess whether national measures that impede cross-border trade are justified as means to secure protection of the environment,[103] to conserve biodiversity,[104] to defend and promote culture and artistic property,[105] to preserve and promote press diversity,[106] to secure respect for human dignity,[107]

[100] Joined Cases C-197/11 and C-203/11 *Eric Libert* EU:C:2013:288.

[101] *cf* the literature cited at n 22.

[102] Case C-441/04 (n 23); Case C-265/12 (n 25).

[103] eg Case 302/86 *Commission v Denmark* EU:C:1988:421; Case C-379/98 *Preussen Elektra* EU:C:2001:160; Case C-573/12 *Ålands Vindkraft AB* (n 64).

[104] Case C-67/97 *Ditlev Bluhme* EU:C:1998:584.

[105] eg Case C-531/07 *Fachverband/ LIBRO* EU:C:2009:276.

[106] Case C-368/95 *Vereinigte Familiapress Zeitungsverlags- und vertriebs GmbH v Heinrich Bauer Verlag* EU:C:1997:325.

[107] Case C-36/02 *Omega Spielhallen* EU:C:2004:614.

to protect the child,[108] to promote concern for animal welfare,[109] to take care of the particular features of sport,[110] or to ensure the survival of small and medium-sized businesses.[111] It is even willing to consider the value in protecting the respect owed to the memory of the deceased, where national rules obstruct the sale of a site to store funeral urns![112] Sometimes the justification is in its particular context sufficiently compelling to be treated as apt to restrain the deregulatory dynamic of free movement law, sometimes it is not, but the point is that the Court pursues the examination even though the Treaty provisions on free movement themselves do not accommodate any explicit direction to take account of such concerns and even though in some cases the Treaty equips the EU with little or no legislative competence to address the matters motivating the national measures. So the Court has ensured that it is open in principle to national (public and private) regulators to draw on the full breadth of their purposes in interfering with the integration of product and service markets in the EU as they seek to demonstrate that they should be treated as justified.

The seriousness of the Court's attachment to reading primary rules with recognition for values beyond those that are textually visible on the terms of the Treaty itself is highlighted by appreciation that what it did to free movement in *Cassis* it has done in a functionally similar way to competition law too. *Albany International* involved affiliation to a sectoral pension fund which was made compulsory by the Dutch authorities at the request of organisations representing employers and workers.[113] Albany wished to attack the request by management and labour as an anticompetitive agreement contrary to what is now Article 101(1) on the basis that the compulsory nature of the scheme shut down opportunities for other providers to compete in the pension insurance market. This was highly significant: if such arrangements fell within the scope of Article 101 the whole array of collective agreements governing labour markets and industrial relations would be open to attack in the name of EU law. The Court closed that door. Restrictions of competition were inherent in such collective agreements, but 'the social policy objectives pursued by such agreements and recognised as important by the Treaty would be seriously undermined' if Article 101 were interpreted to apply to collective action aimed at the improvement of conditions of work and employment.[114] This is a creative interpretation of the scheme and values of the Treaty *as a whole* which allows social dialogue an immunity from competition law. This 'Albany exception' reveals a sensitivity in the Court to the need to limit the destabilising effect of internal market law, although it is admittedly an approach that the Court has been resolutely unwilling to extend beyond the particular circumstances at

[108] Case C-244/06 *Dynamic Medien* (n 73).
[109] Case C-219/07 *Nationale Raad van Dierenkwekers en Liefhebbers* EU:C:2008:353.
[110] Case C-415/93 *Bosman* (n 40).
[111] Case C-464/05 *Maria Geurts* EU:C:2007:631.
[112] Case C-342/17 *Memoria Srl v Comune di Padova* EU:C:2018:906.
[113] Case C-67/96 *Albany International* EU:C:1999:430.
[114] para 59.

stake in *Albany*.[115] A more generally applicable device for softening the interventionism of competition law which also displays clear functional similarities with *Cassis* and the development of free movement law was initiated by the Court in *Wouters*.[116] Rules of the Dutch bar prohibited multidisciplinary partnerships between advocates and accountants. This obviously restricted competition. The Court stated that in applying what is now Article 101(1) TFEU, account must be taken of 'the overall context in which the decision of the association of undertakings was taken or produces its effects'.[117] Directing that account should be taken of the objectives pursued, it added that it 'has then to be considered whether the consequential effects restrictive of competition are inherent in the pursuit of those objectives'.[118] So just as a barrier to inter-State trade which is shown to be justified escapes the prohibition contained in Articles 34 and 56, so too a restriction on inter-State competition which pursues (in short) justified objectives escapes the prohibition found in Article 101(1). In this way, the Court has found no restriction on competition which is incompatible with EU law where sporting bodies impose sanctions on competitors who have been found guilty of doping offences, given the need to safeguard athletes' health, the integrity and objectivity of competitive sport and ethical values in sport.[119]

One cannot miss the Court's concern to read internal market law in a way that is open to non-economic values. Unquestionably the Court enjoys a hugely influential power to determine the shape of the internal market, which, in part because of the Treaty system but also because of its own interpretative choices, allows it to require the setting aside of national choices (the vertical issue) and sometimes in circumstances where its own rulings may not be displaced by political action at EU level (the horizontal issue), but the story of its adjudicative track record is far more complex and nuanced than relentless deregulation and disrespect for local social, moral and ethical choices that touch the market. In *Fransson* the Court declared that '[t]he applicability of EU law entails applicability of the fundamental rights guaranteed by the Charter'.[120] This must cover also internal market law, so the application and interpretation of the free movement and competition rules must be informed by Charter rights and principles, including, for example, Articles 22 (culture), 35 (health), 37 (environment) and 38 (consumer protection). This is reinforced by the transversal or cross-cutting Treaty provisions such as Articles 11, 12 and 168(1) TFEU which mandate that environmental protection, consumer protection and public health (respectively) shall inform the definition

[115] Case C-413/13 *FNV Kunsten Informatie en Media* EU:C:2014:2411; Case C-438/05 *Viking Line* (n 36).

[116] C-309/99 *JCJ Wouters, JW Savelbergh, Price Waterhouse Belastingadviseurs BV v Algemene Raad van de Nederlandse Orde van Advocaten* EU:C:2002:98.

[117] para 97.

[118] para 97.

[119] Case C-519/04 P *Meca-Medina & Majcen v Commission* EU:C:2006:492. See also Case C-1/12 *OTOC* EU:C:2013:127.

[120] Case C-617/10 *Fransson* EU:C:2013:280 para 21.

and implementation of Union policies. The expansive reach of free movement law long ago exploded the notion that the EU deals with market integration while the Member States take care of socially motivated regulation. That dichotomy is false: free movement law cascades over the seawall between integration and regulation. But by virtue of its attentiveness to the availability of justification, free movement law itself becomes more than a site dedicated simply to deregulation: free movement law is not only about free movement (and competition law is not only about competition). The Court makes it so, but the Court has always made it so. The Charter values and those of the transversal Treaty provisions are readily aligned with orthodox justifications long ago embraced in the case law on the law of the internal market.

In an intriguing batch of cases, the Court has been asked to apply free movement law, which the Court itself has described as playing a fundamental role in the EU,[121] to national measures which restrict inter-State trade but which themselves seek to protect national conceptions of social, political and cultural values which are commonly themselves also of fundamental constitutional status, under national or EU law or both. This is to set differently motivated fundamental rights against each other. The Court requires a case-by-case contextually informed assessment to take place: there is no question of elevating economic rights above other types of rights. And the national level of decision-making is explicitly permitted a margin of discretion. There is no brutal deregulation here!

For example in *Schmidberger v Austria*, the Court, asked to consider an obstacle to trade in goods through the Brenner Pass caused by a protest permitted by the Austrian authorities which was aimed at drawing attention to environmental damage, took the view that the protection of fundamental rights of expression and protest counted as a legitimate interest which justified a restriction on an economic fundamental freedom guaranteed by the Treaty.[122] The Court ruled that 'the interests involved must be weighed having regard to all the circumstances of the case in order to determine whether a fair balance was struck between those interests' and it added that '[t]he competent authorities enjoy a wide margin of discretion in that regard'.[123] So the restrictive effect on cross-border trade in goods, though fully acknowledged, was treated as justified. The national authorities, enjoying a wide margin of discretion, were entitled to conclude that a ban on the protest would have been an unacceptable interference with the fundamental rights of the demonstrators.

The Court's readiness to permit justification is structurally consistent with its approach throughout the law governing free movement, but the discourse of 'balancing' adds something new and reflects the sensitivities at stake. This

[121] eg Case 120/78 *Rewe-Zentrale AG* (n 1) para 14; Case C-112/00 *Schmidberger* v *Austria* (n 64) paras 50, 60. Its terminology is admittedly unsystematic: F de Cecco, 'Fundamental Freedoms, Fundamental Rights, and the Scope of Free Movement Law' (2014) 15 *German Law Journal* 383.

[122] Case C-112/00 (n 64).

[123] paras 81–82.

is different in tone from cases of the *Cassis* type, in which the Court is brisk in dismissing the justifiability of rules that are simply inappropriate in an integrating market, but the different tone follows from the different context: genuine conflicts of values fall to be addressed by internal market law in a case like *Schmidberger*. A discourse of 'balancing' allied to a margin of appreciation granted to the regulator, which carries a flavour of general human rights law rather than the more intense, even sceptical, review conventionally associated with the Court's case law in the often protectionist economic heartland of free movement law, is the Court's way to embed sensitivity to the complexity of the calculations at stake in the interplay of economic integration with social and political freedoms. In a structurally similar vein, the Court in *Omega Spielhallen* held that a ban on a game involving simulated killing, 'Laserdrome', on the basis that such practices offended against standards of respect for human dignity that were constitutionally protected in Germany, amounted to a restriction on the free movement of services from the United Kingdom, but that the EU objective of protecting human dignity justified it.[124] This was not EU free movement *versus* protection of human dignity under German law, but instead EU free movement *versus* protection of human dignity under EU law. Today it could confirm this approach by citing Article 1 of the Charter, which expressly embraces human dignity as inviolable, but it is telling of the Court's anxieties that in *Omega*, fully five years in advance of the grant of binding effect on the Charter, the Court was able to shape an EU recognition of a standard of protection in the context of examining the justification advanced according to the particular sensitivities emerging in one Member State. The internal market as a legal concept is porous to divergence in the weight attached to non-economic values, and the Court added explicitly that 'the competent national authorities must therefore be allowed a margin of discretion within the limits imposed by the Treaty'.[125]

These are in formal terms free movement cases not human rights cases: the Court reaches human rights only because there is a free movement issue. In May 2014 the President of the Court, Mr Skouris, speaking in Copenhagen, put it bluntly: 'The Court of Justice is not a human rights court; it is the Supreme Court of the European Union'.[126] It is possible to develop a critique which sees the Court's engagement with human rights as purely instrumental, and dedicated ultimately to market integration. I think this is unconvincing. These cases give room to Member States to justify practices that inhibit free movement because they are motivated by concern for fundamental rights and values: free movement law accommodates such justifications and thereby becomes itself a particular type of human rights law. But the free movement claim itself may sometimes be a means to project a fundamental rights claim, which will in turn challenge and undermine

[124] Case C-36/02 *Omega Spielhallen* [2004] ECR I-9609.

[125] para 31.

[126] Cited by L Besselink, 'The ECJ as the European Supreme Court', available at: verfassungsblog.de/ecj-european-supreme-court-setting-aside-citizens-rights-eu-law-supremacy/.

national practices that are closed to such values. Where a State refuses to recognise same-sex marriage, the natural reaction might be to wonder if Strasbourg might help, but the Grand Chamber ruling in *Coman* reveals the vitality of EU law.[127] Mr Coman, a dual US and Romanian national, married Mr Hamilton, a US national, in Belgium. The question referred to the Court of Justice asked whether Hamilton had a right to reside with Coman in Romania, where, in contrast to Belgium, same-sex marriage is not recognised. Article 21(1) TFEU provided a basis for Coman's free movement claim: he was asserting a right against his own Member State but in circumstances where he had left it and was now returning. This right included a right to lead a normal family life with his spouse, which the Court treated as a gender-neutral term. The Romanian refusal to grant a right of residence could stand only if justified, which the Court did not consider it was. So Member States retain competence to decide who may marry on their territory, but they must exercise that competence within the bounds set by free movement law. This is a structurally familiar approach in EU free movement law – it is the reasoning that underpins the intrusion of free movement law into autonomy to regulate labour relations found in *Viking Line*. The result is not top-down EU legislative rules on the definition of marriage (or of collective labour action), but instead diversity across the Member States conditioned by a bottom-up, litigation-driven adjustment in particular cases of refusal to recognise practice in other Member States. In *Coman*, Romania is not required to open up its marriage laws to all same-sex couples, but it has to accept the consequences of another Member State having chosen to do so. Romania does not have to adopt the Belgian model but it must show 'empathy' for it.[128]

The Court does not assert a general competence to protect fundamental rights, but free movement law opens up scope to protect fundamental rights. It is a model of responsiveness and adaptation, cooperation and toleration. A difference among Member States' values is recognised, but it is managed, rooted in the understanding that, as made very concrete by Mr Coman's travels from east to west and back east again, States in Europe are interdependent, 'like the co-owners of the same constitutional plot'.[129] It is to 'acknowledge the validity of certain forms of bounded identity but simultaneously to reach across boundaries'.[130]

The beauty of free movement law lies in the Court's insistence, in line with the Treaty, that cross-border trading freedom is not absolute but instead must show

[127] Case C-673/16 *Coman* EU:C:2018:385.

[128] K Nicolaidis, 'Mutual Recognition: Promise and Denial, from Sapiens to Brexit' (2017) 70 *Current Legal Problems* 227, 232.

[129] AJ Menéndez, 'United They Diverge? From Conflicts of Law to Constitutional Theory? On Christian Joerges' Theory' ARENA Working Paper (Oslo) No 2 February 2011, 7. This paper correctly heralds the deep impact of Christian Joerges's scholarship in this area.

[130] JHH Weiler, 'Europe: The Case against the Case for Statehood' (1998) 4 *European Law Journal* 43, 61. See also JHH Weiler, 'In Defense of the Status Quo: Europe's Constitutional *Sonderweg*' in JHH Weiler and M Wind, *European Constitutionalism beyond the State* (Cambridge, Cambridge University Press, 2003).

deference both to values promoted through national political processes and to definitive assessment by national courts.[131] The Court does a generally respectful job in balancing the interest in market regulation expressed through (sincere and targeted) national rules against the interest in market deregulation achieved by holding obstructive national rules to be unjustified.[132]

Although it is not in formal terms a human rights court, its engagement with human rights in the context of free movement cases shows that it takes such values seriously. Moreover, looking beyond the vertical implications of its case law to the horizontal implications, it is usually attentive to the need to leave space for political adjustment – in fact, it has been convincingly demonstrated that the Court's judgments generate an intriguingly varied range of responses from the political institutions of the EU.[133]

C. But … What about *Viking Line*?

EU free movement law uses two devices to filter out the poison of deregulation which is insensitive to the value of local regulatory autonomy: first, there are the limits to the reach of the free movement rules examined above in section V.A and, second, even where a national measure is shown to affect inter-State trade, the Court is receptive to sincerely expressed and crafted justification, as explained above in section V.B. These controls reflect, in the first instance, the principle that the EU possesses only the competences conferred on it by its Treaties,[134] which entails that the free movement rules bite only where national practices harm the construction of the EU's internal market, and, in the second, the constitutional commitments made by both the TFEU and the Charter to securing regulatory protection of defined social values within the construction of the internal market.[135] So what about *Viking Line*?

[131] J Zglinski, 'The Rise of Deference: The Margin of Appreciation and Decentralised Judicial Review in EU Free Movement Law' (2018) 55 *Common Market Law Review* 1341. See also J Mulder, 'Responsive Adjudication and the Social Legitimacy of the Internal Market' (2016) 22 *European Law Journal* 597.

[132] *cf* D Damjanovic, 'The EU Market Rules as Social Market Rules: Why the EU Can Be a Social Market Economy' (2013) 50 *Common Market Law Review* 1685; J Schwarze, 'Die Abwägung von Zielen der europäischen Integration und mitgliedstaatlichen Interessen in der Rechtsprechung des EuGH' [2013] *Europarecht* 253: F De Witte, 'Sex, Drugs and EU Law: The Recognition of Moral and Ethical Diversity in EU Law' (2013) 50 *Common Market Law Review* 1545; J Hojnik, 'The EU Internal Market and National Tradition and Culture: Any Room for Market Decentralisation?' (2012) 8 *Croatian Yearbook of European Law & Policy* 117; S Garben, 'The Constitutional (Im)balance between the Market and the Social in the European Union' (2017) 13 *European Constitutional Law Review* 23; M Bartl, 'Internal Market Rationality: In the Way of Re-imagining the Future' (2018) 24 *European Law Journal* 99.

[133] D Martinsen, *An Ever More Powerful Court? The Political Constraints of Legal Integration in the European Union* (Oxford, Oxford University Press, 2015).

[134] Art 5(1) TEU.

[135] eg, public health (Art 35 Charter, Art 168(1) TFEU); environmental protection (Art 37 Charter, Art 11 TFEU); consumer protection (Art 38 Charter, Art 12 TFEU); respect for national identity (Art 4(2) TEU).

The existence of a cross-border dimension in *Viking Line* was plain, so the focus of attention is on the Court's treatment of justification. It was argued above, in examining the ruling, that in *Viking Line* the Court applied an analysis that showed inadequate regard for the place of collective labour action in the market and in society more generally. The wider examination of the Court's case law provided above in section V.B has revealed still more clearly that normally the Court is sensitive to social and political interests in its application of the justification test in free movement law and that, moreover, it builds in an explicit margin of discretion for either the national decision-maker or the referring national court (or both) where fundamental rights and values of differing types come into collision. All this is missing from *Viking Line*.

Viking Line is an aberration, not the norm. It is not (only) that the ruling is imbalanced in its measurement of the strength of the economic claim and the strength of the socio-political claim, it is also that this imbalance is out of line with the Court's own case law. The Court is normally sensitive to the structural imbalance which privileges deregulation by judicial process over re-regulation by legislative intervention, and it accordingly is normally attentive to the vertical and horizontal implications of its ruling. But in *Viking Line* its test significantly favours corporate interests over worker protection. And the Court did not follow the model regularly preferred in the case law considered above: it leaves wholly out of account any margin of appreciation apt to permit recognition of local circumstances by the adjudicating national judge. Moreover it did it in circumstances where there is no serious possibility to readdress the balances at stake through the political process at EU level. The ruling is blind to the safety valve of justification and, in particular, the safety valve of the margin of appreciation to restrain the deregulatory potential of free movement law, thereby to grant space both to local assessment of the virtue of justification in the particular circumstances and to the possibility of political contestation and legislative reappraisal at EU level.

Viking Line should have been decided with a higher level of sensitivity to the vertical and horizontal implications of the Court's choices. And it could have been so decided. So this is my amended version of the ruling: paragraph 90 of *Viking Line* supplemented by recognition of the complexities and sensitivities involved:

> Article 43 EC [now Article 49 TFEU] is to be interpreted to the effect that collective action such as that at issue in the main proceedings, which seeks to induce a private undertaking whose registered office is in a given Member State to enter into a collective work agreement with a trade union established in that State and to apply the terms set out in that agreement to the employees of a subsidiary of that undertaking established in another Member State, constitutes a restriction within the meaning of that article. That restriction may, in principle, be justified by an overriding reason of public interest, such as the protection of workers, provided that it is established that the restriction is suitable for ensuring the attainment of the legitimate objective pursued and does not go beyond what is necessary to achieve that objective. **In making that assessment of the suitability of the restriction and in determining whether it goes beyond what is necessary to achieve the objective, a wide margin of discretion shall be permitted**

> **with a view to ensuring that the promotion of the Community's [now Union's] social purposes is not disproportionately impeded. [The wide margin of discretion shall also be informed by the respect which according to Article 4(2) TEU the Union shall show for the fundamental structures, political and constitutional, of the Member States and by the recognition in Article 28 of the EU Charter of Fundamental Rights of the right of workers to take collective action to defend their interests, while also showing the respect for the autonomy of the social partners which is mandated by Article 152 TFEU.]**[136]

The first added sentence could and should have been included at the time the ruling was delivered; the second (in square brackets) adds in extra balancing concerns in the light of the revisions made to the Treaties with effect from 2009 by the Treaty of Lisbon. Similarly motivated suggestions for rethinking have been pressed on the Court, so far to no avail, by two of its Advocates General – Cruz Villalón in *Santos Palhota and Others*[137] and Trstenjak in *Commission v Germany*.[138] The ambition is to introduce a degree of modesty, even humility, and, most of all, to show greater attentiveness to the horizontal and vertical implications of the Court's stance and the need to leave space for political contestation about the proper scope of collective labour rights. The grant of binding force to the Charter and the increased prominence granted to the social market economy on the entry into force of the Lisbon Treaty in 2009 might eventually provide a convenient cover for the Court to resile from *Viking Line*[139] but there was plenty of material available in the state of EU internal market law existing at the time of *Viking Line* to justify this approach. So I am promoting this *both* as a better presentation of how free movement law should touch sensitive social policy issues *and also* as a better fit with the Court's conventional practice. Such re-balancing would serve to bring the intersection between labour law and EU internal market law into alignment with the general pattern explained above in section V.B whereby sensitive national practices and concerns are treated with care in the light of their impact on the internal market. In fact, *Viking Line* is decided according to a tone which recalls the cases of the early years in which the Court swept aside thoroughly implausible claims to justification

[136] This is taken from S Weatherill, '*Viking* and *Laval*: The EU Internal Market Perspective' 23–39 in M Freedland and J Prassl (eds), *EU Law in the Member States: Viking, Laval and Beyond* (Oxford, Hart Publishing, 2014).

[137] Case C-515/08 *Santos Palhota and Others* EU:C:2010:245.

[138] Case C-271/08 *Commission v Germany* EU:C:2010:183.

[139] *cf*, on re-balancing post-Lisbon, C Semmelmann, 'The European Union's Economic Constitution under the Lisbon Treaty: Soul-searching Shifts the Focus to Procedure' (2010) 35 *European Law Review* 516; N Nic Shuibhne, 'Margins of Appreciation: National Values, Fundamental Rights and EC Free Movement Law' (2009) 34 *European Law Review* 230; S Weatherill, 'From Economic Rights to Fundamental Rights' in S De Vries, U Bernitz and S Weatherill (eds), *The Protection of Fundamental Rights after Lisbon* (Oxford, Hart Publishing, 2013); D Schiek, 'The EU Constitution of Social Governance in an Economic Crisis: In Defence of a Transnational Dimension to Social Europe' (2013) 20 *Maastricht Journal of European and Comparative Law* 185; D Schiek, 'Towards More Resilience for a Social EU: The Constitutionally Conditioned Internal Market' (2017) 13 *European Constitutional Law Review* 611.

made on behalf of public authorities defending anachronistic and sometimes daft practices. It should instead have been decided in the way that the Court has come to handle serious and delicate political questions about priorities which arise in free movement – by setting aside any sense of hierarchy in favour of an economic claim and adding, too, a margin of discretion or appreciation apt to show deference to local political and/or judicial appraisal.

VI. Conclusion

The critical literature on *Viking Line* treats it as insensitive to the legitimate concerns of organised labour. I agree. The critical literature warns that this approach risks converting the EU into a neoliberal project that is insensitive not simply to social values but to democratic contestation itself, and will surely provoke resistance. I agree. But *Viking Line* is atypical. It is not the norm in free movement law – it is an aberration from the norm. The Court is normally sensitive to the vertical and horizontal implications of its case law. This means that the narrative of over-constitutionalisation has bite, but that it should not be exaggerated. And that leads me in turn to scepticism about the more aggressive solutions that are proposed. They may, by overstating the problem, do more harm than good.

The Court possesses, and uses, two devices to protect against over-constitutionalisation. Section V of this chapter, entitled 'How Free Movement Law should be Interpreted and Applied (and Normally is)', explains this. Summarised, the Court is normally attentive to, first, the proper jurisdictional limits of internal market law and, the corollary, to the preserved zone of State autonomy; and, second, once that threshold is crossed, to the need for a porous free movement law. The free movement rules, reflecting the principle of conferral in Article 5(1) TEU, stop where their market-making function is exhausted, and where a national measure is shown to affect inter-State trade the Court, reflecting the constitutional commitments made by both the TFEU and the Charter to securing regulatory protection of defined social values within the construction of the internal market, takes due account of the range of affected values by opening up a broad understanding of justification. These are the two filters or safety valves which prevent free movement law becoming a neoliberal charter which unduly disturbs the vertical distribution of competences and the horizontal distribution of powers in the EU. The Court normally knows its limits.

I believe the court should be trusted *so long as* it consistently embeds these concerns into its interpretation of free movement law. I will not persuade you of this if your objection is to the very fact of a court as an institution making such charged decisions, but given the commitment to creating a transnational internal market for the EU I think that is unavoidable. I will not persuade myself if the Court makes a habit of decisions like *Viking Line*, but I think that is unlikely. It is not deaf to the criticism.

Most of all, I fear that the radical proposal to curtail the risk of neoliberalism by retreat even from *Cassis de Dijon* is to go too far. It would release protectionism. To overthrow *Cassis*, and to offer room to restore national rules on the shape of packets of margarine and on the nature of shallots which would go undisciplined by free movement law, would tear a hole in the fabric of the internal market. It would, moreover, suppress the model of managed cooperation, tolerance and respect for difference which has been deployed in such an agile fashion by the Court in a case like *Coman*, considered in section V.B. To confine free movement law to a mere non-discrimination norm, as proposed in the literature which is critical of over-constitutionalisation considered in section IV of this chapter, over-protects the sphere of local regulatory autonomy; it robs free movement law of its capacity to lock all the Member States into a rule-based system which reviews regulatory choices that generate cross-border implications rather than acceding to aggressive unilateral power-playing.

In the myth, the beauty saves the beast. I want to make that myth reality: I want *Viking Line* to be adjusted, as explained above in section V.C, in order to ensure that the open-textured pattern of justification coupled to a margin of discretion common to free movement law generally also informs the intersection of free movement law with labour law. The beast can be transformed by the magical application of internal market orthodoxy. To travel in the other direction – to overturn *Cassis* and to convert free movement law into a mere non-discrimination norm – would be to transform the beauty into the beast of permitted protectionism and closure to practices preferred elsewhere. It would be the myth in reverse. It would be a tragic tale.

7

Changing the European Union Through Education: What Can the European Union Do for Education, and What Can Education Do for the European Union?

TAMARA PERIŠIN*

'We don't need no education
We don't need no thought control
Hey! Teachers! Leave them kids alone!
All in all you're just another brick in the wall'
Pink Floyd[1]

I. Introduction

Pink Floyd's famous song 'Another Brick in the Wall' and its original video speak of a cruel education system which limits creative and critical thinking, subordinating

* Tamara Perišin, Judge at the Court of Justice of the European Union – General Court, Professor of Law at the University of Zagreb. This paper was originally prepared for the 2018 conference 'The Role of Law and Courts in a Changing European Union', organised by the Jean Monnet Centre of Excellence in Zagreb. Some of the ideas were also presented at the American University, Washington DC, in August 2018, and at the European University Institute in October 2018. I would like to thank the participants of these events for their comments, in particular Koen Lenaerts, Hans Micklitz, John Morijn, Fernanda Nicola, Siniša Rodin, Urška Šadl, Alexander Somek, Philomila Tsoukala and Robert Wai. I am also grateful to Duncan Kennedy and Roberto Unger for earlier discussions which triggered some of the ideas for this chapter. Finally, I am thankful for the research assistance of Alessandro Angelico and Helena Kumpar Zidanič. All opinions expressed herein are personal to the author.

[1] Pink Floyd 'Another Brick in the Wall (Pt 2)' 1979, Harvest (UK) Columbia (USA) © Roger Waters.

students who become faceless and deprived of their individuality. The hierarchy is 'hammering and grinding' them into a mass of 'obedients'. The catchy chorus 'we don't need no education' might sound rebellious and exaggerated, but it makes us think about the kind of education that would be useful both for an individual and for society. It reminds us of the distinction between 'useful knowledge' that teaches us how to act in the existing social set-up and to repeat the existing paradigms, and the 'really useful knowledge' that enables us to critically assess the existing social structure and change it.[2]

This chapter discusses these issues in the context of the changing European Union (EU), and examines whether the topic of education, both general and legal, could have a more prominent role in EU law. It places this discussion in the context of the current times and problems that the EU has been facing. It is well known that the EU has faced unprecedented long-running crises – financial, migration, terrorism, populism and nationalism, Brexit, the global Covid-19 pandemic, to name a few. Overcoming such crises successfully can only be done based on knowledge and sharp, dialectical thinking that tackles each issue from a variety of perspectives, identifying the advantages and disadvantages of the possible solutions. It is worth arguing that the EU should be doing more to ensure this kind of thinking.

In times of crisis, many diverging interests put significant strain on the European integration process and threaten to reverse it, thus undermining the benefits of the EU's existence. It is important to have a population capable of critical thinking and who cannot be misled by populist propaganda or fake news – from information on the spread of viruses, the funding of national health systems, the threats that migration brings, etc. For people to accept more European integration, it is necessary not just to ensure that this process is beneficial to them, but also for everyone to become aware of what the benefits are.

For EU law to continue to achieve its socially relevant and positive aims, the prominent actors in the creation and application of EU law and policies must be critical thinkers. These persons must have a broad understanding of the context in which the EU operates, of the objectives and values that the European legal system serves to protect, while their reasoning should be mindful of any adverse effects that a legal norm, including a judicial decision, might have. In particular, there should be awareness of the distributive effects that law, including case law, could have on non-dominant groups.

This chapter contains two parts. One concerns EU competence in the field of education, and emphasises the correlation between education and the EU's core objectives and powers. The other looks at the substance of education that could be relevant for the EU to regulate.

[2] R Johnson, '"Really Useful Knowledge", 1790–1850' in M Thorpe, R Edwards and A Hanson (eds), *Culture and Processes of Adult Learning* (London, Routledge, 1993).

II. EU Competence in Regulating Education

It is uncontested that education is an important pillar of every society, and will therefore have a vital role in the future of Europe. Still, the question is whether there is anything the EU can and should do in this domain.

It is thus worth presenting the EU's powers that are relevant for education, and particularly to assess the relationship between education and other fields of EU law. This section highlights the interconnection between education and the EU's core objectives, activities and values, such as the establishment of the internal market, EU citizenship and protection of fundamental rights.

A. Complementary Competence in the Field of Education

The Treaty on the Functioning of the European Union (TFEU) gives the EU complementary competence in the field of education aimed at complementing and supporting the action of Member States. The special legal bases for education are Articles 165 and 166 TFEU.

Article 165 TFEU requires the EU to 'contribute to the development of quality education by encouraging cooperation between Member States and, if necessary, by supporting and supplementing their action'. However, there are a number of constraints tied to the exercise of this competence.

First, as regards *the substance of EU measures*, the EU is required to fully respect 'the responsibility of the Member States for the content of teaching and the organisation of education systems and their cultural and linguistic diversity'.[3] Still, this provision does not mean that the EU cannot do anything concerning the content of the teaching, the organisation of education systems or cultural and linguistic diversity. On the contrary, Article 165(2) TFEU specifies that EU action shall be aimed at 'developing the *European dimension in education*' which suggests contributing to the content of education, and it specifies that this can be done 'particularly through the teaching and dissemination of the languages of the Member States' (emphasis added).[4] Further, the EU has the tasks of 'encouraging mobility of students and teachers, by encouraging inter alia, the academic *recognition* of diplomas and periods of study … [and] promoting cooperation between educational establishments' (emphasis added).[5]

Second, as regards *the scope of EU measures*, incentive measures exclude 'any harmonisation of the laws and regulations of the Member States'.[6] It will be shown later that this does not prevent harmonisation affecting education being adopted on another Treaty basis. This is true for any field of EU law, and not just education.

[3] Art 165(1) TFEU.
[4] Art 165(2) TFEU.
[5] ibid.
[6] Art 165(4) TFEU.

As an illustration, Article 168 TFEU entailing the complementary competence for the EU in the field of health similarly excludes any harmonisation.[7] However, Article 114 TFEU which is a legal basis for measures that have as their object the establishment and functioning of the internal market has been used to harmonise issues relating to health (eg, rules on tobacco packaging).[8] Similar examples can be found in other fields as well.[9]

Article 166 TFEU is the legal basis for vocational training. It specifically highlights that the 'Union action shall aim to ... facilitate *adaptation to industrial changes*' (emphasis added).[10] Just as prescribed in Article 165, the Council and the Parliament can adopt measures, but excluding any harmonisation[11] and 'respecting the responsibility of the Member States for the content and organisation of vocational training'.[12]

These two provisions have often been used for adopting measures that complement national education systems, fund relevant EU projects, ensure mobility between Member States, and increase the overall quality of education and training through the exchange of ideas. Most prominently, this provision has been used for the adoption of the Erasmus+ Regulation which covers the renowned programme for the exchange of students, professors and non-teaching staff, Jean Monnet research projects, and creating new curricula on the European Union, etc.[13]

B. Connection between Education and the Internal Market, Citizenship and External Trade

i. Existing Examples of Connection

For a long period, the connection between education and the internal market has been uncontested. In the classic understanding of the EU set-up, the internal market was the core of the European project, and any EU law or policy on education was either a spillover or a complementary activity. While it could be argued that things should be seen the other way around, ie that ensuring progress

[7] The exclusion of harmonisation is provided for in Art 168(5) TFEU.

[8] See Directive 2014/40/EU of the European Parliament and of the Council of 3 April 2014 on the approximation of the laws, regulations and administrative provisions of the Member States concerning the manufacture, presentation and sale of tobacco and related products and repealing Directive 2001/37/EC [2014] OJ L127/1.

[9] eg, the EU does not have conferred competence to regulate animal welfare, but it was possible to contribute to this aim on the basis of a measure adopted under Art 114 TFEU (then Art 95) EC such as Regulation (EC) No 1007/2009 of the European Parliament and of the Council of 16 September 2009 on trade in seal products [2009] OJ L286/36.

[10] Art 166(2) TFEU.

[11] Art 166(4) TFEU.

[12] Art 166(1) TFEU.

[13] Regulation (EU) No 1288/2013 of the European Parliament and of the Council of 11 December 2013 establishing 'Erasmus+': the Union programme for education, training, youth and sport and repealing Decisions No 1719/2006/EC, No 1720/2006/EC and No 1298/2008/EC [2013] OJ L347/50.

would require viewing education as the driving force of progress, and that market strength would be a spillover, this section will merely highlight the strong connection between the market and education.

Many legislative measures relevant for education have been adopted on the legal bases of the internal market and citizenship. Article 165(4) TFEU which provides that a particular legal basis cannot be used for any harmonisation in the field of education must be read in the context of other Treaty provisions. Thus, if conditions for using another legal basis are met, then legislation adopted on that other basis can also affect the content of education. For example, the Professional Qualifications Directive[14] on the recognition of professional qualifications obtained in another Member State has the aim of facilitating the free movement of workers, freedom of establishment and the freedom to provide services, so it was adopted on corresponding legal bases, but it also had effects on educational systems.[15]

Similarly, the Court of Justice has contributed to equalising educational opportunities by interpreting the rules on free movement and/or citizenship in several aspects. First, cases on the recognition of diplomas, such as *Kraus*, interpreted free movement provisions as banning restrictions imposed by States on their nationals using postgraduate academic titles obtained in another Member State.[16] Second, there have also been important cases on access to education of nationals of other Member States. In *Commission v Austria*, additional enrolment requirements for those who had completed secondary education in another Member State were found to constitute indirect discrimination.[17] In *Bressol*, Belgian quotas for non-resident students were found to be contrary to EU citizenship.[18] Third, there is significant case law on financial aid for the children of migrant workers. Some of which, such as *Lair*,[19] *Bernini*,[20] or *Meeusen*,[21] predated the Citizenship Directive[22] and were decided on the basis of free movement rules. Later, *Bidar*[23] and *Förster*[24]

[14] Directive 2005/36/EC of the European Parliament and of the Council of 7 September 2005 on the recognition of professional qualifications (Text with EEA relevance) [2005] OJ L255/22; Directive 2013/55/EU of the European Parliament and of the Council of 20 November 2013 amending Directive 2005/36/EC on the recognition of professional qualifications; and Regulation (EU) No 1024/2012 on administrative cooperation through the Internal Market Information System ('the IMI Regulation') [2013] OJ L354/132.

[15] Now Arts 46, 53(1) and 62 TFEU.

[16] Case C-19/92 *Dieter Kraus v Land Baden-Württemberg* EU:C:1993:125.

[17] Case C-147/03 *Commission v Republic of Austria* EU:C:2005:427.

[18] Case C-73/08 *Bressol v Gouvernement de la Communauté française* EU:C:2010:181.

[19] Case C-39/86 *Lair v Universität Hannover* EU:C:1988:322.

[20] Case C-3/90 *Bernini v Minister van Onderwijs en Wetenschappen* EU:C:1992:89.

[21] Case C-337/97 *Meeusen v Hoofddirectie van de Informatie Beheer Groep* EU:C:1999:284.

[22] Directive 2004/38/EC of the European Parliament and of the Council of 29 April 2004 on the right of citizens of the Union and their family members to move and reside freely within the territory of the Member States amending Regulation (EEC) No 1612/68 and repealing Directives 64/221/EEC, 68/360/EEC, 72/194/EEC, 73/148/EEC, 75/34/EEC, 75/35/EEC, 90/364/EEC, 90/365/EEC and 93/96/EEC [2004] OJ L158/77.

[23] Case C-209/03 *Bidar v London Borough of Ealing* EU:C:2005:169.

[24] Case C-158/07 *Förster v Ib-Groep* EU:C:2008:630.

put this discussion in the context of EU citizenship. Fourth, there have been cases on the right to use a scholarship of one Member State for studies in another Member State. For example, in *Morgan and Bucher* the Court found that such a scholarship cannot be subject to the condition that the studies in another Member State are the continuation of studies in the Member State providing the grant.[25] In *Prinz*, the Court did not allow the grant of a scholarship to be conditioned on three previous years of residence in the Member State granting the scholarship.[26] These are just a few examples of free movement cases having an effect on education.

ii. Possible Regulatory Space at the Intersection of the Internal Market, Citizenship and Education

The connection between the internal market, citizenship and education should not be interpreted too broadly. It should be kept in mind that the EU is based on the principle of the division of competences, and that there is great value in observing the limits of such competences and exercising EU power only subsidiarily to that of Member States. Such division ensures decision-making at levels closer to citizens,[27] regulatory competition and experimentation in searching for better solutions, and a diversity and pluralism of approaches.[28] For education in the EU, great value comes from pluralism of thought, diversity of methods and experimentation in 27 different education systems.

Nevertheless, one could argue that there is still regulatory space for certain new EU rules on education aimed at establishment and functioning of the internal market. While it is clear that the circulation of goods is facilitated by the setting up of common rules, the same should be evident for persons. One should consequently examine whether there are problems in the functioning of the internal market or in the exercise of citizenship rights that could be resolved by measures dealing with education.

[25] Case C-11/06, C-12/06 *Morgan, Bucher v Bezirksregierung Köln* EU:C:2007:626.

[26] Case C-523/11, C-585/11 *Prinz v Region Hannover* EU:C:2013:524.

[27] This is explicitly required by Art 1 TEU.

[28] See K Lenaerts, 'Federalism: Essential Concepts in Evolution – The Case of The European Union' (1998) 21 *Fordham International Law Journal* 746; MW McConnell, 'Federalism: Evaluating the Founders' Design' (1987) 54 *University of Chicago Law Review* 1484; EL Rubin and M Feeley, 'Federalism: Some Notes on a National Neurosis' (1994) 41 *UCLA Law Review* 903; EA Young, 'Protecting Member State Autonomy in the European Union: Some Cautionary Tales from American Federalism' (2002) 77 *New York University Law Review* 1612; EA Young, 'Making Federalism Doctrine: Fidelity, Institutional Competence, and Compensating Adjustments' (2005) 46 *William & Mary Law Review* 1733; K Lenaerts, 'Constitutionalism and the Many Faces of Federalism' (1990) 38 *American Journal of Comparative Law* 205; D Halberstam and RM Hills, Jr, 'State Autonomy in Germany and the United States' (2001) 574 *Annals of the American Academy of Political & Social Sciences* 158; A von Bogdandy, 'The European Union as Situation, Executive, and Promoter of International Law of Cultural Diversity: Elements of Beautiful Friendship' Jean Monnet Working Paper 13/07, available at: www.jeanmonnetprogram.org/papers/07/071301.rtf.

A primary issue that comes to mind is the *brain drain*. Free movement of persons is one of the key features of the EU, allowing for the optimal allocation of resources, and giving more freedom to nationals of EU Member States. Still, it is well known that this market freedom and the related citizenship rights have on many occasions been resisted by certain political and social actors in the so-called 'centre' of Europe, namely in Europe's wealthier countries in the west and north, as they feared that the inflow of workforce would take away the jobs of nationals or allow non-nationals certain social benefits. Mainstream discourse and even academic literature on free movement mostly examine the effects that this movement has on the 'centre', leaving unexamined the undesired consequences for the countries of origin of these persons.[29] The brain drain means that less wealthy EU Member States, after having invested great resources in the education of much needed doctors, nurses and other professionals, are losing them as they seek employment in States with higher incomes.[30] Thus, while free movement and mobility bring many benefits to the EU as a whole, the EU should be mindful that it is the EU set-up that is facilitating this brain drain and that it should act in order to remedy it. The EU has at its disposal some mechanisms for equalising opportunities in the EU and for addressing the negative effects of the brain drain (eg, through projects funded from the Cohesion Fund or EU-wide projects in the field of education), but the persisting differences in economic, educational and other standards raise doubts concerning their sufficiency.[31]

Second, there are *significant educational differences between the EU Member States*. Typically, the Member States in the centre/West have better educational systems than others. This is confirmed both at the school levels by PISA testing,[32] as well as in tertiary education by university rankings.[33] From a market perspective, this means that, on average, people educated in weaker educational systems are, on average, less skilled than those exposed to the better system. If the EU were entirely closed to the world, then either industries needing such less skilled workers would move to Member States where these workers are located or those

[29] See, eg, C Barnard and A Ludlow, '"Undeserving" EU Migrants "Milking Britain's Benefits"? EU Citizens Before Social Security Tribunals' [2019] *Public Law* 260; H Eklund, 'Enlargements, and Displacements of Social Europe: The Example of Sweden' (2018) 14 *European Constitutional Law Review* 114; T Krings, 'A Race to the Bottom? Trade Unions, EU Enlargement and the Free Movement of Labour' (2009) 15 *European Journal of Industrial Relations* 49.

[30] Iris Goldner Lang and Maroje Lang, 'Mračna strana slobode kretanja: kada su u koliziji interesi pojedinca i društva (2019) 1 *Migracijske i etničke teme* 89, available at: papers.ssrn.com/sol3/papers.cfm?abstract_id=3546464.

[31] For some plans on what the EU could do, see the Commission's Policy Report published by the Centre for Strategy and Evaluation Services LLP (CSES) 'Towards a 2030 Vision on the Future of Universities in Europe' (2020), available at: op.europa.eu/en/publication-detail/-/publication/a3cde934-12a0-11eb-9a54-01aa75ed71a1/.

[32] OECD, Programme for International Student Assessment: www.oecd.org/pisa/.

[33] See, eg, *The Times Higher Education Ranking of European Universities for 2020*, available at: www.timeshighereducation.com/student/best-universities/best-universities-europe.

workers would go to where the capital is. Adam Smith's invisible hand[34] and David Ricardo's comparative advantage[35] would solve the problem. However, the problem is not being resolved in this way because industries from Western Europe have not been moving solely to Central and Eastern Europe, but to third countries with an even cheaper labour force. Furthermore, it is due to EU external trade rules that the imports of goods from third countries into the EU is simple. And while the benefits of the internal market and external trade liberalisation for Europe remain undeniable, awareness needs to be raised that these cause distributive effects within the EU and that it is the responsibility in part of the EU to address such issues.

Third, an EU-wide problem is that there is *inequality of education or even of educational opportunities within individual Member States.* Perhaps Brexit shows that some low-skilled workers did not see themselves as benefiting sufficiently from the single market.[36] If workers do not have a proper education themselves, including knowledge of foreign languages, it is not easy to actively exercise free movement rights – either as a worker or a service provider, etc. The internal market is not very useful for those with poor education. These persons also feel left out of political processes which they perceive belong to the elites.[37] There is a sense of disconnect from the EU's economic benefits and/or political processes. The EU needs to confront this problem if it does not want to face internal problems and if it desires to make a more significant contribution elsewhere in the world.

Fourth, many workers throughout the EU are becoming redundant not only due to the internal market or to external trade, but also due to *technological progress.* Machines are taking away some jobs. Changes in education systems are needed to equip people with new skills, allowing them to do the jobs that are not done by machines. Furthermore, many technological changes are being introduced, not just with a view to achieving economic efficiency understood as the lowering of production costs, but for other reasons. For example, the EU's climate change agenda and the 'green transition' require EU industries to become more environmentally friendly and sustainable.[38] Similarly, industry is under pressure to constantly adapt to new circumstances such as the Covid-19 pandemic. Thus, for example, the Commission's 2020 industrial policy which has been modified in response to the crisis mentions the need for lifelong education in order to upskill

[34] Adam Smith, *An Inquiry into the Nature and Causes of the Wealth of Nations* (first published 1776, MetaLibri, 2007), available at: www.ibiblio.org/ml/libri/s/SmithA_WealthNations_p.pdf.

[35] D Ricardo, *On the Principles of Political Economy and Taxation* (London, John Murray, 1821), available at: www.econlib.org/LIBRARY/Ricardo/ricP1.html.

[36] See, eg, S Hobolt, 'The Brexit Vote: A Divided Nation, a Divided Continent (2016) 23(9) *Journal of European Public Policy* 1259.

[37] See eg N Clark, 'Explaining Low Turnout in European Elections: The Role of Issue Salience and Institutional Perceptions in Elections to the European Parliament' (2014) 36 *Journal of European Integration* 343.

[38] I am grateful to Alessandro Angelico for bringing this to my attention.

and reskill 120 million Europeans.[39] Obviously, adaptation requires a great deal of learning and skills which can only be partly acquired through lifelong learning. Therefore, earlier stages of education also need to be designed for persons to become responsive to subsequent education. It is thus relevant to highlight that the competence of the EU derives not only from the needs of the internal market, but also from the express reference in Article 166(2) TFEU that the EU should facilitate adaptation to industrial change.

All this shows that there are acute problems in the functioning of the EU market for which changes in the education system could be a solution.

C. Education as a Fundamental Right under EU Law

The Charter of Fundamental Rights, having the same legal strength as the Treaties, provides in Article 14 that '[e]veryone has the right to education and to have access to vocational and continuing training'.[40] This is quite relevant as this provision binds EU institutions, and potentially requires more action at the EU level for the full realisation of this right.

Still, thus far, the effects of having a fundamental right to education have been relatively modest. The reason lies in that this provision has been understood negatively, ie as precluding States and the EU from hindering someone's education, and not as requiring them to take action. Negative rights are in general quite problematic from a critical perspective. In this respect, Duncan Kennedy's critique of rights is largely based on the problem that most rights are understood as negative, ie as protecting an individual from the action of public authorities.[41] Similarly, Mark Tushnet also drew attention to the fact that rights are typically constructed as negative obligations.[42] In practice, this does not give much meat to the rights. To use a more vivid example, the right to life embodied in the Charter,[43] in the European Convention on Human Rights (ECHR),[44] and national constitutions[45] prohibits Member States and the EU from depriving someone of his or her life, but this right does not in any way create an obligation for the Member States or the

[39] Communication from the Commission to the European Parliament, the European Council, the Council, the European Economic and Social Committee and the Committee of the Regions: A New Industrial Strategy for Europe, COM/2020/102 final, 11.

[40] Art 14(1) and (2) Charter of Fundamental Rights of the EU [2012] OJ C326/02.

[41] D Kennedy, 'The Critique of Rights in Critical Legal Studies' in W Brown and J Halley (eds), *Left Legalism/Left Critique* (Durham NC, Duke University Press, 2002) 214, available at: duncankennedy.net/documents/The%20Critique%20of%20Rights%20in%20cls.pdf.

[42] M Tushnet, 'Essay on Rights' (1984) 62 *Texas Law Review* 1363, 1392.

[43] Art 2 Charter of Fundamental Rights of the European Union [2007] OJ C303/01.

[44] Art 2 European Convention on Human Rights.

[45] eg Art 2(2) Grundgesetz für die Bundesrepublik Deutschland, 23 May 1949 – 'Jeder hat das Recht auf Leben und körperliche Unversehrtheit' [Art 2(2) of the German Basic Law, 23 May 1949 – 'Every person shall have the right to life and physical integrity'].

EU, for example, to save a person drowning in the Mediterranean Sea. According to Kennedy, a radical proposal can more easily be imagined if one puts aside the concept of rights.[46] However, in the field of education it would not even be necessary to go so far because it would be possible simply to give the right to education a more positive meaning and require public authorities to act in order to add fuller content to this right.

A trace of positive content to the right to education is provided in Article 14(2) of the Charter where the right 'includes the possibility to receive free compulsory education'. This is a positive obligation for those bound by the Charter to provide for this free compulsory education. It is not clear from this provision who has the obligation to ensure this right, but according to Article 51(2) the entirety of the Charter is binding on EU institutions and Member States when implementing EU law or more broadly when Member States are acting within the scope of EU law.[47] Article 51(2) provides that the Charter does not entail any change of the powers and tasks of the EU as established by the Treaties. The Charter does not go on to define which levels of education should be compulsory or what that compulsory education should entail.

The importance of having a fundamental right to education stands out when one looks at the comparative context. In the United States, there is no constitutionally guaranteed right to education, and at the same time the American educational system reflects great inequality.[48] The quality of public schools varies, depending in which region they are to be found or even on their neighbourhood because education is funded by local communities. Wealthier ones can invest significantly more than poorer. Further, the high quality of some private schools accentuates the differences between the rich and the poor. Moreover, while many of the best universities and schools have special programmes to help gifted, but underprivileged, students, this remains far from achieving significant equality of opportunity. A recent US case is pertinent with regard to whether the problem of education inequality is a local/state problem or merits protection at the highest level. In *Gary B v Snyder*, a collective action was filed, claiming that students at public schools in Detroit were being denied access to literacy by being deprived of evidence-based instruction and being subject to school conditions that prevent learning.[49] The plaintiffs were arguing that there is a fundamental right to literacy which can

[46] See, eg, D Kennedy, 'Legal Education as Training for Hierarchy' in D Kairys (ed), *The Politics of Law* (New York, Pantheon Books, 1982) where Kennedy states that the 'rights discourse is a trap', and that '[t]his framework is, in itself, a part of the problem rather than of the solution … [since i]t makes it difficult even to conceptualize radical proposals', 62, available at: duncankennedy.net/documents/Legal%20Education%20as%20Training%20for%20Hierarchy_Politics%20of%20Law.pdf.

[47] See, eg, Explanations Relating to the Charter of Fundamental Rights [2007] OJ C303/17.

[48] See, eg, D Bloome et al, 'Educational Inequality, Educational Expansion, and Intergenerational Income Persistence in the United States' (2018) 83 *American Sociological Review* 1215; M Jaeger and K Karlson, 'Cultural Capital and Educational Inequality: A Counterfactual Analysis' (2018) 5 *Sociological Science* 775.

[49] *Gary B et al v Whitmer et al*, 957 F3d 616 (6th Cir 2020).

be derived from the provisions of the US Constitution such as substantive due process and the equal protection requirements of the Fourteenth Amendment. The district court did not accept their arguments. However, a panel of the Court of Appeals gave an opinion finding that there is a right to a 'basic minimum education', and that it has fundamental status.[50] The governor of Michigan then settled the case by investing into public schools in this area.[51] However, just a few days later the full Court of Appeals decided to undertake a rare review of its own case law by rehearing the case.[52] It remains to be seen whether or not the US legal system will embrace the concept of the right to literacy, and this will depend on the balance between progressive and conservative positions on education at the Court of Appeals and the US Supreme Court.

For the EU and this chapter, such a comparative development serves to highlight that, in contrast to the US system where there is a hot legal and political debate on whether the US Constitution guarantees at least some basic level of education, in the EU there is no doubt that the right to education is a fundamental one. This means that the EU has a constitutional duty to guarantee this right, and it is legally allowed to give it meaningful content.

III. Substance of Education in the EU

This section provides several examples from the substance of education that are connected to the EU's aims, policies and legal framework.

First, the most obvious element of general education relevant for the EU is *content concerning the European Union itself*. Kris Grimonprez's academic research has sought to address the fact that Member States differ widely as to the aspects of the EU taught in schools, and that teaching mostly concerns European history, but far less European political and economic integration.[53] As she has argued, the EU Treaties and the Charter could be the basis of citizenship education so as to ensure literacy in this field to complement knowledge of national constitutions.[54] Further, I would argue that it is important for EU-related content to be critically taught

[50] *Gary B et al v Whitmer et al*, 23 April 2020, United States Court of Appeals for the Sixth Circuit: www.opn.ca6.uscourts.gov/opinions.pdf/20a0124p-06.pdf.

[51] Valerie Strauss, 'Michigan Settles Historic Lawsuit after Court Rules Students Have a Constitutional Right to a "Basic" Education, Including Literacy' *Washington Post* (14 May 2020), available at: www.washingtonpost.com/education/2020/05/14/michigan-settles-historic-lawsuit-after-court-rules-students-have-constitutional-right-basic-education-including-literacy/.

[52] Rocco E Testani, 'A Short-Lived Constitutional Right to Education' (*Education Next*, 21 May 2020), available at: www.educationnext.org/short-lived-constitutional-right-to-education-sixth-circuit-rehear-gary-b-whitmer/.

[53] K Grimonprez, *European Union and Education for Democratic Citizenship* (Baden-Baden, Nomos, 2020) 327, citing reports on education in Europe.

[54] ibid 342–44.

rather than presented as dogma or fairy tale. Truly understanding what binds EU people, and awareness of the present and potential benefits of integration, is also pertinent for civic engagement at the EU level and for building European identity.

In this context it is worth mentioning that ideas about the relevance of the European dimension of education are not new, and there has occasionally been political impetus to further push integration in that area. For example, French President Emmanuel Macron, in his Sorbonne speech in September 2017,[55] supported the ideas of creating European Universities – a network of universities across Europe with programmes that have all their students studying abroad and taking classes in at least two languages. These were to become the drivers of educational innovation and a quest for excellence. He proposed creating these ties from high school, and advocated the 'Sorbonne Process' (comparable to the Bologna Process for universities) on the harmonisation and mutual recognition of secondary diplomas and a programme accommodating exchanges. In his view, all these efforts would not only be beneficial for the quality of education, but also for promoting the European identity – one of universalism and multilingualism.

Second, *there is a link between education and the values of the EU mentioned in Article 2 TEU, particularly, democracy, pluralism, non-discrimination, tolerance, rule of law*. Education that fosters the critical thinking of citizens is important to enable citizens to make informed political and other choices, to prevent discrimination on different bases and to ensure civic engagement supportive of the rule of law. This link can be illustrated through two different sets of cases that concern the application of Article 14(3) of the Charter. On the one hand, 'the freedom to set up educational establishments with due respect for democratic principles' is specially mentioned in Article 14(3) of the Charter. This provision has recently been relevant for the Court in deciding *Commission v Hungary*, a case concerning Hungarian measures restricting the functioning of the Central European University and thus hindering the freedoms of an academic institution.[56] On the other hand, the link between education and values entailed in Article 2 TFEU could also be seen in cases on the 'right of parents to ensure the education and teaching of their children in conformity with their religious, philosophical and pedagogical convictions … in accordance with the national laws governing the exercise of such … right'.[57] While there have been no cases on this provision before the EU courts, there is abundant case law of the European Court of Human Rights (ECtHR) on the corresponding provision of the ECHR, namely, Article 2 of Protocol no 1. The ECtHR case law shows that a child's right to receive objective and scientifically founded information taught in an objective, critical and pluralistic manner has precedence over the convictions of parents.[58] Such jurisprudence reflects the fact that the task

[55] Emmanuel Macron, 'Initiative for Europe' (Sorbonne speech, 26 September 2017), available at: international.blogs.ouest-france.fr/archive/2017/09/29/macron-sorbonne-verbatim-europe-18583.html.

[56] Case C-66/18 *Commission v Hungary* EU:C:2020:792.

[57] Art 14(3) of the Charter.

[58] *Dojan v Germany* App no 319/08 (ECtHR, 13 September 2011).

of education is to offer insights which children might not be able to get elsewhere, providing them with the base for being active citizens who understand the values of Article 2 TEU such as tolerance, pluralism, non-discrimination, democracy and the rule of law. Education ought to be about 'breaking down walls', and not about building them, just as Pink Floyd would suggest.

Third, *critical and creative thinking in education is relevant for improving the functioning of the internal market, for the positioning of the EU in external trade and for dealing with the Fourth Industrial Revolution*. EU documents mostly focus on the development of digital skills,[59] but other changes in standard education might also be required. In this field, there have been radically ambitious proposals from academia. For example, Roberto Unger has argued that the EU would have to guarantee high-quality lifelong critical, dialectical and cooperative education based on experimentation[60] enabling the individual to be flexible on the job market and 'to participate in a form of production that increasingly becomes a practice of collective learning and pertinent innovation'.[61] This would enable persons to do jobs that cannot be done by a machine, thus leading to a larger life.[62] In Unger's view, this kind of education should really be the focus of EU efforts, even to the extent that the Treaty should be changed so as to turn the EU upside down, where regulating the market would be left to the Member States so that they could experiment with it, and that the EU should focus on social rights, including education.[63] Similarly, Alexander Somek has argued that '[i]t is essential … that a European Union reverses its perverse federalist make-up. The current combination of free movement conflicting with nationally-conceived social welfare systems is a recipe for political disaster'.[64] In Unger's view, reform of the EU set-up by putting more focus on education is necessary because the current EU structure is beneficial only to a certain proportion of EU citizens who work in 'the most advanced [and small] sectors of the economy: the sectors that are now the favored home of innovation-friendly cooperation and that have become responsible for an increasing part of the creation of new wealth'[65] while 'the vast majority of people [remains] … excluded from [these sectors] as well as from the education which prepares people for them'.[66]

Finally, in the field of law, *education based on critical thinking is highly relevant for lawyers*, including when teaching, studying, creating or applying EU law.

[59] eg, Commission, 'Digital Education Action Plan (2021–2027): Resetting Education and Training for the Digital Age' (European Union, 2021), available at: ec.europa.eu/education/education-in-the-eu/digital-education-action-plan_en.

[60] Roberto Mangabeira Unger's lectures, 'Progressive Alternative: Institutional Reconstruction Today' Harvard Law School, 2014; Roberto Mangabeira Unger, *The Left Alternative* (London, Verso, 2005) 92–93.

[61] Unger, The Left Alternative, ibid.

[62] ibid.

[63] ibid.

[64] A Somek, 'Four Impious Points on Brexit' (2016) 17 *German Law Journal*, Brexit Special Supplement 107.

[65] Unger, *The Left Alternative* (n 60) 89.

[66] ibid.

In all these processes, one has to be aware that there is no objective and neutral law or action, but that each measure has distributive effects. Critical scholars might argue that legal norms typically serve the interests of the dominant groups, but that there are constitutional values that require taking account of others as well. Each legal norm requires balancing between a plethora of interests. In the EU as a transnational legal order, the informed adoption, interpretation and application of rules requires not only a good understanding of the text and telos of the Treaties, but also of the comparative differences between Member States and of the consequences that each rule could have for them. Critical legal discourse on EU law is also important as it should replace uninformed criticism and europhobia. It is only through a critical approach that the true advantages of European integration can become more visible, and change can be brought about in areas where improvements are needed. It is this 'really useful knowledge' that teaches us not only how to reproduce the existing social set-up, but how to change it, which has the potential to ensure continued prosperity.

IV. Concluding Remarks

The EU strives to be able to react to social, economic, migration, environmental, health-related and other changes occurring in the world beyond its direct control. It also seeks to actively promote change in many areas where it considers that progress mandates it. Both responding to and actively bringing about change require suitable education. This chapter has shown that the EU has the competence to undertake measures affecting education – not just on the basis of specific complementary competence, but also on other legal bases. Further, the chapter has proposed that there are several aspects concerning the substance of EU education that are pertinent to the EU, and that have a strong link to EU values, citizenship, the internal market, external trade and fundamental rights.

8

The Origins of the Crisis of Common Values of the European Union

DAMJAN KUKOVEC*

I. Introduction

The European Union (EU; the Union) has changed profoundly since the 1950s, the 1990s and since the 'big bang' enlargement in 2004. It has played a fundamental role in the social, economic and democratic transformation of the Continent. Overcoming several divisions of the Second World War and achieving the integration of the formerly autocratic systems of Spain, Portugal and Greece, the integration of the former Eastern Bloc as well as the general social and economic stabilisation of the Continent are no small feat. Yet, the EU has also been ridden by consecutive crises, including the euro crisis, the migration crisis, Brexit, the rule of law crisis and, as argued, the crisis of common values.

While enabling and encouraging democratisation, the Union's legal structures, lying beneath the veneer of constant transformation, may simultaneously discourage the forces of democracy and the Union's stability. To understand the EU's crises, including the current rule of law crisis, lawyers need to delve into the depths of its functioning. While the EU seems to keep changing with lightning-fast speed, the changes too often reproduce the existing practices, hierarchies and inequalities.[1] It is submitted that this reproduction is at the heart of Europe's crisis and, specifically, is one of the constitutive elements of the current rule of law crisis and the crisis of common values.

Every problem is multifaceted, and one could identify several causes for the current crisis of common values. Some causes may stem from internal histories and the complexities of particular Member States. This chapter identifies Member States' inequality and the legal system's role in its perpetuation as an important

* Judge of the General Court of the European Union.

[1] D Kukovec, 'Taking Change Seriously: The Rhetoric of Justice and the Reproduction of the Status Quo' in D Kochenov, G de Búrca and A Williams (eds), *Europe's Justice Deficit?* (Oxford, Hart Publishing, 2015) 324–30, available at: www.bloomsburycollections.com/book/europes-justice-deficit; D Kukovec, 'Hierarchies as Law' (2014) 21 *Columbia Journal of European Law* 131.

element in the destabilisation of the EU and, specifically, in the current crisis. By ignoring the role played by law in the perpetuation of hierarchy, inequality, as well as in their wider social repercussions, the EU keeps addressing and treating the symptoms of its crises rather than the actual disease. Neglect of the real forces of its disintegration leads the Union to enact inadequate and counterproductive policies, preventing a fuller realisation of its immense normative and integrative potential, at best, and leading to its disintegration, at worst.

II. The Crisis of Values in the EU

The EU is built on a set of values stemming from the Enlightenment and modern legal thought. Article 2 of the Treaty on European Union (TEU) sets out the fundamental values of the EU. It states that the Union is founded on the values of respect for human dignity, freedom, democracy, equality, the rule of law and respect for human rights, including the rights of persons belonging to minorities. These values are common to the Member States in a society in which pluralism, non-discrimination, tolerance, justice, solidarity and equality between women and men prevail.

In recent years, some Member States have more or less openly confronted the EU on the interpretation of many of these values.[2] The European Commission commenced several infringement procedures against Poland for alleged violations of judicial independence.[3] Similarly, national courts in Poland have started making requests for preliminary rulings on the issue of the rule of law, culminating in the ever-richer jurisprudence of the Court of Justice on judicial independence.[4] The measures of the Polish authorities have also been disquieting courts across Europe which have started to make preliminary references concerning the situation.[5]

[2] See D Kochenov, 'EU Law without the Rule of Law: Is the Veneration of Autonomy Worth It?' (2015) 34 *Yearbook of European Law* 74; L Pech and K Lane Scheppele, 'Illiberalism Within: Rule of Law Backsliding in the EU' (2017) 19 *Cambridge Yearbook of European Legal Studies* 3. Wojciech Sadurski has argued that since 2015 Poland's leading party has been dismantling the major checks and balances of the Polish state and subordinating the courts, the civil service, and the media to the will of the executive. W Sadurski, *Poland's Constitutional Breakdown* (Oxford, Oxford University Press, 2019).

[3] Order C-441/17 R *European Commission v Republic of Poland (Białowieża forest)* EU:C:2017:877; Order C-619/18 R *European Commission v Republic of Poland (Independence of the Supreme Court – Interim measures)* EU:C:2018:1021; Order C-791/19 R *European Commission v Poland (Independence of the Disciplinary Chamber of the Supreme Court)* EU:C:2020:277; Case C-619/18 *European Commission v Poland (Independence of the Supreme Court)* EU:C:2019:531; Case C-192/18 *European Commission v Poland (Independence of the ordinary courts)* EU:C:2019:924; Case C-791/19 *European Commission v Poland (Disciplinary regime for judges)* EU:C:2021:596.

[4] Joined Cases C-585/18, C-624/18 and C-625/18 *AK et al (Independence of the disciplinary chamber of the Supreme Court)* EU:C:2019:982; Joined Cases C-558/18 and C-563/18 *Miasto Łowicz and Prokurator Generalny* EU:C:2020:234; Case C-824/18 *AB et al (Appointment of judges to the Supreme Court – Actions)* EU:C:2021:153.

[5] Case C-216/18 *PPU LM (Deficiencies in the system of justice)* EU:C:2018:586. The High Court of Ireland had in 2018 requested a preliminary ruling in the context of the European arrest warrant. The Irish Court was concerned with the existence of a real risk that the person in respect of whom a

Several of these cases reveal challenges to the core values of the EU. The judiciary's independence from other branches of the government has been instrumental in the historic construction of the EU[6] and is an inherent part of the ontology and axiology of its autonomous legal order.[7] It is of vital importance to the preliminary reference procedure, which has made the EU the supranational polity it is today.[8] Some of the claims thus go against the essence of the EU's architectural structure.[9] The Court of Justice has developed impressive case law on the affirmation of the rule of law. This importantly solidifies the EU as the leader in the enforcement and development of the jurisprudence of the rule of law.

However, the proposals to address the crisis have been profoundly legalistic, divorcing the legal system from social reality. Calls for the enhanced affirmation and enforcement of core European values by European and national institutions, setting up scoreboards of adherence to the legal system, and withholding funding in the case of violation of the rule of law principles may seem to be important tools to address the current crisis. The origins of the rule of law crisis in this narrative appear to be fully external to law. By ignoring the deep structure of the current crisis, attempts to fix it address the symptoms rather than identifying and seriously addressing the disease. A legal process based on a combination of waving the banner of righteousness and threats thus risks a political and academic spectacle that could serve better its individual participants rather than seriously identifying and resolving the underlying problem.

One of the factors for such an approach may be an oversight of the rule of law crisis as an emanation of a larger crisis of values. 'The rule of law crisis' is a

European arrest warrant has been issued would, if surrendered to the issuing Polish judicial authority, suffer a breach of his fundamental right to an independent tribunal. It consequently enquired if such a real risk permits the executing judicial authority to exceptionally refrain from giving effect to that European arrest warrant. The Court of Justice emphasised that the criminal courts of other Member States must meet the requirements of effective judicial protection, including their independence and impartiality. However, it concluded that implementation of the European arrest warrant mechanism may be suspended only in the event of a serious and persistent breach by one of the Member States of the principles set out in Art 2 TEU, determined by the European Council under Art 7(2) TEU. As long as such a decision has not been adopted, as it had not been adopted concerning Poland, the executing judicial authority may refrain to give effect to a European arrest warrant issued by another Member State only in exceptional circumstances, after carrying out a specific and precise assessment of the particular case. This careful judgment from 2018 has since been topped by the Court of Amsterdam and the Supreme Court of Ireland asking the Court whether, in light of the *Xero Flor* case of the European Court of Human Rights, Polish courts are still proper 'courts'. see Joined Cases C-354/20 PPU *L* and C-412/20 PPU *P* EU:C:2020:1033, and a request for a preliminary ruling in C-480/21 *WO, JL v Minister for Justice and Equality*.

[6] JHH Weiler, 'The Transformation of Europe' (1991) 100 *Yale Law Journal* 2403.

[7] D Kukovec, 'The Court of Justice of the European Union for Hedgehogs' (2021) Jean Monnet Working Paper 1/21, 30–32, available at: jeanmonnetprogram.org/wp-content/uploads/JMWP-01_Damjan-Kukovec.pdf.

[8] KJ Alter, 'Who Are the "Masters of the Treaty"? European Governments and the European Court of Justice' (1998) 52 *International Organization* 121. Judicial independence is clearly the core tenet of any democratic system of government, stemming, in the EU, from constitutional traditions common to the Member States. K Lenaerts, 'New Horizons for the Rule of Law within the EU' (2020) 21 *German Law Journal* 29, 30–31.

[9] Kukovec, 'The Court of Justice of the European Union for Hedgehogs' (n 7) 32.

misrepresentation of the reality and breadth of the crisis. The current re-evaluation of values by the Eastern periphery is not limited to judicial independence or the values underlying the rule of law. We are witnessing a far wider crisis of common values. Withdrawal from the Council of Europe Istanbul Convention on preventing and combating violence against women and domestic violence,[10] cracking down on LGBTIQ communities,[11] resisting the migrant quotas,[12] insistence on logging in the Natura protected forest,[13] and last, but certainly not least, rejection of the supremacy of EU law[14] all point to a wider crisis of common values in the Union. These challenges are a far cry from the post-1989 period lasting to the honeymoon after joining the Union in the early 2000s, when the new peripheral Member States would do anything to honour the common values of the Union.

Why is the Union faced with a crisis of common values as it unfolds before our eyes? The Polish government has supported its measures on judicial independence by a variety of constitutional pluralism arguments,[15] arguments akin to cultural relativism. The idea that the principle of the judiciary's independence depends largely on its specific cultural understanding is a mirror image of the argument that the current situation is due to Central or Eastern Europe's cultural and social backwardness.[16] The latter is implicitly or explicitly cited as a reason for other challenges to the common values of the Union. The revolt against the EU legal system, however, requires a deeper legal and psychological explanation, seeking the real directing forms of human development in the very place where the intellectual

[10] Council of Europe Convention on preventing and combating violence against women and domestic violence [2011] No 210.

[11] 'Poland: Crackdown on LGBT Activists' (*Human Rights Watch*, 7 August 2020), available at: www.hrw.org/news/2020/08/07/poland-crackdown-lgbt-activists; 'Poland LGBT Protests: Three Charged with Hanging Rainbow Flags off Statues' *BBC News* (5 August 2020), available at: www.bbc.com/news/world-europe-53673411.

[12] Joined Cases C-643/15 and C-647/15 *Slovakia and Hungary v Council* EU:C:2017:631; Joined Cases C-715/17, C-718/17 and C-719/17 *European Commission v Poland, Hungary and the Czech Republic* EU:C:2020:257.

[13] Case C-441/17 *Commission v Poland (Białowieża Forest)* EU:C:2018:255.

[14] Judgment of the Polish Constitutional Court P 7/20 (14 July 2021), K 3/21 (7 October 2021); Romanian Constitutional Court Decision No 390 of 8 June 2021, and the press release of the Romanian Constitutional Court, issued on 23 December 2021.

[15] See Chancellery of the Prime Minister, 'White Paper on the Reform of the Polish Judiciary' (2018) White Paper, available at: www.statewatch.org/media/documents/news/2018/mar/pl-judiciary-reform-chanceller-white-paper-3-18.pdf. See also J Scholtes, 'Abusing Constitutional Identity' (2021) 22 *German Law Journal* 534.

[16] For the background of this problem, see D Kukovec, 'Whose Social Europe? The Laval/Viking Judgments and the Prosperity Gap' Harvard Law School, 2011 Working Paper 3, available at: iglp.law.harvard.edu/wp-content/uploads/Writing%20Workshop%20Papers/Kukovec_WhoseSocialEurope.pdf. There is ample evidence that the Polish legal tradition is deeply anchored in Western legality. See, for instance, R Mańko, 'Artur Kozak's Juriscentrist Concept of Law: A Central European Innovation in Legal Theory' (2020) 45 *Review of Central and East European Law* 334. Moreover, the backlash against the power of courts is a global phenomenon and even countries with a venerable rule of law tradition, such as the United Kingdom, are not immune to it. 'Concerns about Judges' Powers Must Be Heeded, Says Attorney General' *BBC News* (12 February 2020), available at: www.bbc.com/news/uk-politics-51474169.

pride of man would least wish to find it.[17] In other words, we, lawyers, need to dig beneath the surface and bore into the foundations of the reality of living in the Union.

The EU, as well as other liberal democracies around the world, are facing what Friedrich Nietzsche termed 'the slave revolt',[18] which occurs when the subordinate groups start challenging the totality of values of the system. The rebellion against the values of liberal democracy of the EU as enshrined in Article 2 TEU is widespread, and its causes should be addressed. It is submitted that the EU has been significantly underestimating the power of frustration stemming from persistent inequalities. The regional wage inequality in the EU is staggering. In 2014, the highest median gross hourly earnings in euros were recorded in Denmark (€25.52), Ireland (€20.16) and Sweden (€18.46). By contrast, the lowest median gross hourly earnings in euros were registered in Lithuania (€3.11), Romania (€2.03) and Bulgaria (€1.67). The highest national median gross hourly earnings were thus 15 times higher than the lowest when expressed in euros; when adjusted for price levels by converting to the purchasing power standard, the highest average was five times higher than the lowest average, with Denmark and Bulgaria again representing the extremes at either end of the range.[19]

It took West Germany 20 years to have its 'Wirtschaftswunder' and to overtake France and the United Kingdom. Thirty years after the fall of the Berlin Wall, no such prospect of closing the gap exists for Eastern Europe, including for the parts of Eastern Europe which topped the world's development rankings before the Second World War, such as Latvia or the Czech Republic. In 1991, according to the World Bank, Hungary's GDP per capita was $US 3,333 and Austria's was $US 22,356. By 2015, Hungary's GDP had risen to $US 25,581, while Austrian GDP had risen to $US 47,824. Although the gap has narrowed considerably, Hungary and other Eastern European countries have only cut the lead in half, at best. 'We closed the gap somehow, but now it is just plateaus',[20] is a common lament. The failure of Eastern Europe to replicate the German and Irish miracles has generated considerable disappointment and a corresponding swerve away from liberalism.[21]

[17] Friedrich Nietzsche, *On the Genealogy of Morals: A Polemic. By Way of Clarification and Supplement to My Last Book, 'Beyond Good and Evil'* (Douglas Smith trans, Oxford, Oxford University Press, 1998).

[18] Nietzsche (n 17) 11.

[19] 'Wages and Labour Costs – Gross Wages/Earnings' (*Eurostat*, March 2021), available at: ec.europa.eu/eurostat/statistics-explained/index.php?title=Wages_and_labour_costs.

[20] J Feffer, *Aftershock: A Journey into Eastern Europe's Broken Dreams* (London, Zed Books, 2017) 187. National populists are drawing their votes from the mass of Eastern Europe's left-behind. Such parties 'channel the frustration of the losers of the transition', argues Feffer. Ivan Krastev argues that massive depopulation raises fears of Eastern nations' disappearance and fuels anti-immigrant sentiment. I Krastev and S Holmes, 'Explaining Eastern Europe: Imitation and its Discontents' (2018) 29 *Journal of Democracy* 117.

[21] Ivan Krastev explains well the sentiment in Eastern Europe which has led to profound frustration and consequently to nationalism and illiberalism. For countries emerging from communism, the post-1989 imperative to 'be like the West' has generated discontent for countries emerging from communism and even a 'return of the repressed', as the region feels old nationalist stirrings and new demographic pressures. He argues that the origins of the region's current illiberalism are emotional and

While EU membership has brought immense benefits to the European periphery in terms of economic and social development, the centre has also profited from successive enlargements of the EU. The European periphery is economically uncompetitive in the existing legal structure. Much of the wealth in Europe flows from poorer countries to richer ones – not the other way around. Starting with the brain drain. The 'sending' peripheral regions of Europe are losing high skills and competencies to the advantage of central 'receiving' regions as a result of permanent emigration.[22] Between 2009 and 2015, Romania lost half its doctors. The profits Western European companies make in Central and Eastern Europe far outstrip the public funding that is transferred to the East. From 2010 to 2016, Hungary, Poland, the Czech Republic, and Slovakia received EU funds roughly equivalent to 2 to 4 per cent of their gross domestic product. But the outflow of profits and property incomes to the West from these countries over the same period ranges from 4 to 8 per cent of GDP.[23] The central distributional problem in the Union is how the rules of the game – the law – of the European Union are set and how those in a structurally subordinate position feel they can in fact affect the legal and political course of the Union.[24]

III. 'Ressentiment' at the Origin of the Crisis of Values

Hierarchical plateaus and the perception of a never-ending second-class status spark revolt. The genealogy of the revolt against the Union in the form of the crisis of values can be traced back to Nietzsche's notion of 'ressentiment'. Ressentiment is the central concept of Nietzsche's argument on the genealogy of morals. Nietzsche specifically describes how Christian morality developed as a revolt against the moral values of the Roman Empire.[25] Yet, he develops the notion of ressentiment

pre-ideological, rooted in rebellion at the humiliations that accompany a project requiring acknowledgment of a foreign culture as superior to one's own. The demographic collapse further contributes to illiberalism. The collapse results from ageing populations, low birth rates and massive outmigration – which manifests as a fear that the arrival of unassimilable foreigners will dilute national identities and weaken national cohesion. Krastev and Holmes (n 20).

[22] 'What Solutions to Population Decline in Europe's Regions?' (*European Parliament News*, 20 April 2021), available at: www.europarl.europa.eu/news/en/headlines/society/20210414STO02006/what-solutions-to-population-decline-in-europe-s-regions; European Parliamentary Research Service (EPRS) and Monika Kiss, 'Demographic Outlook for the European Union 2021' (Publications Office, 2021) PE 690.528, available at: data.europa.eu/doi/10.2861/429257.

[23] Clotilde Armand, 'Eastern Europe Gives More to the West Than It Gets Back' *Financial Times* (12 February 2020), available at: www.ft.com/content/39603142-4cc9-11ea-95a0-43d18ec715f5.

[24] D Kukovec, 'Law and the Periphery' (2015) 21 *European Law Journal* 406; D Kukovec, 'Economic Law, Inequality, and Hidden Hierarchies on the EU Internal Market' (2016) 38 *Michigan Journal of International Law* 56.

[25] See Nietzsche (n 17).

as a general psychological phenomenon that springs up regularly in history, such as, for example, before and during the French Revolution.[26]

Ressentiment is a psychological reaction based on hierarchical subordination, be it material or spiritual. It arises out of competition for social dominance and a coveted good. It is a reactive mode of feeling which negates the active and spontaneous affirmation of values of the privileged ruling class.[27] In other words, it is revengeful and malicious ill-will directed to other agents, notably to stronger rivals.[28] Ressentiment is a process in which frustrated dominated people generate *a struggle for values*.

Ressentiment should not be equated with resentment, which is a response to someone who fails to discharge a moral obligation towards me.[29] Neither should ressentiment be equated with envy. The source of envy is another's possession of a material or spiritual value. While the desire to harm the envied other is a part of envy, just as it is a part of ressentiment, the essential difference between ressentiment and envy is that with ressentiment there is a perception that the other, the stronger rival, has actively *harmed* me. The fact that someone has hitherto caused me harm, however, is not an essential element of envy.

Before 1989 the feeling of Eastern Europeans towards those who were fortunate enough to have remained on the western side of the Berlin Wall may have been envy. Much later on, it turned into ressentiment. With ressentiment, the stronger rivals are the object of revenge. The East was moved into the Western orbit after 1990, yet left in a profoundly subordinate position. The fact that an enormous gap persists between Eastern and Western Europe and that several Eastern countries' countryside stays mired in the past is not a question of perception, but of 'stubborn facts'.[30] The life chances of a child are still profoundly dependent on where they are born in the EU. Born in the periphery, a person is likely to have a shorter life and work in a less productive society with lower life chances and opportunities than if born in socially similar circumstances in the centre.[31]

Ressentiment results from such frustrations – from the agents' inability to get what they will. There is a close connection between suffering – an experience of frustration, thwarted desire – and a sense of impotence. Having ressentiment plays a remedial role in driving out of mind the original pain that gave rise to it.[32] Ressentiment follows from the repeated failure of strategies and from the habitual ineffectiveness of those who are subordinated.[33] It is a response to doubts, stemming from a desire to prove oneself, and to demonstrate that one can do

[26] ibid.
[27] ibid, 142, explanatory note 22.
[28] ibid.
[29] G Elgat, *Nietzsche's Psychology of Ressentiment: Revenge and Justice in 'On the Genealogy of Morals'*, 1st edn (New York, Routledge, Taylor & Francis Group, 2019).
[30] Feffer (n 20) 31.
[31] Kukovec, 'Law and the Periphery' (n 24) 408–09.
[32] Elgat (n 29) 100–13.
[33] Nietzsche (n 17).

something. The subordinated, unable to get a higher rank of power, seek revenge. Revenge may become spiritual or imaginary and takes the form of a re-evaluation of values.[34] The challenge to commonly accepted values is a central element of the revenge. The current crisis of common values is, in Nietzsche's words, 'the grand politics of revenge' of those who feel harmed and unable to change the system.

IV. The Role of Law in Ressentiment and Anomie

EU law itself plays a fundamental role in the revolt against the Union's common values. The disparity between the lofty ideals on the one hand and the harsh reality on the other and the lack of possibilities to challenge it sparks Nietzsche's ressentiment and the rejection of the fundamental value system in totality. This can occur every time the legal, seemingly technical, provisions of EU law, in the name of fundamental common values, give preference to some to the detriment of others. In the context of the Union, this sparks a challenge to the common values as set out in Article 2 TEU. The famous *Laval* judgment of the Court of Justice[35] and its follow up provide an example or an allegory of the hierarchical struggle of the European periphery, which sparks the process of ressentiment and the re-evaluation of common values.

The Court of Justice in 2007 ruled that a blockade by the Swedish trade union of the Latvian company Laval, which was paying its workers less than the Swedish minimum wage, had violated Laval's freedom of movement of services. The judgment was followed by unprecedented academic criticism, accusing the Court of giving preference to the provisions of free movement over workers' rights.[36] The judgment was understood as a mistake and a testament to the Court's purported neoliberal philosophy.

The *Laval* judgment was deemed to be largely in favour of the European periphery, despite the fact it condemned 'social dumping'. Following the judgment, the Posted Workers Directive was amended[37] in terms much less favourable to the European periphery. The amendments introduced into the Posted Workers Directive included the application to posted workers of all the mandatory elements of remuneration (instead of the 'minimum rates of pay'), and for postings longer than 12 or 18 months also the application of an extended set of terms and conditions of employment of the receiving Member State. This is a clear trend towards the 'host Member State' rules, unthinkable in other fields, such as, for example, free movement of goods, if the internal market was to survive. Importantly, it clearly reduced the competitive advantage of companies and workers of the periphery.

[34] Harm is the lowest common denominator of the legal system, the central element in the domain of law. See Kukovec, 'Taking Change Seriously (n 1) 145–46.

[35] Case C-341/05 *Laval un Partneri* EU:C:2007:809.

[36] Kukovec, 'Law and the Periphery' (n 24).

[37] The original Directive 96/71/EC was amended by Directive 2018/957 [2018] OJ L173/16.

Poland and Hungary introduced legal actions against the European Parliament and the Council, requesting the Court of Justice to annul the amended Posted Workers Directive.[38]

The Court of Justice dismissed both actions in their entirety, deferring to the legislator who rationally articulated the goals of the level playing field and protection and equal treatment of workers. Given the changed circumstances of enlargement, the Court concluded that it was open to the EU legislature to adjust the balance inherent in that Directive so that competition between the undertakings posting workers to that Member State and the undertakings established in that State should develop on a more level playing field.[39] In several host Member States, substantial differences in remuneration had come to light between workers employed by undertakings established in those Member States and the workers who were posted there, which created a competitive imbalance, argued the European Parliament. Both the Advocate General and the Court of Justice concluded that the EU legislature complied with the requirements of the principle of proportionality without manifestly exceeding its broad discretion when it chose a suitable measure for the attainment of the aims pursued.[40]

The legal actions introduced by Poland and Hungary well portray the lack of the effective agency of actors of the periphery. Their position could be understood as the usual situation of one of the Member States (or a minority) being outvoted by the majority in the legislative or other policymaking process. This a frequent and normal state of affairs in the EU. The *Weiss* case[41] or the older Tobacco advertising case[42] in which Germany was unsatisfied by being left in the minority are two of the most famous examples of this vital element of the construction of the EU. Qualified majority voting was an important step towards the development of an ever closer Union[43] and remains a key element of its functioning. Sometimes you win, sometimes you lose, for the benefit of everyone. Yet, when harm imposed on some parts of the general public is repetitive, structural, and social hierarchies

[38] European Parliament and Council Directive (EU) 2018/957 of 28 June 2018 amending Directive 96/71/EC concerning the posting of workers in the framework of the provision of service [2018] OJ L173/16; Case C-620/18 *Hungary v Parliament and Council* EU:C:2020:1001; Case C-626/18 *Poland v Parliament and Council* EU:C:2020:1000.

[39] *Hungary v Parliament and Council* (n 38) para 64.

[40] ibid, paras 126–29. The Court further examined the plea concerning an alleged infringement of Art 56 TFEU and, more specifically, the claim that the amending Directive removes the competitive advantage enjoyed by the service providers established in some Member States, in terms of costs. The Court stated that the amending Directive, in order to achieve its objective, undertakes a re-balancing of the factors affecting the competitiveness of undertakings established in various Member States. However, that Directive does not remove any competitive advantage which the service providers in some Member States may enjoy, since it in no way has the effect of eliminating all competition based on cost, such as the productivity or efficiency of those workers.

[41] Case C-493/17 *Weiss and Others* EU:C:2018:1000.

[42] Case C-376/98 *Federal Republic of Germany v European Parliament and Council of the European Union* EU:C:2000:544.

[43] See Weiler (n 6).

cannot be adequately challenged,[44] ressentiment develops, as in the case of the European periphery's lack of agency and power. The weak feel impotent and start a re-evaluation of common values.

The amendments made peripheral companies, those from poorer Member States, less competitive. Posting of workers was one of the few instances of a clear comparative advantage of the periphery in the internal market.[45] The posting of (cheaper) workers helps the far weaker peripheral companies penetrate the competitive markets of the centre of the EU and reduces unemployment in the periphery. It should also not be forgotten that peripheral workers, posted or not, always earn less than workers of the centre, not because of higher exploitation in the periphery, but because they live and work in poorer societies. After the completion of works, the posted workers return to the periphery, having earned money and experience. While some workers who are posted may earn more as a result of the amended Directive, workers of the periphery are generally posted less frequently than they would be if they were more competitive. The posting of workers, ensuring greater employment of workers from the periphery and the connected positive ripple effects on its social and economic development,[46] including on increased workers' salaries, was importantly limited. The amended Posted Workers Directive thus contributes to peripheral unemployment and to disabling its genuine economic development. The fact that this is a mere example of far greater structural subordination[47] does not make this case a normal instance of a 'win-some-lose-some' situation resulting from qualified-majority voting. It is part of a pattern that the periphery is locked into that leads to ressentiment.

Grave socio-economic challenges facing peripheral regions have not been missed by one of the co-legislators. According to the European Parliament, there is serious depopulation of the European east and European south. Sharp declines in population, especially in Eastern and Southern Europe, are due to the combination of intra-EU migration from these areas and low fertility rates. There is the serious problem of brain drain. The 'sending regions' are losing high skills and competencies to the advantage of the 'receiving regions' as a result of permanent emigration.[48]

It should be noted that the situation as described by the European Parliament is also due to the adopted amendments to the Posted Workers Directive. Instead of giving peripheral workers temporary jobs and experience in the centre, which

[44] For the inability of the periphery to effectively compete in the EU internal market, see Kukovec, 'Hidden Hierarchies' (n 24); for an example of the frustration of Eastern Europeans, see Feffer (n 20).

[45] See Kukovec, Whose Social Europe?' (n 16).

[46] See Kukovec, 'Law and the Periphery' (n 24); Kukovec, 'Hidden Hierarchies' (n 24).

[47] See Kukovec, 'Hidden Hierarchies' (n 24); see also a recent statement to this effect by the Romanian Minister of Finance, *Financial Times* (28 November 2018), available at: www.ft.com/content/35a31080-f322-11e8-ae55-df4bf40f9d0d.

[48] 'What Solutions to Population Decline in Europe's Regions?' (*European Parliament News*, 20 April 2021), available at: www.europarl.europa.eu/news/en/headlines/society/20210414STO02006/what-solutions-to-population-decline-in-europe-s-regions; European Parliamentary Research Service (EPRS) and Monika Kiss (n 22).

they could bring back home once the work is completed, the amended Directive effectively gives the jobless of the periphery a choice between being jobless or to permanently move from the periphery to the centre. This leads to the devastating depopulation of peripheral areas with a limited economic and social future, fuelling extremism in the periphery as well as in the centre where worries about excessive immigration lead to social tensions.

The European Parliament's proposed solution to depopulation is improving local public transport as well as easing access to healthcare and the internet in the periphery. It is difficult to conceive that such solutions sustainably address the depopulation of regions on the outskirts of the Union on a downward spiral[49] when there is no economic activity and no jobs which would ensure prosperity and human dignity and when there is legislation in place perpetuating this situation. Can the jobless and depressed truly usefully use public transport and the internet?

The mistaken policy, however, is only part of the problem. The disintegration of common values that results in such legislation is a serious challenge to the stability of the Union and is a real generator of the crisis of values. The distress to the axiological unity of the Union has resulted from the fact that the amendments to the Posted Workers Directive were argued to be guided by the principle of equal treatment, fair competition and protection of workers. Promoting these values as normative reasons for measures resulting in actual impoverishment fuel ressentiment. The understanding of harm in the legal system that does not acknowledge the harms to the periphery breeds the impotence of peripheral actors. Equal treatment, fair competition and the protection of workers cannot be argued to be the guiding line when some are given the opportunities to prosper and some, the unprivileged, are not.[50]

Moreover, independently of ressentiment, the legal system, when harming some actors under the pretext of common values, itself vitally contributes to their disintegration. When the values of the legal system that are hailed as universal are in fact partial, common standards and values break down. When measures are adopted in the name of values such as the protection of workers, equal treatment or fair competition, which lead to results opposite to what those values profess, a condition of instability develops.

Émile Durkheim called a situation of instability due to a breakdown of common values an 'anomie'.[51] The application of a universal norm from a single perspective against the background of a deep social and economic split, such as the centre-periphery split,[52] leads to anomie. The value of the 'protection of workers' is individualised when the position of workers of the periphery is not adequately

[49] G Myrdal, *Economic Theory and Underdeveloped Regions* (Urbana-Champaign, Duckworth, 1957).
[50] Kukovec, 'Law and the Periphery' (n 24).
[51] Émile Durkheim, *Suicide: A Study in Sociology* (1897).
[52] See Kukovec, 'Law and the Periphery' (n 24).

considered in the context of the posting of workers. The amended Posted Workers Directive ensured protection of workers, equal treatment and fair competition for workers and companies of the centre. The individualisation of goals and values causes social conflict which leads to a sense of futility and lack of purpose.[53]

In a society where proclaimed common values openly harm some, those common values and common meanings are effectively no longer available. Individuals no longer abide by the rules imposed by society, and they openly question the totality of hitherto common values. In other words, society loses the power to impose rules on individuals (or on individual Member States) to ensure social harmony. Common values disintegrate as a result of ressentiment and anomie produced by the legal system itself. EU law, and the particular articulation of its values, thus reveals itself as an important pillar of the Union's (in)stability.

To preserve the power and adherence to the common values of the Union, a new narrative is needed for the Union, one based on an acknowledgement that the EU is split along centre-periphery lines and that common values cannot be used to mask this split. The narrative should be based on a changed understanding of harm, one that consciously acknowledges the harm imposed on peripheral actors.[54] This narrative should not perpetuate an economic, spiritual, legal and political underclass, but rather allow such status and harm to be effectively challenged at every opportunity. The aim of this narrative does not necessarily mean injecting more money into the less developed regions and countries, but rather giving them fair competitive opportunities to develop. If the Union's normative power is to survive, vested short-term economic interests will have to give way to the long-term interests of cohesion and stability, and the law needs to transparently support this development.

V. Conclusion

Law plays a powerful role in the stability of Europe. Infusing the EU legal system with moral pronouncements and calls for the increased decisiveness of EU institutions, all the while ignoring the hierarchical structure of the Union, scratch the surface of the problem rather than address the deep structure of profound imbalances of power and the genealogy of the most destabilising forces in the EU. The former approach lacks an adequate legal and social appreciation of the reality of life in the EU, the role of law and lawyers in the crisis, as well as the context and background of litigation before the Court of Justice.

The rule of law crisis is a symptom of a larger hierarchical power struggle and the concomitant rejection of common values. Through this lens, regional

[53] S Serpa and C Miguel Ferreira, 'Anomie in the Sociological Perspective of Émile Durkheim' (2018) 2 *Sociology International Journal*.

[54] Kukovec, 'Taking Change Seriously' (n 1); Kukovec, 'Law and the Periphery' (n 24).

inequality coupled with the legal impotence of certain groups represents a cancer of the EU. As Nietzsche notes: 'From powerlessness … hatred grows to take on a monstrous and sinister shape, the most cerebral and most poisonous form'.[55]

The European periphery has come full circle from an uncritical acceptance of common policies and values of the Union to their forceful rejection. Ressentiment can be detected within other liberal democracies, including in the United States and in the United Kingdom, where it importantly led to Brexit.[56] In the international realm, parallels can be drawn with a struggle for values by Russia, Turkey and China vis-a-vis the liberal democracies. Within the EU, the struggle bears even greater importance as it directly affects the Union's existence. At the same time, the remedies within the Union are far more readily available than in the international realm.

The crisis of values is serious. Instead of waving the banner of righteousness, lawyers need to address the anti-structural reformism of the EU. The transformations of Europe have been transformations of European institutional structures which one way or another contribute to the reproduction of the existing distribution of material and spiritual values in the Union.[57] Lawyers should take a closer look at the perpetuation of inequality through the legal system underlying the gloss of constant betterment and change.

[55] Nietzsche (n 17) 19.

[56] D Kukovec, 'The Legal Profession's Responsibility for Brexit' in T Ahmed and E Fahey (eds), *On Brexit* (Cheltenham, Edward Elgar Publishing, 2019).

[57] ibid.

9

Towards 'Judicial Passivism' in European Union Migration and Asylum Law?*

IRIS GOLDNER LANG**

I. Introduction

The title of this text suggests that in the past several years the Court of Justice (CJEU) has been showing signs of passivism in some of its most prominent cases relating to the 2015/2016 refugee influx into the European Union (EU). Such behaviour of the Court will be labelled as 'judicial passivism'. The aim of this chapter is, first, to define the term 'judicial passivism', second, to identify examples of the Court's passive behaviour and, third, to determine the reasons for such behaviour and its impact on the future development of EU law in general and EU migration and asylum law in particular.

The term 'judicial passivism' stands at the heart of this discussion and calls for a precise definition. However, unlike the term 'judicial activism', 'judicial passivism' has not been used in relation to EU law. In order to understand its meaning, it is necessary to briefly address and define the term 'judicial activism'.

In EU law, judicial activism is most often understood as cases where the judiciary oversteps its judicial powers.[1] The problem with this definition is that the

* This text is based on a blog post by Iris Goldner Lang, 'Towards "Judicial Passivism" in the EU and Asylum Law?' (*Odysseus*, 24 January 2018), available at: https://eumigrationlawblog.eu/towards-judicial-passivism-in-eu-migration-and-asylum-law-preliminary-thoughts-for-the-final-plenary-session-of-the-2018-odysseus-conference/. I am grateful to Professor Philippe De Bruycker and Advocate General Tamara Ćapeta for their valuable comments on the text.

** Jean Monnet Professor of EU Law, Holder of the UNESCO Chair on Free Movement of Persons, Migration and Inter-Cultural Dialogue and Vice Dean, University of Zagreb – Faculty of Law.

[1] For discussions on judicial activism of the Court of Justice and in general, see H Rasmussen, *On Law and Policy in the European Court of Justice: A Comparative Study in Judicial Policymaking* (Dordrecht, Nijhoff, 1986); M Cappelletti, 'Is the European Court of Justice "Running Wild?"' (1987) 12 *European Law Review* 3; M Dawson, B de Witte and E Muir (eds), *Judicial Activism at the European Court of Justice* (Cheltenham, Edward Elgar Publishing, 2013); JHH Weiler, 'The Court of Justice on Trial – A Review of Hjalte Rasmussen: On Law and Policy in the European Court of Justice' (1987) 24

delimitation of the CJEU's powers often lies in the eye of the beholder. In other words, a case which one person might define as an example of the Court transgressing its powers (activism) might be seen by somebody else as an example of the Court staying within its boundaries, and the other way around. The perception of the existence or non-existence of judicial activism would partly depend on the ideology, beliefs and the background of the person you ask. It is also difficult, if not impossible, to tear the case away from its political and social setting. If we start from the premise that a judge is *homo politicus* and that he or she does not decide a case in a vacuum, every case is bound to carry a policy, social and political message.[2]

Defining and determining cases of judicial passivism is equally problematic. Despite the fact that one might semantically consider judicial passivism as the opposite of judicial activism, this text will argue that judicial passivism is just a subcategory of judicial activism. In this regard, a self-standing definition of judicial passivism would apply to cases where the CJEU is consciously (actively) not using its powers where it could, due to the political and social sensitivity of the case, often combined with the ambiguity of the legal text. By remaining silent, the Court is sending a message to the EU institutions, its Member States and other political actors in the EU that a different interpretation would require legislative amendments.

This phenomenon can happen in one of the two following ways. First, 'judicial passivism in its narrow sense' would refer to cases where the Court chooses not to decide on the issue by declaring that it lacks jurisdiction. In other words, by identifying a certain situation as falling outside the scope of EU law, the CJEU is not addressing the substance of a given case and is actively choosing not to act. Second, 'judicial passivism in the extensive sense' would also encompass situations where the Court is using its judicial (eg, interpretative) role, but it does so in a manner which deviates from the teleological interpretation to which the Court has accustomed us over the past decades of its adjudication. Significantly, judicial passivism in both its narrow and extensive sense can be understood as the flipside of judicial activism – as the Court's conscious decision not to decide, or to decide in a strict, formalist way.

The phenomenon of judicial passivism will be discussed by looking at several judgments of the CJEU in the area of migration and asylum: the judgments on

Common Market Law Review 555; A Arnull, 'The European Court and Judicial Objectivity: A Reply to Professor Hartley (1996) 112 *Law Quarterly Review* 411; P Neill, *The European Court of Justice: A Study in Judicial Activism* (London, European Policy Forum, 1995); DK Kmiec, 'The Origin and Current Meanings of Judicial Activism' (2004) 92 *California Law Review* 1942; M Dawson, 'How Does the European Court of Justice Reason? A Review Essay on the Legal Reasoning of the European Court of Justice' (2014) 20 *European Law Journal* 423.

[2] On indeterminacy of law and the importance of ideology in legal reasoning, see T Ćapeta, 'Ideology and Legal Reasoning at the European Court of Justice' in T Perišin and S Rodin (eds), *Transformation or Reconstitution of Europe: The Critical Legal Studies Perspective on the Role of Courts in the European Union* (Oxford, Hart Publishing, 2018); N Bačić Selanec, 'A Realist Account of European Union Citizenship' (PhD dissertation, University of Zagreb, 2019).

the EU–Turkey Statement,[3] the judgment on humanitarian visas in *X & X*,[4] and the judgments on the Western Balkans route in *AS* and *Jafari*.[5] These judgments encourage us to reassess the role of the Court for the future course of EU integration, in general, and for EU migration and asylum law, in particular. They open up the question of the Court's role and responsibility in the context of the past years of the refugee influx into Europe and in terms of the consequent and future legal and policy developments. In this regard, the text will connect the judgments on the EU–Turkey Statement and in *AS* and *Jafari* with the February/March 2020 developments at the Greek–Turkish border and the EU leaders' reaction thereto. It will also consider the future behaviour of the Member States and the CJEU by discussing the implications of the judgment of the European Court of Human Rights (ECtHR) in *ND and NT*.[6]

II. Judicial Passivism in the Narrow Sense

There are strong arguments to view the Orders of the General Court on the legality of the EU–Turkey Statement as examples of judicial passivism in its narrow sense. When asked to review the legality of the Statement, the General Court declared that it lacked jurisdiction to hear and determine the cases and, accordingly, dismissed them. The actions were brought in April 2016 by two Pakistani nationals and an Afghan national. They travelled from Turkey to Greece, where they applied for asylum, claiming that they risked persecution if they returned to their respective countries of origin. Fearing that they might be returned to Turkey if their asylum applications were rejected, they decided to challenge the legality of the EU–Turkey deal before the CJEU. In their submission they made a number of claims: that the deal is incompatible with EU fundamental rights, that Turkey is not a safe third country, that the Temporary Protection Directive should have been used in the existing situation,[7] that the EU–Turkey deal is actually an international agreement which fails to comply with the relevant Treaty articles, and that the prohibition of collective expulsion is being breached by the deal.

In its judgments, the General Court accepted the arguments put forward by the EU institutions, which claimed that they were not the authors of the Statement, but that it was a measure concluded by the EU Member States. The Court, therefore, ascertained that the EU–Turkey Statement was not concluded by the European Council, but by the heads of state or government of the EU Member States,

[3] Orders of the General Court in Cases T-192/16, T-193/16 and T-257/16 *NF, NG & NM v European Council* EU:T:2017:128; EU:T:2017:129; and EU:T:2017:130.
[4] Case C-638/16 PPU *X & X v État belge* EU:C:2017:173.
[5] Case C-490/16 *AS v Slovenia* EU:C:2017:585; Case C-646/16 *Jafari* EU:C:2017:586.
[6] *ND and NT v Spain* Apps nos 8675/15 and 8697/15 (ECtHR, 13 February 2020).
[7] Council Directive 2001/55/EC [2001] OJ L 212/12 on minimum standards for giving temporary protection in the event of a mass influx of displaced persons and on measures promoting a balance of efforts between Member States in receiving such persons and bearing the consequences thereof.

as actors of international law, and the Turkish Prime Minister. Therefore, the Court concluded that the EU–Turkey Statement could not be considered to be an act of an EU institution pursuant to Article 263 of the Treaty on the Functioning of the European Union (TFEU).[8] Consequently, the Court declared that it lacked jurisdiction to review the Statement's legality and decided not to rule on the issue whether it was a political statement (as suggested by the European Council, the Council and the Commission) or an agreement producing binding legal effects.

This text will not enter into a discussion of the content of the EU–Turkey Statement or of the arguments put forward by the General Court to support its finding that the EU–Turkey Statement is not an EU act.[9] This would require much more space, and a considerable amount of ink has already been spilled on this.[10] This text starts from the premise that there is room for a different reading of the EU–Turkey Statement (from the one given by the General Court), supporting the view that it should be considered as an EU act. One of the strong arguments in favour of such a reading is the European Road Transport Agreement (ERTA) doctrine,[11] which establishes the rule that once the EU implements a common policy in a certain field, the EU Member States no longer have the right 'to undertake obligations with third countries which affect those rules or alter their scope'.[12]

By failing to fulfil its judicial function of reviewing the legality of the EU–Turkey Statement, according to Article 263 TFEU, the General Court has actively chosen not to decide on the substance of the cases. In this sense, the judgments on the EU–Turkey Statement can be viewed as examples of judicial passivism, which has far-reaching effects both for EU migration and asylum law and for the future development of EU law in general. The Court's conscious decision not to decide has enabled the EU–Turkey Statement to endure and has allowed for similar agreements to be concluded with third countries outside the scope of EU law and exempt from the judicial review of the CJEU. In this sense, the Court's behaviour could be explained as its desire to accommodate itself to political reality and the Member States' intentions, without having to rule on their compliance with EU law. However, it is doubtful that avoiding scrutinising the EU–Turkey Statement can or should be reconciled with the judicial function. Giving carte blanche to the

[8] Art 263 TFEU provides that '[t]he Court of Justice of the European Union shall review the legality of legislative acts, of acts of the Council, of the Commission and of the European Central Bank, other than recommendations and opinions, and of acts of the European Parliament and of the European Council intended to produce legal effects vis-à-vis third parties. It shall also review the legality of acts of bodies, offices or agencies of the Union intended to produce legal effects vis-à-vis third parties'.

[9] European Council, 'EU–Turkey Statement' (*European Council*, 18 March 2016), available at: www.consilium.europa.eu/en/press/press-releases/2016/03/18/eu-turkey-statement/.

[10] For a discussion on the EU–Turkey Statement, see I Goldner Lang, 'Human Rights and Legitimacy in the Implementation of EU Asylum and Migration Law' in S Vöneky and GL Neuman (eds), *Human Rights, Democracy, and Legitimacy in a World of* Disorder (Cambridge, Cambridge University Press, 2018).

[11] Case 22/70 *Commission v Council* (European Road Transport Agreement) EU:C:1971:32.

[12] T Spijkerboer, 'Bifurcation of Mobility, Bifurcation of Law. Externalization of Migration Policy Before the EU Court of Justice' (2018) 31 *Journal of Refugee Studies* 216.

EU institutions and Member States not only sends the wrong message that it is all right to have your cake and eat it, but it could also tie the Court's hands to rule on similar agreements in the future.

In the meantime, the applicants appealed and the case was decided by the CJEU's higher instance, the Court of Justice, which again did not go into the substance of the case.[13] However – unlike the General Court – the Court of Justice avoided reducing its institutional powers by excluding a whole category of cases from its jurisdiction and influence. The Court did this by dismissing the appeals as manifestly inadmissible in their entirety.[14] It corroborated its decision by stating that the appeals were incoherent, since their reasoning was not clear and precise and since they only made general assertions that the General Court had disregarded a number of EU principles, without indicating precisely enough the contested elements of the Court's Orders.[15] In this way, both instances of the CJEU avoided responding to the question of the compatibility of the EU–Turkey Statement with EU law and its human rights standards.

Several weeks after the General Court's decisions on the EU–Turkey Statement, the Grand Chamber of the Court of Justice issued its judgment on humanitarian visas in *X & X*. There are strong arguments suggesting this ruling represents another example of the Court's passivism in the narrow sense, ie that the Court should have decided that the case was governed by EU law, but it remained passive. The case concerned a Syrian couple and their three minor children, living in Aleppo, who submitted applications for visas with limited territorial validity on the basis of Article 25(1)(a) of the Visa Code, at the Belgian Embassy in Beirut.[16] They stated that the purpose of humanitarian visas would be to enable them to reach Belgium and apply for asylum there. They stressed the precarious security situation in Syria and pointed out that, as Orthodox Christians, they were at risk of persecution on account of their religious beliefs. They also emphasised that they could not register as refugees in Lebanon and were therefore forced to return to Syria.

In this case, the Court was asked to rule whether the term 'international obligations' contained in Article 25(1)(a) of the Visa Code covers the rights guaranteed by the Charter – in particular its Article 4 (prohibiting torture and inhuman and degrading treatment) and Article 18 (on the right to asylum) – and whether it also covers obligations binding Member States in the light of the European Convention on Human Rights (ECHR) and the Geneva Convention. In the case

[13] For a later decision of the Court of Justice in the appeals procedure, see Joined Cases C-208/17 P to C-210/17 P *NF and Others v European Council* EU:C:2018:705.

[14] ibid para 30.

[15] ibid para 16.

[16] Regulation (EC) No 810/2009 of the European Parliament and of the Council of 13 July 2009 establishing a Community Code on Visas (Visa Code) [2009] OJ L243/1. Art 25(1)(a) of the Visa Code states: 'A visa with limited territorial validity shall be issued exceptionally, in the following cases: when the Member State concerned considers it necessary on humanitarian grounds, for reasons of national interest or because of international obligations, to derogate from the principle that the entry conditions laid down in Article 5(1)(a), (c), (d) and (e) of the Schengen Borders Code must be fulfilled'.

of a positive answer, in its second question, the referring court wanted to know whether a Member State to which an application for a humanitarian visa with limited territorial validity has been made is required to issue the visa, where a risk of infringement of Article 4 and/or 18 of the Charter is established.

The crux of the case – for the purpose of the discussion on judicial passivism – is that the Court did not answer the questions. It noted that the Visa Code establishes procedures and conditions for issuing visas not exceeding 90 days in any 180-day period. The Court then ascertained that the Syrian family applied for humanitarian visas with a view to applying for asylum in Belgium and to being granted a residence permit with a period of validity not limited to 90 days. It therefore concluded that such applications fall outside the scope of the Visa Code and are solely within the scope of national law. Consequently, the Court determined that the situation was not governed by EU law and that the provisions of the Charter did not apply.

However, in the context of the discussion on judicial passivism, the judgment in *X & X* significantly differs from the judgments on the EU–Turkey Statement. As pointed out previously, in the judgments on the EU–Turkey Statement, the Court took a formalist approach when arguing that the situation fell outside the scope of EU law. This judgment was not based on the nature and the effects of the Statement, but on the (EU institutions') view that the signatories of the Statement were not the EU institutions, but its Member States. Having stated that the EU–Turkey Statement was not an EU act, the Court ascertained that it lacked jurisdiction to rule on the question.

On the other hand, in *X & X*, the Court cannot be accused of refraining from the discussion of the object and purpose of X & X's applications, the Visa Code and EU asylum law in general. The Court examined the (in)applicability of the Visa Code to the applications for humanitarian visas made by the Syrian family, and it did this in a non-formalist, teleological manner. The Grand Chamber made an effort to argue that classifying the applications in question as applications for humanitarian visas, pursuant to Article 25(1)(a) of the Visa Code would be contrary to EU law on several levels. First, such a classification would be opposed to the objective of the Visa Code, as stated both in the Code itself and in the TFEU.[17] Second, deciding that the applications of the Syrian family are covered by Article 25 of the Visa Code would be contrary to Article 79(2)(a) TFEU. Finally, it would be contrary to the general structure of EU asylum law, in particular Articles 1 and 3 of the Dublin Regulation and Article 3(1) and (2) of the Asylum Procedures Directive.[18] In other words, in the Court's view, the purpose of the applications was contrary to the

[17] *X & X* (n 4) paras 40–41.

[18] ibid para 49. Dublin Regulation: Regulation 604/2013, of the European Parliament and of the Council of 26 June 2013 establishing the criteria and mechanisms for determining the Member State responsible for examining an application for international protection lodged in one of the Member States by a third-country national or a stateless person (recast) [2013] OJ L180/31. Asylum Procedures Directive: Directive 2013/32/EU of the European Parliament and of the Council of 26 June 2013 on common procedures for granting and withdrawing international protection [2013] OJ L180/60.

purpose of the Visa Code.[19] Consequently, the CJEU concluded the Visa Code did not apply to the situations and neither did any other EU law instrument.

There are divergent views as to the correctness of the Court's logic. For example, in his Opinion in this case, AG Mengozzi followed a completely different line.[20] He deemed the situation to be governed by the Visa Code and, therefore, by EU law, including if it were held that the applications were rightly refused.[21] He further contended that 'by adopting a decision under Article 25 of the Visa Code, the authorities of a Member State implement EU law for the purposes of Article 51(1) of the Charter and are, therefore, required to respect the rights guaranteed by the Charter'.[22] He concluded that a Member State is required to issue a humanitarian visa if there are substantial grounds to believe that the refusal to issue that document would deprive that national of a legal route to seek international protection in that Member State.[23] However, no matter which stance one takes it is evident that by its judgment in *X & X*, the Court sends a message to the EU legislators that an opposite conclusion would require legislative amendments to current EU asylum law.

III. Judicial Passivism in the Extensive Sense

The aim of the preceding discussion of the judgments on the legality of the EU–Turkey Statement and of the judgment in *X and X* was to explain judicial passivism in its narrow sense. On the other hand, an examination of the cases of *AS* and *Jafari* in the following paragraphs serves as the starting point for the conceptualisation of judicial passivism in its extensive sense.[24] As stated previously, an extensive understanding of judicial passivism would also encompass cases where the Court accepts to decide the case, but it does so in a formalist way, without taking into consideration the overall purpose and scheme of the relevant norms, the factual circumstances of the case and the intentions of the Member States, as the masters of the Treaties.

The judgments of the Grand Chamber of the Court of Justice in *AS* and *Jafari* are the Court's reaction to the non-application of the Dublin State of first entry rule[25]

[19] *X & X* (n 4) para 47.
[20] Case C-638/16 PPU *X & X* ECLI:EU:C:2017:93, Opinion of AG Mengozzi.
[21] ibid para 61.
[22] ibid para 84.
[23] ibid para 163.
[24] For a detailed account of *AS* and *Jafari*, *Mengesteab* and the Western Balkans route, see I Goldner Lang, 'Croatia and EU Asylum Law: Playing on the Sidelines or at the Centre of Events?' in V Stoyanova and E Karageorgiou (eds), *The New Asylum and Transit Countries in Europe During and in the Aftermath of the 2015/2016 Crisis* (Leiden, Brill, 2018).
[25] Art 13(1) of the Dublin Regulation stipulates that the Member State responsible for examining an asylum application is the State whose border the asylum applicant first crossed irregularly when coming from a third country. If asylum rules do not apply to a third-country national, the entry conditions of a third-country national to the territory of a Member State are regulated by Art 6(1) of the

across the Western Balkans route in 2015/16.[26] Between September 2015 and March 2016, more than 700,000 people passed along the Western Balkans route, which involved a voyage from the Middle East, across Turkey and Greece to FYROM, Serbia, Hungary, Croatia (upon the Hungarian closure of its border with Serbia), Slovenia and Austria, mostly ending up in Germany. The migrants on the route were not applying for asylum either in the EU Member State of their first entry (Greece) or in the Western Balkans countries, among them Croatia as the second EU Member State on the Western Balkans route. Instead, they were transiting through several EU and non-EU States until they came to the EU Member State of their desired destination (mostly Germany) and applied for asylum there. On the other hand, Greece, Croatia and other countries on the Western Balkans route did not apply the Schengen Borders Code and, thus, they did not prevent the entry of irregular migrants into their respective territories, but facilitated their further movement to other States along the route. The transit of migrants on the Western Balkans route was organised by the States along the way, which sometimes (allegedly), contrary to the Eurodac Regulation, did not fingerprint and register the migrants before further transit.

Clearly, there was a tacit agreement between the Western Balkans States and the migrants transiting the route not to apply the Dublin rules. Further, there was an agreement among the States on the Western Balkans route to organise and run the route contrary to the Dublin rules. The route was both authorised and facilitated by the authorities of both the EU Member States and third countries on the route, which organised transportation along the way. This was the direct consequence of two factors. First, it was prompted by German willingness to take all the migrants

Schengen Borders Code, which stipulates that the third-country national has to have a valid travel document and a valid visa. Third-country nationals should also be able to justify the purpose and conditions of their intended stay and show that they have sufficient means of subsistence, both for the duration of the intended stay and for the return journey. Exceptionally, a third-country national who does not fulfil one or more of the above conditions may be granted entry on humanitarian grounds, on grounds of national interest or because of international obligations. However, as will be shown in the analysis of the CJEU's judgment in *AS* and *Jafari*, the exception based on humanitarian grounds was not applicable to the developments on the Western Balkans route.

[26] For the developments on the Western Balkans route, see S Šelo Šabić and S Borić, 'At the Gate of Europe: A Report on Refugees on the Western Balkan Route' (Friedrich Ebert Stiftung, SOE Dialog Südosteropa, 2017) 11, available at: library.fes.de/pdf-files/bueros/kroatien/13059.pdf; 'Balkan States Attempt to Limit Numbers of Refugees Claiming Asylum' *Guardian* (20 January 2016), available at: www.theguardian.com/world/2016/jan/20/balkan-states-attempt-to-limit-numbers-of-refugees-claiming-asylum; Jennifer Rankin, 'Austria Dismisses Criticism of Its Plan to Limit Daily Refugee Numbers' *Guardian* (18 February, 2016), available at: www.theguardian.com/world/2016/feb/18/austria-dismisses-criticism-of-its-plan-to-limit-daily-refugee-numbers; Jennifer Rankin, 'Croatia and Slovenia Impose Limits on Refugee Numbers' *Guardian* (26 February, 2016), available at: www.theguardian.com/world/2016/feb/26/croatia-slovenia-limits-refugee-numbers-europe-greece; Peter Teffer, 'Balkan Countries Close Borders to Economic Migrants' (*EuObserver*, 20 November, 2015), available at: euobserver.com/migration/131192. The Dublin state-of-first entry rule, which dominates the Dublin Regulation and is its weakest link, provides that in the vast majority of cases, the Member State in charge of determining an asylum claim will be the State of the applicant's first entry into the Union.

and examine their asylum claims itself. The States on the route were allowing entry and transit of migrants as long as Germany was ready to accept them on its territory. Second, the Western Balkans route was the direct consequence of the States' realisation that the alternative to not allowing migrants' entry into their respective territories would have been to leave hundreds of thousands of migrants stranded at national borders in degrading conditions which would have led to a humanitarian catastrophe and to the respective States' breach of Article 3 of the ECHR and Article 4 of the Charter.[27]

The joined cases *AS* and *Jafari* concerned a Syrian and two Afghan nationals, respectively, who were taking the Western Balkans route in 2015/16 and ended up in Slovenia and Austria respectively, where they applied for asylum. Slovenia and Austria refused to examine their asylum applications, taking the position that Croatia was responsible for the examination, as the State of first entry into the EU, not counting Greece which had been exempt from Dublin transfers due to systemic deficiencies in its asylum system.

In its judgments, the Court of Justice ruled that the entries of AS and the Jafari sisters must be regarded as 'irregular crossings' within the meaning of Article 13(1) of the Dublin Regulation 'irrespective of whether the crossing was tolerated or authorised in breach of the applicable rules or whether it was authorised on humanitarian grounds by way of derogation from the entry conditions generally imposed on third-country nationals'.[28] According to the Court, the fact that such a crossing took place in the context of the arrival of an unusually large number of third-country nationals could not affect the irregular character of the crossing.[29] The only instance where the responsibility of the State of irregular crossing could be precluded would be the case where Dublin transfers to that State could lead to a risk of inhuman and degrading treatment of the transferee, within the meaning of Article 4 of the Charter.[30]

Even though the Court did not explicitly incriminate Croatia – by characterising the crossing of the Croatian border as irregular – it indirectly stated that Croatia was responsible for examining the asylum applications of AS and the Jafari sisters and thereby implied that Croatia was responsible for examining the applications for international protection of the vast majority of the 700,000 persons crossing its borders during the 2015/16 migration wave (apart from those who would fall under the preceding criteria for determining the responsible Member State, stipulated by Articles 8–12 of the Dublin Regulation).[31]

[27] Art 3 ECHR and Art 4 of the Charter prohibit torture and inhuman and degrading treatment. In that respect, see the statement of AG Sharpston in Case C-490/16 *AS v Slovenia* and Case C-646/16 *Jafari* EU:C:2017:443, Opinion of AG Sharpston para 174.

[28] *Jafari* (n 5) para 92.

[29] ibid para 93.

[30] ibid para 101.

[31] ibid paras 74–76. It is surprising that Croatia did not intervene either in the written or oral stage of the court proceedings, despite the fact that this case was of importance to it.

Why can the judgments in *AS* and *Jafari* serve as an example of judicial passivism in its extensive sense? The Grand Chamber of the Court made a visible effort to discuss the substance of the cases and elaborated its judgments with many, often technical, details. Despite this, these judgments can be viewed as an example of a formalist interpretation, which disregards, first, the overall purpose and scheme of the Dublin Regulation and EU asylum law; second, the factual circumstances on the Western Balkans route; and third, the intentions of at least those EU Member States which took part in the organisation of the route. In this sense, the Court's (unusual?) reluctance to show flexibility in its interpretation and to depart from the strict reading of the Dublin Regulation deviates from Recital 5 of the Regulation (as pointed out in AG Sharpston's Opinion)[32] which calls for the application of 'objective, fair criteria both for the Member State and for the person concerned' when determining the Member State responsible for the examination of the asylum application. Furthermore, the Court denies the inapplicability of the State of first entry rule on the factual circumstances of a mass influx of persons across the Western Balkans route. Finally, when defining the term 'irregular crossing' in relation to Article 13(1) of the Dublin Regulation, the Court disregards the fact that the route was both authorised and facilitated by the States on the route, including the EU Member States linked to the dispute, which challenges the applicability to the situation of the term 'irregular crossing'.

All these arguments question the correctness and rectitude of the Court's formalist approach. In addition, even if we start from the premise that the Court's literal interpretation of the Dublin Regulation is the correct one, its automatic presumption that the criterion of 'irregular crossing' contained in Article 13(1) of the Dublin Regulation (ie, the State of first entry rule) is applicable to the case is rebuttable. As explained previously, AS and the Jafari sisters first entered the EU via Greece, so Greece was the State of first entry. However, Dublin transfers to Greece could not take place as of 2011, due to systemic deficiencies in its asylum system. However, as pointed out in AG Sharpston's Opinion, there is nothing in Article 13(1) to suggest that 'responsibility under that provision transfers to the second Member State of entry'.[33] Such understanding of the Dublin Regulation is additionally supported by the Opinion of AG Villalón in the earlier case of *Abdullahi*,[34] where AG Villalón suggested that once the Member State which should have been responsible, based on the criterion of 'irregular crossing', has been excluded, a different criterion has to be applied.[35]

This logic starts from the premise that the criterion of 'irregular crossing', contained in Article 13(1) of the Dublin Regulation, has been exhausted by the fact that the first irregular crossing into the EU took place in Greece and that Dublin transfers to Greece could not take place due to the systemic deficiencies

[32] Opinion of AG Sharpston (n 27).
[33] ibid.
[34] Case C-394/12 *Shamso Abdullahi v Bundesasylamt* EU:C:2013:813.
[35] Case C-394/12 *Shamso Abdullahi v Bundesasylamt* EU:C:2013:473, Opinion of AG Villalón.

in its asylum system. Consequently, the same criterion could no longer be applied in finding the next Member State of irregular crossing on the Western Balkans route. If so, the Member State of the asylum application would have to allocate responsibility for examining the asylum application based on the following criteria contained in the Dublin Regulation, in their hierarchical order: visa waiver[36] and application in an international transit area of an airport.[37] If none of the Member States could be designated based on these two criteria, the responsible Member State would be the first one in which the asylum application was lodged, based on Article 3(2) of the Dublin Regulation.[38] Additionally, in his Opinion in *Abdullahi*, AG Villalón also pointed out the judgment in *NS*, where the Court referred to the transferring Member State's obligation to apply one of the 'following' criteria for determining the responsible Member State.[39]

However, in *AS* and *Jafari*, the Court chose to take a different avenue, thus departing from both the Opinion of AG Sharpston in *AS* and *Jafari* and from the Opinion of AG Villalón in *Abdullahi*. From that perspective, the rulings in *AS* and *Jafari* can be viewed as an act of scolding Croatia and the other EU Member States on the Western Balkans route and a warning not to repeat such behaviour in the future.

However, it is no coincidence that on the same day as its judgments in *AS* and *Jafari* – 26 July 2017 – the Grand Chamber of the Court of Justice issued another important judgment in *Mengesteab*, which concerned an Eritrean national requesting asylum in Germany.[40] Here, the Court limited the practical effects of its judgments in *AS* and *Jafari* by declaring that a Dublin transfer cannot take place upon the expiry of the three-month period after the application for international protection has been lodged. According to the Court, that period starts to run before a formal asylum application has been lodged if a written document confirming the request for international protection has been received by the competent authority or if only the main information contained in such a document has reached the authority. In practical terms, this means that, at the time the judgments in *AS* and *Jafari* and *Mengesteab* were issued, the three-month period had already expired for the vast majority of migrants who crossed the Western Balkans route in 2015/16 and that, consequently, Dublin transfers to Croatia were not possible for most of those who passed through Croatia on their way to Western European States, where they eventually applied for asylum.

In its judgment in *Mengesteab*, the Court of Justice first ascertained that the asylum applicant may rely on the expiry of the three-month period, even if the requested Member State is willing to take charge of him.[41] The Court then

[36] Art 14(1) of the Dublin Regulation.
[37] Art 15 of the Dublin Regulation.
[38] Art 3(2) of the Dublin Regulation.
[39] Case C-411/10 *NS and Others* EU:C:2011:865 para 107.
[40] Case 670/16 *Mengesteab* EU:C:2017:587.
[41] ibid para 62.

continued by stating that a take-charge request cannot legitimately be made more than three months after the asylum application has been lodged, even if the request is made within two months of a receipt of a Eurodac hit.[42] Finally, and most importantly, the Court concluded that an asylum application 'is deemed to have been lodged if a written document, prepared by a public authority and certifying that a third-country national has requested international protection, has reached' the responsible authority or 'if only the main information contained in such a document, but not the document or a copy thereof, has reached that authority'.[43]

The combination of the Court's formalist approach to the Dublin Regulation in *AS* and *Jafari* and its flexible interpretation of the three-month time limit in *Mengesteab* has a twofold effect. First, it sends the message to all EU Member States that they have to comply with the strict reading of the Dublin Regulation, regardless of the factual circumstances, and a message to the Member States as legislators that the application of the Dublin Regulation, as it now stands, leads to absurd and dangerous results in cases of mass influx. At the same time, it precludes any immediate, dangerous consequences of the rulings in *AS* and *Jafari*, by excluding their application for the majority of migrants who transited the Western Balkans route in 2015/16, thereby indirectly recognising the humanitarian and political sensitivity of the cases. The Court's ruling in *Slovakia and Hungary v Council*, decided on 6 September 2017, adds to the equation the principle of solidarity by confirming joint Member State responsibility for the mandatory relocation of the agreed quotas of asylum seekers from Greece and Italy.[44] In this way, all four judgments can be viewed together as the Court's attempt to strike the right balance between competing interests and responsibilities in the EU.[45]

However, striking the right balance by delivering a 'package of judgments' cannot make up for the shortcomings of individual judgments contained in that package. There is no doubt that the judgments in *AS* and *Jafari*, on their own, have a strong effect on the development of EU asylum law and on the subsequent behaviour of EU Member States when faced with the possibility of a new refugee

[42] ibid para 74.

[43] ibid para 103.

[44] Joined Cases C-643/15 and C-647/15 *Slovakia and Hungary v Council* EU:C:2017:631. Mandatory relocation was based on Council Decision (EU) 2015/1601 of 22 September 2015 establishing provisional measures in the area of international protection for the benefit of Italy and Greece [2015] OJ L248/80. For a critique of this judgment, see H Labayle, 'Solidarity Is Not a Value: Provisional Relocation of Asylum-seekers Confirmed by the Court of Justice (6 September 2017, Joined Cases C-643/15 and C-647/15 Slovakia and Hungary v Council)' (*Odysseus*, 11 September 2017), available at: eumigrationlawblog.eu/solidarity-is-not-a-value-provisional-relocation-of-asylum-seekers-confirmed-by-the-court-of-justice-6-september-2017-joined-cases-c-64315-and-c-64715-slovakia-and-hungary-v-council/. On solidarity in EU asylum law, see I Goldner Lang, 'The EU Financial and Migration Crises: Two Crises – Many Facets of Solidarity' in A Biondi, E Dagilyte and E Küçük (eds), *Solidarity in EU Law: Legal Principle in the Making* (Cheltenham, Edward Elgar Publishing, 2018); M Garlick, 'Solidarity under Strain: Solidarity and Fair Sharing of Responsibility in Law and Practice for the International Protection of Refugees in the European Union' (PhD thesis, Radboud University Nijmegen, 2016).

[45] Speech by Judge Siniša Rodin organised by the UNESCO Chair on Free Movement of People, Migration and Inter-Cultural Dialogue at the Faculty of Law, University of Zagreb, 31 October 2017.

influx: it is inconceivable that the EU Member States would again authorise and facilitate a new Western Balkans route in the case of a future refugee influx.

IV. The Impact of 'Judicial Passivism' on the Future: Developments at the Greek–Turkish Border and *ND and NT*

The early 2020 developments at the Greek–Turkish border, as the external EU border, confirm the statement that the Western Balkans route is not likely to be repeated ever again. The EU's political and practical reactions to the attempt of thousands of migrants to cross the Greek–Turkish border in February and March 2020 can only be understood as the result of the interaction of four factors: the EU Member States' experience of the Western Balkans route and their fear of its reoccurrence; the fear, especially, of frontline Member States – such as Greece, Croatia and Hungary – of turning into hotspots; the judicial reaction to the Western Balkans route, as conveyed by the CJEU in its decisions on the EU–Turkey deal and in *AS* and *Jafari*; and the judicial reaction to collective expulsion and 'pushbacks', as articulated by the ECtHR's judgment in *ND and NT*. Each of these factors will be explained in turn below, preceded by a brief outline of the developments at the Greek–Turkish border.

Since the implementation of the EU–Turkey Statement in March 2016 up until 28 February 2020, the Greek–Turkish border had been mostly closed, with Turkey hosting around 3.6 million Syrian refugees (out of a total of over four million refugees).[46] On 28 February 2020 Turkey announced that it would no longer stop refugees and migrants trying to cross the Greek–Turkish border and entering the EU.[47] According to the Greek media, the following day more than 4,000 people repeatedly tried to cross the Greek border. However, the border was opened only on the Turkish side, as the Greek police stopped everybody who tried to cross the border by using tear gas and rubber bullets.[48] The situation continued to escalate in the following weeks, with tens of thousands of people gathering on the Turkish side of the border, after having been reportedly taken there by Turkish buses.[49]

[46] European Commission, 'The EU Facility of Refugees in Turkey', updated March 2020, available at: ec.europa.eu/neighbourhood-enlargement/sites/near/files/frit_factsheet.pdf.

[47] Euractiv with Reuters, 'Turkey Says Will Not Stop Syrian Refugees Reaching Europe after Troops Killed' (*Euractiv*, 28 February 2020), available at: www.euractiv.com/section/justice-home-affairs/news/turkey-says-will-not-stop-syrian-refugees-reaching-europe-after-troops-killed/.

[48] Georgi Gotev and Sarantis Michalopoulost, 'Erdogan Drops the "Human Bomb" on EU' (*Euractiv*, 29 February 2020) www.euractiv.com/section/global-europe/news/erdogan-drops-the-human-bomb-on-eu/; Sarah Dadouch, 'Syrian Migrants Trying to Reach Greece from Turkey Find Their Dreams Evaporating as Border Guards Push Them Back' *Washington Post* (2 March 2020), available at: www.washingtonpost.com/world/turkey-greece-migrants-refugees/2020/03/02/c74ba9f8-5c8e-11ea-ac50-18701e14e06d_story.html.

[49] Helena Smith, 'Greece Hopes EU–Turkey Talks Will Ease Tension over Refugee Crisis' *Guardian* (16 March 2020), available at: www.theguardian.com/world/2020/mar/16/.

At the same time, Greece decided to suspend all asylum applications for one month.[50] The Greek border conduct was strongly supported and praised by EU leaders.[51] The President of the European Commission, Ursula von der Leyen, openly thanked Greece as Europe's 'shield' in blocking entry to the EU and promised financial and material support, as well as the deployment of Frontex.[52] On top of this, at the time of writing this text, the Commission has refused to release a preliminary legal assessment into the Greek decision to temporarily freeze all asylum applications.[53] In the meantime, the number of people trying to cross the border considerably decreased, partly since they realised that they would not be able to enter the EU and partly due to the coronavirus crisis.

The reaction of EU leaders to the possibility of a new refugee/migrant influx reveals their determination to prevent the Western Balkans route from happening again. As outlined above, this reaction was motivated by several factors. First, it was prompted by the EU's experience of the hugely disruptive effect of the 2015/16 refugee influx on the functioning of EU migration and asylum policy and on the EU as a whole, by its security concerns, and xenophobic fears. Second, the rigid reaction was additionally induced by the fear held by front line Member States – such as Greece and Croatia, the latter of which was at that time presiding the EU – that, in the case of a new influx, they would have to conduct the initial processing of all asylum applications by themselves if the German non-paper on the reform of the Common European Asylum System (CEAS) – which argues in favour of mandatory initial assessment of asylum applications at the external EU borders – received sufficient support in the EU.[54]

Additionally, the EU's conduct at the Greek–Turkish border was probably also prompted by the behaviour of two European courts – the Court of Justice and the ECtHR. Only the combination of Member States' fears combined with their belief that their actions would not be judicially condemned can explain the rigidity

[50] Helena Smith, 'Child Dies off Lesbos in First Fatality since Turkey Opened Border' *Guardian* (2 March 2020), available at: www.theguardian.com/world/2020/mar/02/child-dies-as-boat-carrying-migrants-capsizes-off-lesbos.

[51] Paul Antonopoulos, 'Greece Did an Excellent Job in Guarding Europe's Border, Says German Minister' *Greek City Times* (18 April 2020), available at: greekcitytimes.com/2020/04/18/greece-did-an-excellent-job-guarding-europes-border-says-german-minister/.

[52] See the remarks by President von der Leyen at the joint press conference with Kyriakos Mitsotakis, Prime Minister of Greece, Andrej Plenković, Prime Minister of Croatia, President Sassoli and President Michel of 3 March 2020, available at: ec.europa.eu/commission/presscorner/detail/en/STATEMENT_20_380. See also Jennifer Rankin, 'Migration: EU Praises Greece as "Shield" after Turkey opens border' *Guardian* (3 March 2020), available at: www.theguardian.com/world/2020/mar/03/migration-eu-praises-greece-as-shield-after-turkey-opens-border. For the activities of Frontex in Greece, see Frontex News Release, 'Frontex Launches Rapid Border Intervention on Greek Land Border' (*Frontex*, 13 March 2020), available at: frontex.europa.eu/media-centre/news-release/frontex-launches-rapid-border-intervention-on-greek-land-border-J7k21h.

[53] Nikolaj Nielsen, 'EU Commission Keeps Asylum Report on Greece Secret' (*EuObserver*, 21 April 2020), available at: euobserver.com/migration/148119.

[54] The German non-paper entitled 'Outline for Reorienting the Common European Asylum System' (*Statewatch*, 13 November 2019), available at: www.statewatch.org/news/2019/dec/eu-asylum-FoodForThought-GermanNoPaper.pdf.

of the measures, accompanied by the political discourse dominated by security concerns and fears of uncontrolled migration and secondary movements.

As regards the Luxembourg Court, its avoidance to adjudicate on the legality of the EU–Turkey deal enabled the deal to endure and for Turkey to use it and the migrants it hosts to blackmail the EU. Had the CJEU decided to examine the substance of the case, it is likely it would have had to annul the EU–Turkey deal due to its non-compliance with EU law. The non-existence of the deal does not mean that there would be no influx, but it would have taken place under different circumstances and it would not have been encouraged by the Turkish authorities, as they would have no incentive to do so. In addition, the CJEU's reluctance to decide on the substance of the deal in 2017 and 2018 was an assurance to Member States that the Court would also not annul the deal in the future and that it is safe to reinstate it.

Besides, the CJEU's judgments in *AS* and *Jafari* highlighted the fragility of solidarity in the EU. It sent a clear message to EU Member States that – if confronted with a new refugee influx into their territories – each Member State would have to deal with the consequences on their own, based on a strict reading of the Dublin State of first entry rule and with the slim chance of relocation to other Member States.

On the other hand, the ECtHR's judgment in *ND and NT* was viewed by EU Member States as a signal that blocking migrants from entering Greece in certain situations would receive judicial approval in the case of a reference to the Strasbourg (and perhaps also the Luxembourg) Court. The ECtHR's Grand Chamber judgment in *ND and NT* of 13 February 2020 can be viewed as the Strasbourg Court's endorsement of Member States' use of force and other deterrent activities when confronted with the possibility of a new migration influx, in a situation similar to the one at the Greek–Turkish border. The ECtHR's ruling sends a strong signal to the CJEU – should it be confronted with a similar case – to rule that Member States' collective expulsion or 'pushbacks' of refugees and migrants who try to enter the EU irregularly, outside the border crossing points, and in big numbers and by using force is not contrary to EU law. The case concerned the immediate return to Morocco of two nationals of Mali and Côte d'Ivoire who arrived in Morocco in March 2013 and stayed in a migrants' camp close to the Spanish enclave of Melilla until 13 August 2014, when they attempted to enter the Spanish territory by climbing the fences surrounding Melilla, together with two groups of altogether more than 600 individuals. As they reached the Spanish ground, they were apprehended by the Spanish police, who handcuffed them and handed them over to the Moroccan authorities, without undertaking any identification procedure and without enabling ND and NT to explain their personal circumstances.

The Strasbourg Court decided that the lack of an individualised removal procedure did not violate either Article 4 of Protocol No 4 (prohibition of collective expulsion) to the ECHR or Article 13 ECHR (right to an effective remedy), as it was the consequence of the applicants' own conduct. According to the Court, the applicants chose not to make use of the official entry procedures to enter the

Spanish territory lawfully.[55] Instead, they took advantage of the fact that they were part of a large group of individuals which used force in its attempt to cross the border. Consequently, the Court concluded that the lack of individual removal decisions could be attributed to the applicants' unlawful behaviour.

The judgment in *ND and NT* can be seen as the ECtHR's departure from its ruling in *Hirsi*, where the Court decided that the interception at sea by the Italian authorities of Somali and Eritrean migrants, who were travelling from Libya, and their sending back to Libya violated Article 3 ECHR, as they faced a risk of being arbitrarily returned to their countries of origin.[56] However, the ruling in *ND and NT* does not give carte blanche to collective expulsions, but states that this is justified if it is the consequence of the applicant's own conduct, which is the case if two conditions are met. First, what needs to be considered is whether the respective State provides 'genuine and effective access to means of legal entry, in particular border procedures for those who have arrived at the border'.[57] If the answer to the first question is positive, then one needs to examine whether there is an 'absence of cogent reasons why the applicant did not make use of official entry procedures, which were based on objective facts for which the respondent State was responsible'.[58]

However, the Court does not explain the criteria for establishing the State's responsibility in a situation where the applicant does not make use of the official entry procedures, such as asking for asylum at the official border crossing point. It seems logical that the existence of a deal with the neighbouring State, like the EU–Turkey Statement, which has the effect of stopping individuals from getting to the border, would make that Member State responsible.[59] When applied to the Greek situation, this could indicate the existence of Greek responsibility in a situation where the applicant could not use the official entry procedures because he or she was prevented from doing so by Turkey, based on the EU–Turkey Statement.

The judgment left a number of other open questions. First, it was not clear whether the Court's evaluation of the legality of expulsion applies only to cases where migrants had arrived en masse or also to cases where they had arrived individually. Neither was it clear whether the same rule would apply if migrants did not use force, but just peacefully approached the border. In other words, until the judgment in *MK and Others v Poland*,[60] it was unclear whether the Court would

[55] However, it was pointed out by Ambassador Tomáš Boček, Special Representative of the Secretary General on migration and refugees, to Spain, and Dunja Mijatović, the Commissioner for Human Rights of the Council of Europe, that 'persons from sub-Saharan Africa were effectively prevented by Moroccan authorities from approaching regular border crossing points' (*ND and NT* (n 6) paras 58 and 143).

[56] *Hirsi Jamaa and Others v Italy* App no 27765/09 (ECtHR, 23 February 2012).

[57] *ND and NT* (n 6) para 201.

[58] ibid.

[59] However, it is not clear why the ECtHR stated that 'even assuming that difficulties existed in physically approaching this border crossing point on the Moroccan side, no responsibility of the respondent Government for this situation has been established before the Court'.

[60] *MK and Others v Poland* App nos 40503/17, 42902/17 and 43643/17 (ECtHR, 23 July 2020). For a discussion on *MK and Others v Poland*, see further below.

have ruled differently if an individual attempted to cross the border in a situation where there was no security threat, and what criteria the Court would use to measure the existence of such a threat.

The judgment in *ND and NT* has serious implications. Most importantly, it sends a signal to EU Member States that under certain conditions it is not illegal, under the Convention human rights standards, to collectively push back third-country nationals who try to enter the EU, without individually assessing their status and knowing whether they are economic migrants or refugees. It could encourage similar behaviour in the future. Most likely, the judgment contributed to the Greek and other EU leaders' reactions to the Greek border crisis in early 2020 and it could again encourage similar behaviour in the event of a new influx. It is also possible that – if confronted with a similar case – the Luxembourg Court will be influenced by the ECtHR's judgment and decide that collective expulsion in circumstances similar to those in *ND and NT* does not violate EU law, including the Charter of Fundamental Rights.

Nevertheless and despite its many shortcomings and ambiguities, the judgment explicitly confirms the prohibition of *refoulement*, as an absolute right enshrined in Article 3 ECHR.[61] However, it remains unclear how the Spanish authorities could have known, at the time they conducted the pushbacks, that their conduct would not result in *refoulement*, considering that the pushbacks took place without first assessing the (non-)existence of ND's and NT's need for protection.[62] On the other hand, the judgment has no effect on Member States' obligations based on the Geneva Convention and EU law, both of which bind States to respect the principle of *non-refoulement*. Taking all this into consideration, the judgment in *ND and NT* does not change the fact that returning individuals at the EU border remains contrary to the letter of the law, unless they are not in need of protection, which, in return, can only be determined by examining individual circumstances on a case-by-case basis or by first examining whether the individual will have access to an adequate asylum procedure in the receiving State.

The ECtHR's judgment in *MK and Others v Poland* confirms this.[63] In this case, involving Russian nationals who attempted to flee from Chechnya and cross the Terespol border between Poland and Belarus, the Strasbourg Court indicated that if a State removes an asylum seeker to a third country without examining the asylum request on the merits, it must first review whether the individual will have access to an adequate asylum procedure protecting him or her against *refoulement* in the receiving third country.[64] Since this was not the case, the Court concluded

[61] *ND and NT* (n 6) para 232.

[62] For a critique of the judgment from the perspective of the principle of *non-refoulement*, see A Lübbe, 'The Elephant in the Room: Effective Guarantee of Non-Refoulement after ECtHR ND and NT?' (*Verfassungsblog*, 19 February 2020), available at: verfassungsblog.de/the-elephant-in-the-room/.

[63] *MK and Others* (n 60). Ulrike Brandl, 'The ECtHR Adjusts Its Case Law in MK vs Poland' (*Odysseus*, 11 September 2020), available at: eumigrationlawblog.eu/a-human-right-to-seek-refuge-at-europes-external-borders-the-ecthr-adjusts-its-case-law-in-m-k-vs-poland/.

[64] *MK and Others* (n 60) paras 172 and 173.

that the Polish authorities violated Article 3 ECHR and it unveiled the existence of a systematic administrative practice of pushbacks of asylum seekers at the border with Belarus.[65]

V. Concluding Remarks

The preceding text has aimed to define and determine cases of 'judicial passivism' in the area of EU migration and asylum law and determine its practical and political implications. The text puts forward the proposition that judicial passivism is a subcategory, or the flipside, of judicial activism. It is applicable to cases where the Court consciously decides not to use its judicial power where it could. The Court does this either by claiming that the case falls outside the scope of EU law and that it therefore lacks jurisdiction to decide on the substance of the case ('judicial passivism in the narrow sense'), or by deciding in a strict, formalist way, without taking into consideration the overall purpose and scheme of the relevant norms, the factual circumstances of the case, and the intentions of the Member States ('judicial passivism in the extensive sense'). The CJEU's judgments on the EU–Turkey Statement, on humanitarian visas in *X & X*, and on the Western Balkans route in *AS* and *Jafari* have served to illustrate judicial passivism in its narrow and extensive sense, respectively. The discussion has shown that, whichever type of judicial passivism was at issue, such passivism is the result of a conscious (active) judicial decision and, therefore, sends a conscious message to the EU institutions, Member States and other political actors. The Court's passivism lies, first, in the political and social sensitivity of the cases, backed by frequent ambiguity of the legal text, and, second, in the Court's view that EU political institutions, and not the Court, should take on the responsibility to act. Most importantly, the effects of judicial passivism are far-reaching, both in terms of the further development of EU migration and asylum law and in terms of the future behaviour of the EU institutions and its Member States, as shown by the February/March 2020 developments at the Greek–Turkish border.

[65] ibid para 186.

10

A Path to Ending Irregular Migration Control: Evaluating Judicial Review of the European Union's Migration and Border Control Through Externalisation*

SAM KOPLEWICZ,** ALFRED BRIDI*** AND
MONA HAGHGOU STRINDBERG****

I. Introduction

In recent years, the European Union (EU) has faced the difficult reality of an influx in migration. In response, it has exercised more competence in the area of migration and border control. Its policy, along with that of relevant Member States, has been to externalise migration management to third countries. The actions by the EU, at the direction of the EU, and knowingly financed by the EU, have resulted in violations of the Charter of Fundamental Rights (EU Charter) and other international human rights obligations. The Court of Justice of the European Union (CJEU), as well as the other EU institutions or Courts, have been unable or unwilling to curtail this problematic policy. The absence of EU accountability for this policy has led to an avoidable expansion of humanitarian issues. There are several routes for the Court to review this policy, including cases brought by EU institutions, arising from national courts through preliminary hearings, initiated by

* The authors would like to thank the editors of this book for their guidance and support, Selena Parnon and Mark Davies for their edits, and Kester Siegrist for the research that made the paper possible.

** Director of Voter Protection at the Florida Democratic Party, Term Member at the Council on Foreign Relations, and former Fulbright Visiting Researcher at the University of Zagreb's Faculty of Law.

*** Immigration Counsel at Scale LLP and Term Member at the Council on Foreign Relations.

**** Attorney at law, Advokat Mona Haghgou Strindberg AB.

individuals as actions of annulment or actions for damages. An assessment of these possible approaches reveals that there is a lack of political will for some to be realised while others face legal hurdles that bar a realistic chance. The option that appears to have the most potential is an action brought by an individual for damages.

Over the last decade, the EU and its Member States have struggled to collectively respond to the inflow of migrants, who include both bona fide refugees and economic migrants. The challenge arises mainly due to 'irregular migration', or individuals or families entering EU territory without passing through normalised migration points of entry. The two most significant paths for this type of entry are, on the one hand, in the Eastern Mediterranean on the Aegean Sea via Turkey or by land through Bulgaria or Greece and, on the other, in the Central Mediterranean through North Africa (primarily Libya) over the Mediterranean Sea to Italy, Spain or Malta. This is not a new struggle, but one that hit a peak in the summer of 2015 and throughout the period commonly referred to as the 'migration crisis'. While there have been attempts at writing legislation to address this, the rise of right-wing political parties in several Member States founded on xenophobic sentiments has made collective EU responses difficult. The result has been a centrifugal force outward of responsibility vis-a-vis migrants and legal obligations.

Inside the EU, this has meant implementing the Dublin Regulation, which places the responsibility of processing and hosting potential refugees on the peripheral Member States, many of which are already under financial strain. The enormous numbers of potential refugees and inaction to take on EU-wide responsibility has meant continuously deteriorating migrant conditions and increasingly exclusionary practices against migrants. Several Member States on the EU's external borders, both along the Eastern and Central Mediterranean routes, have reportedly performed 'pushbacks', the practice of either sending migrants to their host country or country of transit without doing the required protection analysis. While this is an explicit violation of the international law principle of *non-refoulement*, to which all Member States are subject, it is still commonly practised.[1]

Externally, it has meant assisting, funding and training third countries to prevent these migrants from reaching EU territory. At first, Member States like Italy attempted *non-entrée* practices, which stopped potential refugees before landing on their territory in order to ostensibly avoid having to process their asylum claims or violating the principle of *non-refoulement*. However, in 2012 the European Court of Human Rights (ECtHR) found this practice to violate the principle of *non-refoulement*. As a next step, Member States and EU bodies began drafting agreements with third countries to help mitigate the flow of migrants. While this approach has limited the number of migrants entering EU territory, it

[1] Lydia Gall, 'Dispatches Violent Pushbacks on Croatia Border Require EU Action' (*Human Rights Watch*, 29 October 2020), available at: www.hrw.org/news/2020/10/29/violent-pushbacks-croatia-border-require-eu-action#.

has caused an increasingly dire humanitarian crisis in these third countries, which, similar to the peripheral Member States, are already under significant strain. In many cases both groups of countries started off with weaker economies and were already hosting more refugees.

While there have been numerous attempts to bring these internal and external human rights violations before courts, the CJEU has avoided ruling on the fundamental rights of asylum seekers. Rather than address the clear fundamental rights violations, which could land responsibility for the EU's collapse on the Court, the Court has avoided applying a fundamental rights analysis on the current migration political approach. One of this book's editors has aptly coined this as 'judicial passivism'.[2] In any governmental structure, the judiciary is wise to limit itself so as not to wade into the arena of the legislative branch. However, the Court's silence has led to further violations of fundamental EU principles and significant loss of life, the remedies for which should not be delayed for political debate.

In this chapter, we will assess the EU's growing competence in migration policy as well as its practices of externalised immigration management to third countries outside EU territory. We will demonstrate how this shift has resulted in an unchecked and deteriorating humanitarian situation, with a particular focus on Libya. The chapter also reviews other legal attempts to curtail this policy and potential routes that can be taken to remedy these violations before the CJEU. We will argue that the CJEU should cease to shy away from the legal remedies established through the Treaties, as well as to argue in favour of the Court's constitutional and humanitarian imperative to do so. In essence, not acting undermines the non-majoritarian nature of the Court's role in the EU system and undercuts the very principles on which the EU was founded in exchange for the political whims of the day.

II. The EU as an Emerging Actor in Migration Policy

The EU was created in the wake of a military and humanitarian disaster the scale of which the world had never seen. The project's founding commitment to human rights, the rule of law and free movement – 'the cornerstones of the EU's ethical and legal *acquis*'[3] – has had an important impact well beyond the club's expanding borders. Despite the Union's express obligation to promote these values internally and externally,[4] its recent record in this area is mixed. In the past three decades,

[2] I Goldner Lang, 'Towards "Judicial Passivism" in European Union Migration and Asylum Law?', ch 9 in this volume.

[3] Parliament Resolution of 15 January 2020 on human rights and democracy in the world and the European Union's policy on the matter [2020] 2019/2125(INI), para B. See also: Parliament Resolution of 5 April 2017 on addressing refugee and migrant movements: the role of EU External Action [2017] 2015/2342(INI) para R.

[4] Consolidated Version of the Treaty on European Union [2012] OJ C326/47, Arts 2, 21.

the number of forcibly displaced people worldwide has doubled from 40 million in 1990 to approximately 80 million today.[5] According to the United Nations (UN), in 2000 there were around 150 million international migrants and today there are 272 million.[6] A portion of these people are on the move due to conflict, persecution and other life-threatening reasons, but many are also on the move seeking a better life and prosperity. Europe and EU Member States, as destination countries, have not escaped the impact of this increase in migration.

The EU's reaction to increased migration trends brought with it a more harmonised approach and one that externalised operations to third countries. The EU's policy to address migration through containment with its neighbours is hardly new, with evidence of EU actors requiring their neighbours to contain migrants in exchange for financial benefit occurring as early as 2004.[7] As will be outlined below, increased inaction and delegation of responsibility have become the Bloc's formal migration management approach since the EU's 2016 deal with Turkey. That agreement sought to contain European-bound migrants in Turkey based on a 'one-for-one' resettlement policy[8] and in exchange for a €3 billion 'Facility for Refugees in Turkey'.[9] It has been criticised from its signing[10] to today[11] and, more importantly, has left tens of thousands stranded in inhumane conditions inside Turkey,[12] on Greek islands,[13] on the Greek-Turkish border[14] and at sea.[15] It has also meant Turkey taking a hard line on its southern border with Syria, meaning those attempting to flee war have been trapped in one of the most dangerous areas

[5] United Nations High Commissioner for Refugees, 'Figures at a Glance' (UNHCR, 18 June 2020), available at: www.unhcr.org/en-us/figures-at-a-glance.html.

[6] International Organization for Migration, *World Migration Report 2020* (IOM, 2019), available at: www.un.org/sites/un2.un.org/files/wmr_2020.pdf.

[7] 'How Libya Kept Migrants Out of EU – At Any Cost' *The Week* (5 April 2011), available at: www.theweek.co.uk/6515/how-libya-kept-migrants-out-of-eu-at-any-cost. See also, generally, British Prime Minister Tony Blair's 2004 'deal in the desert' with Colonel Muammar Gadaffi of Libya.

[8] Commission, 'Second Report on the progress made in the implementation of the EU–Turkey Statement' COM (2016) 349 final.

[9] European Council, 'EU–Turkey Statement' (European Council, 18 March 2016), available at: www.consilium.europa.eu/en/press/press-releases/2016/03/18/eu-turkey-statement/.

[10] Interview with Aurélie Ponthieu, Humanitarian Advisor, MSF (*Médecins Sans Frontières Analysis*, 18 March 2016), available at: msf-analysis.org/refugee-crisis-eus-deal-turkey-no-solution/.

[11] Kati Piri, 'Blame Europe, Not Just Turkey, for Migration Deal Collapse' (*Politico*, 5 March 2020), available at: www.politico.eu/article/blame-europe-not-just-turkey-for-migration-deal-collapse/.

[12] Katy Fallon and Ans Boersma, '"There Is No Future": The Refugees Who Became Pawns in Erdoğan's Game' *Guardian* (8 May 2020), available at: www.theguardian.com/global-development/2020/may/08/erdogan-turkey-refugees-pawns-game.

[13] Lefteris Papadimas, 'Fed-up Lesbos Islanders, Migrants Stuck Waiting for Europe to Decide' (*Reuters*, 12 September 2020), available at: www.reuters.com/article/us-europe-migrants-greece-lesbos-islande-idUSKBN2640BM.

[14] 'Caught in a Political Game: Asylum-Seekers and Migrants on the Greece/Turkey Border Pay the Price for Europe's Failures' (EUR 01/2077/2020, Amnesty International, 2020), available at: www.amnesty.org/en/documents/eur01/2077/2020/en/.

[15] Aurélie Ponthieu, 'Humanity Diverted at Sea: Europe Exchanges Migrants Lives for Votes' (*Médecins Sans Frontières Analysis*, 15 June 2018), available at: msf-analysis.org/humanity-diverted-sea-europe-exchanges-migrants-lives-votes/.

of the country and conflict. Libya is our primary focus of the assessment here, given its volatile and dangerous political situation and the fact that its position as a prime migrant departure area has now shifted to being among the direst migrant detention areas in the world.

The Lisbon Treaty and the Stockholm Programme, in particular, helped move the EU toward a more cohesive body when it came to international action, especially around border control. The Stockholm Programme called for the accelerated use of all its existing instruments and increased coordination,[16] which was a boon to agencies like the European Border and Coast Guard Agency (Frontex) and the European Border Surveillance System (Eurosur).[17] This programme called equally for the creation of 'a comprehensive partnership with the countries of origin and of transit in order to encourage the synergy between migration and development'.[18] The plan outlined a focus on increased integrated cooperation with the most relevant countries in Africa and Eastern and South-Eastern Europe.[19] In particular, the Programme emphasised Mobility Partnerships as the 'main strategic, comprehensive and long-term cooperation framework for migration management'.[20] This meant moving border control competence towards the EU, but still sharing it with Member States.

By establishing a High Representative for the EU in Foreign Affairs and Security Policy, establishing a Permanent President of the European Council, and defining the EU as an international body that could conclude agreements with third countries, the Lisbon Treaty set the stage for more cohesive international action by the EU. Such action frequently stemmed from another European framework that integrated and delegated EU migration management, the Global Approach to Migration and Mobility (GAMM). With the stated goal of a 'coherent and comprehensive migration policy for the EU',[21] the EU committed more than €1 billion on 400 migration projects between 2004 and 2013.[22] Mobility Partnerships, which are typically between a third country, the EU and Member States, were a significant part of its implementation. Although intended as comprehensive instruments, Mobility Partnerships predominantly focus on irregular migration.[23] Even though the GAMM and other EU migration frameworks present fundamental rights and

[16] M Takle, 'The Treaty of Lisbon and the European Border Control Regime' (2012) 8 *Journal of Contemporary European Research* 280.

[17] The Stockholm Programme – An Open and Secure Europe Serving and Protecting the Citizens (EC 17024/09, 2 December 2009) s 5.1.

[18] ibid, s 6.

[19] ibid, s 6.1.1.

[20] ibid.

[21] Commission, 'The Global Approach to Migration and Mobility' (Communication) COM(2011) 743 final, 2.

[22] ibid.

[23] Paula García Andrade, Iván Martín and Sergo Mananashvili, *EU Cooperation with Third Countries in the Field of Migration* (Study, European Parliament Policy Department C: Citizens' Rights and Constitutional Affairs, 2015) 22, 30–33.

protection as priorities, these Mobility Partnerships lack enforcement mechanisms to ensure conformity with fundamental rights.[24]

As migration flows increased, eventually reaching a feverish pitch during the summer of 2015, so did the EU's attention and efforts to combat the influx. The EU Agenda on Migration was meant to meet the moment through the further unification and externalisation of migration policy. One of its four pillars to improve migration management was to support third countries in maintaining their own borders.[25] Implementation reports of the Agenda do not evaluate the impact on the rights of third-country nationals,[26] sometimes excluding the assurance of humanitarian imperatives and fundamental rights in third countries.[27] The text and official comments make the primary focus of these partnerships clear: stemming the flow of migrants. The European Council explicitly stated that 'cooperation on readmission and return will be a key test of the partnership between the EU and [its] partners'.[28]

Recent years have seen the emergence of an EU practice to negotiate European Union Readmission Agreements (EURAs) alongside other associated deals for leverage.[29] EURAs aim to create a legal framework for forced returns that allow border authorities to handle transfers of third-country nationals swiftly, without the involvement of diplomatic contacts.[30] Today, EU Readmission Agreements are made up of a complex web of interconnected instruments that range from visa facilitation to development aid.[31] While there is an assumption that the EU and Member States will not conclude return agreements with third countries who do not meet safe third-country standards, the Commission itself has '[m]any doubts … about the conclusions of EURAs with countries with weak human rights and international protection records'.[32] As the Directorate General for the External Policies of the Union points out, these Readmission Agreements are particularly problematic, since these EU level arrangements are concluded with no input from the Parliament and their non-legally binding nature means there are no specific means of remedying possible human rights violations.[33] Furthermore, there is no post-return monitoring of the situation of returnees

[24] Violeta Moreno-Lax, *EU External Migration Policy and the Protection of Human Rights* (PE 603.512, European Parliament, 2020) 24–31.

[25] Commission, 'A European Agenda on Migration' (Communication) COM(2015) 240 final, 11.

[26] Moreno-Lax, *EU External Migration Policy and the Protection of Human Rights* (n 24) 22–23.

[27] Commission, 'State of Play of Implementation of the Priority Actions under the European Agenda on Migration' (Communication) COM(2016) 85 final, 15.

[28] Council of the European Union, *External Aspects of Migration – Monitoring Results* (EC 10822/16, 4 July 2016).

[29] Moreno-Lax, *EU External Migration Policy and the Protection of Human Rights* (n 24) 24–31.

[30] ibid.

[31] See generally, M Giuffré, 'The Obligation to Readmit and the Relationship between Interstate and EU Readmission Agreements' in F Ippolito and S Trevisanut (eds), *Migration in Mare Nostrum: Mechanisms of International Cooperation* (Cambridge, Cambridge University Press, 2016).

[32] Commission, 'Evaluation of EU Readmission Agreements' (Communication) COM(2011) 76 final, 12.

[33] Moreno-Lax, *EU External Migration Policy and the Protection of Human Rights* (n 24) 27.

that would guarantee treatment in line with fundamental rights in order to avoid direct or chain *refoulement*.[34] Yet, still no mechanism is in place to provide judicial review for those whose rights are impacted by the execution of these agreements.

Similar to formal arrangements, the EU also favours cooperation through informal channels, taking the form of 'working arrangements' between Frontex or other EU agencies and police corps of third countries, for instance bolstering joint patrol operations and collaboration regarding pre-emptive controls. Frontex has standing working arrangements with 18 countries.[35] Notably, neither the partner State's record nor the likelihood of its violation of human rights is considered in negotiating these agreements, which include training, providing technical assistance and conducting joint operations to stem migration flow.[36] While these operations have been effective in reducing the number of migrants reaching EU territory, there is currently no effective remedy and check on whether the activities born from these agreements comply with fundamental rights.[37] In line with this approach, the new European Board and Coast Guard Regulation (2019)[38] has a clause that requires that '[w]hen implementing [working agreements], Member States shall assess and take into account the general situation in the third country on a regular basis'.[39] However, the Regulation does not outline the level of detail for these reviews or consequences.[40] It should be noted that the recent allegation against Frontex, regarding the agency's involvement in pushbacks of asylum seekers by the Greek border and their cover-up which caused the European Commission to call for an urgent extraordinary meeting of the agency's board, has resulted in increased scrutiny of the agency. Member States and the European Commission established a special committee to investigate incidents and interpret European regulation on 'Interception in the territorial sea'.[41]

On top of these agreements, there is a complex multi-actor approach used to establish the externalised, and with it more forceful, prevention of migration to the EU. For example, Italy, Malta and EU bodies have all contributed to the relationship and goals of their partnership with Libyan actors preventing migrants

[34] ibid 26.

[35] Frontex, 'Working Arrangements with non-EU Countries' (*Frontex*), available at: frontex.europa.eu/about-frontex/key-documents/?category=working-arrangements-with-non-eu-countries.

[36] M Fink, 'Frontex Working Arrangements: Legitimacy and Human Rights Concerns Regarding "Technical Relationships"' (2012) 28 *Utrecht Journal of International and European Law* 20.

[37] Regulation 2019/1896 of the European Parliament and of the Council of 13 November 2019 on the European Border and Coast Guard and repealing Regulations (EU) No 1052/2013 and (EU) 2016/1624 [2019] OJ L295/1.

[38] On the limitations of the Frontex complaints mechanism (Regulation 2019/1896) for lack of compliance with effective remedy standards, see V Moreno-Lax, *Accessing Asylum in Europe: Extraterritorial Border Controls and Refugee Rights under EU Law* (Oxford, Oxford University Press, 2017).

[39] Regulation 2019/1896 (n 37) Art 72(3).

[40] ibid.

[41] European Council on Refugees and Exiles, 'Frontex: Critique and Scrutiny Continues' (*ECRE Weekly Bulletin*, 4 December 2020), available at: www.ecre.org/frontex-critique-and-scrutiny-continues/.

from reaching the EU. In February 2017, Italy and Libya signed a Memorandum of Understanding which included Italy's commitment to fund detention centres.[42] Separately, in July of that year, an EU project was awarded to the Italian coastguard, channelling over €90 million over two years to strengthen the Libyan coastguard's maritime surveillance and rescue capacity.[43] The complexity and multi-pronged, non-binding nature of these agreements that are enforced outside EU territory have created a legal grey area so EU and Member State actors avoid legal culpability. The EU's recent action and omissions have had life or death impacts on scores of non-citizens in and around the Mediterranean Sea, with failures to live up to human rights, the law of the sea obligations, and guarantees to ensure humanitarian access becoming far more common.

III. Systemic Humanitarian Issues Stemming from the EU's Cooperation with Libya

In this section, we will focus specifically on Libya to illustrate Europe's policy. As one of the countries with the greatest number of migrants coming from or through it to Europe, one that hosts some of the worst human rights violations emanating from EU policy, and one that has not yet had a landmark case in regard to that policy, we thought it an appropriate case study for a possible shift in the EU's policy.

Though frequently a destination for foreign migrants arriving to profit from its strong economy, Libya has a long history of detaining and profiting from migrants. Under Colonel Gaddafi's regime, migrants were captured and only liberated once their fines and their journeys home were paid.[44] After the collapse of Gaddafi, militia groups and military councils took over government-controlled migrant detention centres, with the oversight of these centres falling to the Ministry of the Interior's Directorate for Combating Illegal Migration (DCIM) established in 2012. A part of the DCIM's mandate was for the militia-run centres to be integrated into the state apparatus.[45] The business of migration was a lucrative one for Libyan militias, which profited from the transport of wealthier Syrian migrants until 2015. When Syrian traffic dropped significantly as a result of the EU–Turkey deal and other factors, Libyan militia groups pivoted to profiting from the growth and maintenance of migrant detention centres – both official and unofficial. Despite the degrading political climate in Libya, the EU strengthened

[42] Moreno-Lax, *EU External Migration Policy and the Protection of Human Rights* (n 24) 44.

[43] EU Trust Fund for Africa, 'DEC – Support to Integrated border and migration management in Libya' (EU Trust Fund for Africa, 2017), available at: eutf.akvoapp.org/en/project/7601/.

[44] Arezo Malakooti, 'The Political Economy of Migrant Detention in Libya: Understanding the Players and the Business Models' (*Global Initiative Against Transnational Organized Crime*, 2019), available at: globalinitiative.net/migrant-detention-libya/.

[45] ibid.

its ties with the Government of National Accord in 2015 to curb migration from Libya. With the establishment of the EUNAVFOR MED Operation Sophia, the EU sought to contribute 'to the disruption of the business model of human smuggling and trafficking networks in the Southern Central Mediterranean' through cooperation with the Libyan Coast Guard.[46] This stance was framed as pragmatism and as a way to avoid acting as the frequently dismissed 'pull factor' in the Mediterranean.[47] This policy has run counter to official Council of the EU reports which have highlighted how detention centres are 'under the control of militias with serious human rights violations'.[48] Moreover, the United Nations Support Mission in Libya (UNSMIL) has reported on 'unlawful killings, in particular the execution of individuals taken captive or detained/abducted, and assassinations of those voicing disagreement are reported in all conflict areas and by most major groupings of armed actors in Libya committed either by government forces or armed groups and tolerated by the Government'.[49]

Despite the recent slowing of active combat, an array of humanitarian issues continues to face migrants, namely access to healthcare, food security, housing conditions, water and sanitation.[50] An alarming 70 per cent of migrants in Libya had limited or no access to health services in 2020 amid the Covid-19 pandemic, according to the International Organization for Migration (IOM),[51] and 15–25 per cent of the country's population were in extreme need of access to primary and secondary healthcare services (1,663,000 people).[52] Refugees, migrants and asylum-seekers are also exposed to alarming levels of violence and exploitation in Libya[53] at the hands of a range of actors, from state officials to criminal gangs, including violence, sexual violence, arbitrary detention in

[46] Council Decision on a European Union military operation in the Southern Central Mediterranean (EUNAVFOR MED) [2015] OJ L122/31.

[47] Lorenzo Pezzani and Charles Heller, 'Blaming the Rescuers' (London, University of London, 2017), available at: blamingtherescuers.org/report/; and Maria Gabrielsen Jumbert, 'The "Pull Factor": How It Became a Central Premise in European Discussions about Cross-Mediterranean Migration' (*Oxford Border Criminologies Blog*, 24 March 2020), available at: www.law.ox.ac.uk/research-subject-groups/centre-criminology/centreborder-criminologies/blog/2020/03/pull-factor-how.

[48] European External Action Service, 'EUBAM Libya Initial Mapping Report Executive Summary' (Working document, EEAS(2017) 0109), available at: www.statewatch.org/media/documents/news/2017/feb/eu-eeas-libya-assessment-5616-17.pdf.

[49] ibid.

[50] International Organization for Migration, 'Libya's Migrant Report' (IOM, 2020), available at: displacement.iom.int/system/tdf/reports/DTM_R30_Migrant_Report.pdf?file=1&type=node&id=9067. Specifically on housing, see also, International Organization for Migration, 'A Long Way From Home: Migrants' Housing Conditions in Libya' (IOM, 2020), available at: dtm.iom.int/reports/libya-%E2%80%94-long-way-home-%E2%80%93-migrants%E2%80%99-housing-conditions-libya-23-nov-2020.

[51] IOM, 'Libya's Migrant Report' (n 50).

[52] United Nations Office for the Coordination of Humanitarian Affairs, 'Humanitarian Response Plan: Libya' (OCHA, 2020), available at: reliefweb.int/report/libya/libya-humanitarian-response-plan-2020-enar.

[53] Michaël Neuman, 'Libya: The Forgotten Ones' (*Médecins Sans Frontières*, 2 March 2020), available at: www.msf-crash.org/en/blog/camps-refugees-idps/libya-forgotten-ones.

inhumane conditions, torture and ill-treatment, financial exploitation and forced labour.[54] Official EU documents describe reports about these detention centres that highlight 'gross human rights violations and extreme abuse and mishandling of detainees, including sexual abuse, slavery, forced prostitution, torture and maltreatment … The trafficking of migrants for organs has also been reported'.[55] The IOM estimates 600,000 migrants in Libya could have been victims of abuse and human rights violations in 2018 alone.[56]

Given the abundance of evidence illustrating that Libya is not a safe third country for these refugees, many who reach ships take their chance crossing the Mediterranean to Europe. The goal of these crossings is to be rescued and brought to a port of safety (ie Europe) per international law, which obliges all vessels to rescue those in distress – regardless of the character of the vessel in question.[57] The EU's border agency, Frontex, in the Central Mediterranean has focused on security over humanitarian concerns, with priorities ranging from anti-smuggling to border control. Indeed, the Frontex chief, Fabrice Leggeri, stated that the EU 'cannot have provisions for proactive search-and-rescue action. This is not in Frontex's mandate, and this is in my understanding not in the mandate of the European Union'.[58]

Early 2017 saw migration flows continue at peak levels until traffic drastically dropped in mid-2017, in large part because of the 2017 Memorandum of Understanding (MoU) signed by Italy and Libyan forces to curb migration.[59] This agreement marked the beginning of EU and Italian training, funding, equipping and operationally assisting the Libyan Coast Guard in search, rescue and disembarkation.[60] The day after the signing of the MoU, the Malta Declaration was

[54] Benjamin Bathke, 'Hunger, Forced Labor, Torture: Shocking Conditions in Libyan Detention Camps' (*InfoMigrants*, 15 July 2019), available at: www.infomigrants.net/en/post/18164/hunger-forced-labor-torture-shocking-conditions-in-libyan-detention-camps.

[55] European External Action Service, 'EUBAM Libya Initial Mapping Report Executive Summary' (n 48).

[56] International Organization for Migration, 'Libya 2018 Humanitarian Compendium' (IOM, 2018), available at: humanitariancompendium.iom.int/appeals/libya-2018.

[57] While international law calls for the delivery of those rescued to a port of safety, there is no such default port assigned *ex ante*. Considerations for the designation of a port of safety include the legal framework of States under international maritime law and refugee law; the pressing safety and humanitarian concerns of those rescued; the safety concerns of the rescuing vessel and the crew; the number of persons rescued and the consequent need to ensure prompt disembarkation; the technical suitability of the port in question to allow for disembarkation; the need to avoid disembarkation in the country of origin for those alleging a well-founded fear of persecution; and the financial implications and liability of shipping companies engaged in undertaking rescue operations. The decision of where to be disembarked is one that not only affects the material status of these third-country nationals, but also their legal rights.

[58] Patrick Kingsley and Ian Traynor, 'EU Borders Chief Says Saving Migrants' Lives "Shouldn't Be Priority" for Patrols' *Guardian* (22 April 2015), available at: www.theguardian.com/world/2015/apr/22/eu-borders-chief-says-saving-migrants-lives-cannot-be-priority-for-patrols.

[59] Anja Palm (trans), 'Memorandum of Understanding on Cooperation in the Fields of Development, the Fight against Illegal Immigration, Human Trafficking and Fuel Smuggling and on Reinforcing the Security of Borders between the State of Libya and the Italian Republic' (2017), available at: eumigrationlawblog.eu/wp-content/uploads/2017/10/MEMORANDUM_translation_finalversion.doc.pdf.

[60] ibid Art 2.

adopted by the European Council, which underlined that 'in Libya, capacity building is key for the authorities to acquire control over the land and sea borders and to combat transit and smuggling activities'.[61] Despite the IOM and UN Secretary General's reports on 'slave markets' in Libya in April[62] and August 2017,[63] respectively, further EU funding was provided through the EU Emergency Trust Fund for Africa (EUTFA) as expressed in a Joint Statement by the High Representative of the EU Foreign Affairs and Security Policy and several EU Member States.[64] Projects such as the 'Support to Integrated border and migration management in Libya', which bolstered the operational capacity of Libyan authorities to conduct maritime surveillance, received €91.3 million in EUTFA funding.[65] As of June 2018, 213 of the 3,385 total Libyan Coast Guard and Navy personnel have taken part in EU-administered training seminars as part of EUNAVFOR MED.[66] In August 2018, 12 patrol boats and €1,370,000 for training maintenance were given to the Libyan Coast Guard by the Italian government.[67] What this codified was Leggeri's statement: the emphasis of search and rescue operations, not by NGOs but the European-trained Libyan Coast Guard, was on border control at the expense of humanitarian and legal considerations. This conformed with the terms of the Hirsi judgment and exacerbated NGO restrictions on search and rescue activities via the prohibitive Code of Conduct for NGOs.[68] While NGOs accounted for 38 per cent of rescues in 2017 and 40 per cent in the first half of 2018,[69] NGOs

[61] European Council, 'Malta Declaration by the Members of the European Council on the External Aspects of Migration: Addressing the Central Mediterranean Route' (European Council, 3 February 2017), available at: www.consilium.europa.eu/en/press/press-releases/2017/02/03/malta-declaration/.

[62] Giuseppe Loprete, 'IOM Learns of "Slave Market" Conditions Endangering Migrants in North Africa' (IOM, 11 April 2017), available at: www.iom.int/news/iom-learns-slave-market-conditions-endangering-migrants-north-africa.

[63] Report of the Secretary-General on the United Nations Support Mission in Libya (S/2017/726, 22 August 2017).

[64] Addressing the Challenge of Migration and Asylum (Joint Statement, 28 August 2017), available at: www.bundesregierung.de/resource/blob/997532/603824/5c1dee9e40e743517ceb883c98c543d9/2017-08-28-statement-refugee-migration-english-data.pdf?download=1.

[65] Achilles Skordas, 'A "Blind Spot" in the Migration Debate? International Responsibility of the EU and Its Member States for Cooperating with the Libyan Coastguard and Militias' (*EU Immigration and Asylum Law and Policy*, 30 January 2018), available at: eumigrationlawblog.eu/a-blind-spot-in-the-migration-debate-international-responsibility-of-the-eu-and-its-member-states-for-cooperating-with-the-libyan-coastguard-and-militias/.

[66] European External Action Service, 'EUBAM Libya Revised Mapping Report on Border Management, Law and Criminal Justice Systems in Libya' (EU Restricted Document ST 7598 2018 INIT) 61, on file with Human Rights Watch as referenced at SHADE MED conference, Rome, 19–20 June 2018.

[67] Italian Chamber of Deputies, 'Cessioni di unità navali alla Libia' (*Decreti legge*, 6 August 2018) DL 84/2018.

[68] 'Italy's Code of Conduct for NGOs Involved in Migrant Rescue: Text' (*Euronews*, 8 March 2017), available at: www.euronews.com/2017/08/03/text-of-italys-code-of-conduct-for-ngos-involved-in-migrant-rescue.

[69] Isabella Lloyd-Damnjanovic, 'Criminalization of Search-and-Rescue Operations in the Mediterranean Has Been Accompanied by Rising Migrant Death Rate' (Migration Policy Institute, 9 October 2020), available at: reliefweb.int/report/world/criminalization-search-and-rescue-operations-mediterranean-has-been-accompanied-rising.

were largely blocked by the EU, which favoured the Libyan Coast Guard over outlawed foreign ships in an expanded Libyan search and rescue zone.[70]

Since then, approximately 42,500 refugees and migrants have been rescued/intercepted at sea by the Libyan Coast Guard. Tragically though, the risk of crossing increased significantly once NGOs were effectively outlawed from conducting search and rescue operations, with mortality increasing from 2.8 per cent to 7 per cent since mid-June 2018,[71] with 564 migrants dying in June 2018 alone.[72] Those who did not perish en route were then disembarked in Libya[73] despite UNSMIL's assessment to the UN Security Council that it 'cannot be considered as a safe port for disembarkation' under international law.[74] As reported by InfoMigrants, 'the [Libyan] coast guard in the Mediterranean is efficient; it is not as good, however, at abiding by the law',[75] with the chances of dying in waters off the Libyan coast increasing from one in 42 in 2017 to one in 18 in 2018, according to the United Nations High Commissioner for Refugees (UNHCR).[76]

In August 2016, the European Council extended the mandate of the European Union Border Assistance Mission in Libya (EUBAM Libya) until August 2017 and approved a budget of €17 million for that period, with a specific EU mission of 'providing advice and capacity-building in the area of criminal justice, migration, border security, and counter-terrorism'.[77] The particular emphasis of this extended mandate was 'to address law enforcement aspects of irregular migration, smuggling of migrants and trafficking of human beings [and] would be conducted at the request of the legitimate Libyan authorities, with their full ownership'.[78] Between 2017 and 2019, flights by the EU border agency Frontex

[70] 'Libya Navy Bars Foreign Ships from Migrant "Search and Rescue" Zone' *Daily Mail* (10 August 2017), available at: www.dailymail.co.uk/wires/afp/article-4779316/Libya-navy-bars-foreign-ships-migrant-search-rescue-zone.html.

[71] Matteo Villa, 'Outsourcing European Border Control: Recent Trends in Departures, Deaths and Search and Rescue Activities in the Central Mediterranean' (*Oxford Border Criminologies Blog*, 11 September 2018), available at: www.law.ox.ac.uk/research-subject-groups/centre-criminology/centreborder-criminologies/blog/2018/09/outsourcing.

[72] United Nations High Commissioner for Refugees, 'Mediterranean Crossings Deadlier Than Ever, New UNHCR Report Shows' (UNHCR, 3 September 2018), available at: www.unhcr.org/news/press/2018/9/5b8935964/mediterranean-crossings-deadlier-new-unhcr-report-shows.html.

[73] Eric Reidy, 'The legal battle to hold the EU to account for Libya migrant abuses' (*The New Humanitarian*, 10 August 2020), available at: www.thenewhumanitarian.org/analysis/2020/08/10/Libya-migrant-abuses-EU-legal-battle.

[74] Briefing of Acting SRSG Stephanie Williams to the Security Council on the situation in Libya (2 September 2020), available at: unsmil.unmissions.org/sites/default/files/acting_srsg_stephanie_williams_briefing_to_the_security_council_02_sep_2020_1.pdf.

[75] Benjamin Bathke, 'When Helping Hurts – Libya's Controversial Coast Guard, Europe's Go-to partner to Stem Migration' (*InfoMigrants*, 24 July 2019), available at: www.infomigrants.net/en/post/18196/when-helping-hurts-libya-s-controversial-coast-guard-europe-s-go-to-partner-to-stem-migration.

[76] UNHCR, 'Mediterranean Crossings Deadlier Than Ever' (n 72).

[77] European Council, 'EUBAM Libya: Mission Extended, Budget Approved' (European Council, 4 August 2016), available at: www.consilium.europa.eu/en/press/press-releases/2016/08/04/eubam-libya-mission-extended/.

[78] ibid.

almost doubled the size of the EU aerial mission. Under the law of the sea, its pilots were bound to contact whichever ship was best placed to assist any boats in distress. As Libyan maritime presence grew in the Mediterranean, European coordinators gave preference to ships that would take those they rescued back to North Africa, even though European courts and the UN's refugee and migration agencies all agreed that Libya was not a safe country.[79] To avoid contact with migrant vessels and related rescue responsibilities, since March 2019, surveillance drones have been deployed to capture relevant information on smuggling/distress incidents. Details have then been communicated to the Libyan Coast Guard for their intervention, through the intermediation of the Italian authorities, who act as 'a communication relay'.[80] As a result, intercepted 'boat migrants' have been pulled back to Libya, disregarding *non-refoulement* and related safeguards.[81]

This violation of *non-refoulement* and the practice of delegated *refoulement* via the Italian trained and supported Libyan Coast Guard have been criticised by several courts, including in pending cases before the ECtHR, by the UN Human Rights Committee and by the UN Committee Against Torture. This argument is equally the rationale for an International Criminal Court (ICC) inquiry.[82] The deterioration of migrant conditions and violations of international law, including fundamental human rights and the law of the sea, are doubly disappointing in the Central Mediterranean context when compared with the humanitarian commitments enshrined in the MoU, most notably that the '[p]arties commit to interpret and apply the present Memorandum in respect of the international obligations and the human rights agreements to which the two Countries are parties'.[83] Article 3 even establishes a dedicated committee to monitor the commitments taken, though the rights of third-country nationals remain in doubt.

Interception at sea and disembarkation in Libya have led to a marked increase in migrants held in Libyan detention camps. As early as 2017, the conditions in Libya even alarmed the EU's migration commissioner, Dimitri Avramopoulos, who noted, 'the appalling and degrading conditions in which some migrants are

[79] Daniel Howden, Apostolis Fotiadis and Zach Campbell, 'Revealed: The Great European Refugee Scandal' *Guardian* (12 March 2020), available at: www.theguardian.com/world/2020/mar/12/revealed-the-great-european-refugee-scandal.

[80] Letter from Paraskevi Michou to Fabrice Leggeri, Executive Director, European Border and Coast Guard Agency (18 March 2019), available at: www.statewatch.org/media/documents/news/2019/jun/eu-letter-from-frontex-director-ares-2019)1362751%20Rev.pdf.

[81] Human Rights Watch, 'No Escape from Hell: EU Policies Contribute to Abuse of Migrants in Libya' (*Human Rights Watch*, 21 January 2019), available at: www.hrw.org/report/2019/01/21/no-escape-hell/eu-policies-contribute-abuse-migrants-libya.

[82] *SS and others v Italy* App no 21660/18 (ECtHR, 11 November 2019); Global Legal Action Network, 'Communication to the United Nations Human Rights Committee in the case of SDG against Italy' (Communication, 18 December 2019); Centre Suisse pour la Défense des Droits des Migrants, 'Information Submitted under Article 20 of the Convention against Torture and Other Cruel, Inhuman or Degrading Treatment or Punishment' (Communication, 25 June 2020); Omer Shatz and Juan Branco, 'EU Migration Policies in the Central Mediterranean and Libya (2014–2019)' (Communication to the Office of the Prosecutor of the International Criminal Court Pursuant to the Article 15 of the Rome Statute, 3 June 2019).

[83] Palm (n 59) Art 5.

held in Libya'.[84] When the EU renewed the three-year term of the agreement in February 2020, Amnesty International stated this 'confirms Italy's complicity in torture of migrants and refugees' and is a 'shameful display of how far EU governments are prepared to go to keep refugees and migrants from Europe's shores'.[85] A year earlier, Human Rights Watch produced a report outlining the EU policies' contribution to abuses of migrants in Libya.[86] Notably, neither the training and assistance documentation nor disembarkation guidance provided by Italy to Libya under the terms of the MoU is in the public domain. Although the EU ensures 'a particular focus on human rights',[87] reports from the UN Secretary General[88] and others have been confirmed by the UN Security Council's Panel of Experts on Libya, which pointed to the Libyan 'coastguard [being] directly involved in … grave human rights violations, [including] executions, torture and deprivation of food, water and access to sanitation … [as well as] enslavement of sub-Saharan migrants'.[89] Despite this, funds are sent from the EU to Libya in the form of cooperation packages worth €120 million.[90] These packages are supplemented by 'short-term assistance through various funding instruments' with the aim of achieving '[i]mproved security conditions on the ground and political stability'.[91]

Overall, the EU has spent €700 million to support Libya through a variety of funding instruments.[92] The EU's efforts to prevent loss of life at sea through strengthened border control, increased militarisation and a focus on anti-smuggling instead of humanitarian action have resulted in more people drowning as the crossing by sea has only become even deadlier. Italy, despite being a signatory to a deal that claims to '[consider] the obligations deriving from international customary law and agreements to which the Parties are bound',[93] has failed in its human rights responsibility under the EU Charter, a key document in the EU's human rights commitments according to Article 6 of the Treaty on European

[84] AFP, 'EU Working Without "Letup" to Help Migrants in Libya' (*Euractiv*, 24 November 2017), available at: www.euractiv.com/section/justice-home-affairs/news/eu-working-without-letup-to-help-migrants-in-libya/.

[85] Amnesty International, 'Libya: Renewal of migration deal confirms Italy's complicity in torture of migrants and refugees' (Amnesty International, 30 January 2020), available at: www.amnesty.org/en/latest/news/2020/01/libya-renewal-of-migration-deal-confirms-italys-complicity-in-torture-of-migrants-and-refugees/.

[86] Human Rights Watch, 'No Escape from Hell' (n 81).

[87] European External Action Service, 'EU–Libya relations' (European External Action Service, 3 February 2021), available at: eeas.europa.eu/headquarters/headquarters-homepage_en/19163/EU-Libya%20relations.

[88] Report of the Secretary-General on the United Nations Support Mission in Libya (S/2018/140, 12 February 2018).

[89] Letter dated 1 June 2017 from the Panel of Experts on Libya established pursuant to resolution 1973 (2011) addressed to the President of the Security Council (S/2017/466, 1 June 2017).

[90] 'Council conclusions on Libya, adopted by the Council at its 3516th meeting held on 6 February 2017' (Annex) 5321/17.

[91] ibid.

[92] EU Emergency Trust Fund for Africa, 'Factsheet: EU Support on Migration in Libya' (EUTF, October 2020), available at: ec.europa.eu/trustfundforafrica/sites/euetfa/files/eutf-factsheet_2020-libya_2710.pdf.

[93] Palm (n 59).

Union (TEU). This flagrant and continued violation of the principle of *non-refoulement* is a direct result of Europe and Italy's training of the Libyan Coast Guard. Even though many have tried through advocacy and legal action, little has been effective in curtailing this approach to migration.

IV. Current Attempts to Remedy the Problem

Many have attempted to review these policies through different courts, but have not been successful. Rarely does the argument fail due to substantive considerations; instead, it regularly fails due to jurisdictional or admissibility considerations. Bringing cases in front of courts with geographic restrictions is difficult since much of the impact occurs in third countries or international waters. This limits asylum seekers' opportunities to bring suit. The agreements themselves also raise admissibility questions due to their stated soft law status. Essentially, because they are said to be voluntary and are concluded outside the framework established by the Treaty on the Functioning of the European Union (TFEU), the CJEU has stated that they are not within the Court's competence to review.[94] As a result, those harmed by EU externalisation of migration are left without a proper remedy.

The prohibition of *refoulement* in international human rights law is absolute, protecting any individual from being returned to another state where there would be a real risk to their right to life, to freedom from torture or cruel, inhuman or degrading treatment or punishment, and to liberty and security of person, 'irrespective of their criminal record or the danger they may pose to the security of the host state'.[95] In primary EU law, the principle of *non-refoulement* is enshrined in Article 19(2) of the EU Charter which provides that '[n]o one may be removed, expelled or extradited to a state where there is a serious risk that he or she would be subjected to the death penalty, torture or other inhuman or degrading treatment or punishment'. Furthermore, Article 4 of the EU Charter provides that '[n]o one shall be subjected to torture or to inhuman or degrading treatment or punishment'. EU Member States have ratified the Geneva Convention, which defines the situations in which a State must grant refugee status to persons who apply for it, and the rights and responsibilities of those persons.[96] In the Refugee Convention, '[n]o Contracting State shall expel or return ('*refouler*') a refugee in

[94] Joined Cases C-208/17 P to C-210/17 P *NF and Others v European Council* EU:C:2018:705.

[95] European Asylum Support Office, 'Asylum Procedures and the Principle of *Non-refoulement*' (Judicial analysis, 2018) 28; see, eg, UN Committee against Torture, views of 28 April 1997, *Gorki Ernesto Tipia Paez v Sweden*, UN Doc CAT/C/18/D/39/1996 para 14.5; UN Committee against Torture, views of 21 June 1999, *MBB v Sweden*, UN Doc CAT/C/22/D/104/1998 para 6.4; ECtHR, judgment of 15 November 1996, Grand Chamber, *Chahal v United Kingdom* App no 22414/94 paras 79 and 80; ECtHR, judgment of 28 February 2008, Grand Chamber, *Saadi v Italy* App no 37201/06 para 127; and ECtHR, judgment of 17 January 2012, *Omar Othman (Abu Qatada) v United Kingdom* App no 8139/09.

[96] Convention relating to the Status of Refugees [1951] UNTS 189/137, Art 1.

any manner whatsoever to the frontiers of territories where his life or freedom would be threatened'.[97] *Refoulement* is also prohibited when the returning State must have been aware that the destination State might further send the individual to another State where there is a risk of ill-treatment; known as 'indirect' or 'chain *refoulement*'.[98] Although the EU is not a party to the Geneva Convention, the EU is indirectly bound to the Convention by Article 78 TFEU and Article 18 of the EU Charter.

The current situation in Libya stemming from the 2017 MoU between Italy and Libya[99] is comparable with the 2012 case of *Hirsi Jamaa and others v Italy*, regarding Italian patrol boats intercepting asylum seekers and migrants at sea and returning them to Libya.[100] The applicants before the ECtHR alleged, in particular, that their transfer to Libya by the Italian authorities had violated Article 3 of the Convention for the Protection of Human Rights and Fundamental Freedoms (the Convention) and Article 4 of Protocol No 4.[101] The applicants further argued that the failure to assess their complaints fell short of the Convention's requirements. The Italian Interior Minister on the other hand argued that the transfer in question was pursuant to the 2009 Italy–Libya bilateral agreements to combat clandestine immigration. In 2012, the ECtHR ruled that the practice violated multiple articles of the Convention and found that Italy's 'pushback' under the bilateral agreements specifically breached the principle of *non-refoulement* and protections against collective expulsion.[102]

Another attempt to challenge the EU's involvement in human rights violations was made in 2016 when three similar applications for annulment were lodged under Article 263 TFEU with the General of the Court of Justice the European Union directed against the European Council. The applicants, two Pakistani nationals and an Afghani national, requested the Court to annul the 'EU–Turkey Statement' which was issued following the meeting of 18 March 2016 of the Members of the European Council and their Turkish counterpart.[103] The applicants challenged

[97] ibid Art 33.1.

[98] European Asylum Support Office (n 95) 28; see also *Soering v The United Kingdom*, 1/1989/161/217; UN Committee against Torture, General Comment No 1 on the Implementation of Article 3 of the Convention in the Context of Article 22, see fn 47, para 2; and *Mr Husain Ibrahimi and Mr Mohamed Abasi v The Secretary of State for the Home Department* [2016] EWHC 2049, 5 August 2016.

[99] Italy–Libya 2017 Memorandum of Understanding, English translation, available at: eumigrationlawblog.eu/wp-content/uploads/2017/10/MEMORANDUM_translation_finalversion.doc.pdf.

[100] *Hirsi Jamaa and Others v Italy* App no 27765/09 (ECtHR, 23 February 2012). See also, 'The Legal Battle to Hold the EU to Account for Libya Migrant Abuses', available at: www.thenewhumanitarian.org/analysis/2020/08/10/Libya-migrant-abuses-EU-legal-battle.

[101] Convention for the Protection of Human Rights and Fundamental Freedoms [1950] UNTS 213/221, Art 13.

[102] *Hirsi Jamaa and Others v Italy* (n 100).

[103] Case T-192/16 *NF v European Council* EU:T:2017:128; Case T-193/16 *NG v European Council* EU:T:2017:129; Case T-257/16 *NM v European Council* EU:T:2017:130. See also 'EU–Turkey Statement' (n 9).

the legality of the deal, claiming that it 'produces legal effects adversely affecting the applicants' rights and interests … render[ing] them at risk of *refoulement* to Turkey or "chain *refoulement*" to Pakistan or Afghanistan', which compelled them to make applications for international protection in Greece against their will.[104] The European Council, though, successfully argued that the Court lacked jurisdiction to hear and determine the actions, leading to the General Court holding that the EU–Turkey deal could not be challenged directly before EU courts due to it being a product of Member State action rather than that of an EU institution.[105] The Court found that the fact that proper procedures were not followed indicated that it was not an action that arose through the Treaties and was therefore not attributable to the EU. Consequently, in an action brought under Article 263 TFEU, the Court does not have jurisdiction to rule on the lawfulness of an international agreement concluded by the Member States.[106] The Court thus declared it lacked jurisdiction to hear and determine the actions pursuant to Article 263 TFEU and, accordingly, dismissed them.

More recent attempts to challenge illegal EU actions have taken a creative approach. In April 2020, applicants sought to hold the EU accountable for its involvement in Libya using the complaint mechanism in the Court of Auditors (ECA).[107] The Global Legal Action Network and two Italian legal organisations filed a complaint to the ECA alleging that due to their financial support the EU and its Member States share responsibility for human rights abuses taking place in Libya in violation of EU budget and constitutional law. The ECA does not have legal powers, but audit and advisory powers. According to its own website, '[t]he European Court of Auditors mission is to contribute to improving EU financial management, promote accountability and transparency, and act as the independent guardian of the financial interests of the citizens of the Union'.[108] More recently,

[104] Council of the European Union, Cases before the General Court of the European Union, T-192/16 *NF v European Council*, T-193/16 *NG v European Council*, T-257/16 *NM v European Council* (EC 9897/16, 7 June 2016). In support of their request, the applicants raised a number of additional pleas, including: the failure to comply with the procedures set out in Art 218 TFEU and Art 78(3) TFEU; the failure to apply Council Directive 2001/55/EC; incompatibility with EU fundamental rights (namely Arts 1, 18 and 19 of the EU Charter); invalidity pursuant to ECtHR and CJEU case law confirming the serious flaws at all levels of the Greek asylum system, including lack of an effective remedy and deficient reception facilities; violation of direct and indirect refoulement protections; invalidity based on the unlawful naming of Turkey as a safe country; and invalidity due to breach of the collective expulsion prohibition.

[105] It equally held that the nature of the EU's presence via the President of the European Council and President of the European Commission was merely informal.

[106] General Court of the European Union, 'Orders of the General Court in Cases T-192/16, T-193/16 and T-257/16 *NF, NG and NM v European Council*' (Press Release No 19/17, 28 February 2017).

[107] 'Complaint to the European Court of Auditors Concerning the Mismanagement of EU Funds by the EU Trust Fund for Africa's "Support to Integrated Border and Migration Management in Libya" (IBM) Programme' (Global Legal Action Network, Association for Juridical Studies on Immigration, and Italian Recreational and Cultural Association, 27 April 2020).

[108] European Court of Auditors, 'Mission and Role', available at: www.eca.europa.eu/en/Pages/MissionAndRole.aspx.

it has broadened its role as it 'increasingly resembles a think-tank since it now puts forward policy recommendations'.[109] The Court of Auditors can therefore issue a recommendation that might go to curtailing this activity, but will not in itself have the power to stop the practice.

Further cases in the European courts have alleged that through its financial, material and operational support, Italy has 'contactless control' over those individuals intercepted by the Libyan Coast Guard, thus performing jurisdiction over them.[110] In yet another claim, the EU and Member States were accused before the ICC of committing crimes against humanity due to their role in the deaths of migrants and refugees in the Mediterranean Sea.[111]

V. Possible Legal Remedies that can be Brought in Front of the CJEU

With the human rights violations committed by Libyan authorities in Libya and the Libyan search and rescue zone well documented, as well as the EU and Member States' explicit support – financially, in kind and through capacity building and other cooperation mechanisms – what consequences, if any, could arise from the EU's execution of this policy?

The EU is based on the principles of the rule of law, in which the administration must be accountable for conduct that is not in accordance with the law. The Union has legal obligations to ensure that its actions do not violate human rights, not only in its internal, but in its external action. Unlike Article 1 of the ECtHR or Article 2 of the International Covenant on Civil and Political Rights, Article 51(1) TEU makes it clear that the Charter applies whenever EU organs exercise their competencies. Moreover, there are examples of the CJEU applying the Charter to extra-territorial action with the Common Foreign and Security Policy.[112] Furthermore, the CJEU has long held that the Union's Member States and institutions cannot avoid review of the conformity of their acts with EU principles.[113] This has become enshrined in Article 47 of the EU Charter and recently confirmed by the Court in PPU, *FMS*.[114] In that case, the Court ruled that Article 47 guarantees third-country nationals access to a court due to their detainment. Currently,

[109] P Stephenson, 'Reconciling Audit and Evaluation? The Shift to Performance and Effectiveness at the European Court of Auditors' (2015) 6 *European Journal of Risk Regulation* 79. See also Case C-539/09 *European Commission v Federal Republic of Germany* EU:C:2011:733.

[110] *SS and others v Italy* (n 82).

[111] Shatz and Branco (n 82).

[112] Case T-494/10 *Bank Saderat Iran v Council of the European Union* EU:T:2013:59.

[113] Joined Cases C-402/05 P and C-415/05 P *Kadi and Al Barakaat International Foundation v Council and Commission* EU:C:2008:461.

[114] Joined Cases C-924/19 PPU and 925/19 PPU *FMS and Others v Országos* EU:C:2020:367.

potential asylum seekers do not have a clear option for an effective judicial remedy against EU institutions or bodies' actions that violate an individual's fundamental rights.[115]

Some of the hurdles to bring a case include jurisdiction, standing, political will and narrowly tailored legal standards. We will address these questions below by discussing the non-binding nature of the agreements with third countries, the possible routes to bring a case on externalisation of migration before the Court, and the extent of the Court's jurisdiction.

Many have articulated the EU's culpability in the human rights violations happening in third countries, yet a hurdle to check these actions has been the CJEU deciding that it cannot review those agreements. There are several ways the Court would have the opportunity to review this policy, but successfully bringing one of these actions has been an essential challenge. These routes include actions of annulment brought by one of the privileged applicants (an institution of the EU), an action brought by a Member State, an action brought in a national court (possibly reaching the CJEU through a preliminary ruling), an action of annulment brought by an individual, and an action for damages. While discussing these possible routes, we will highlight the political realities of these actions successfully being heard by the Court.

One legal hurdle to reviewing the externalisation policy is the method by which the agreements are concluded. As discussed above, in the instance of the EU–Turkey Statement, the General Court found that the agreement was not one between an EU institution and Turkey, but rather the Member States and Turkey. To come to this conclusion, the Court examined whether the agreement was concluded within the defined procedures set out by the Treaties. According to Article 263 TFEU, the CJEU only has competence to review the legality of legislative acts of EU institutions meant to produce legal effects.[116]

There has been significant criticism of the Court's approach in this case. The main problem is that this approach allows for a 'quasi' or 'soft-law' approach to agreements with third countries. Even though these agreements are negotiated and executed by EU actors, the fact that they do not follow proper EU procedures has meant that they can avoid formal legal review. As a matter of fact, these instruments do take on legal effects in that third countries and the EU intend to, and do assent to and execute them and, as a result, the Court could change its approach. In *European Parliament v Council of the European Union*, it was held that simply stating that an agreement is non-binding (or if it is framed as guidelines) cannot hide the fact that the action required has legal effects.[117] However, the Court's ruling

[115] S Progin-Theuerkauf, 'Asylum and Return: The Gnandi Case, or a Clarification of the Right to an Effective Remedy?' [2019] *European Papers* 4/1 359, available at: www.europeanpapers.eu/en/europeanforum/asylum-and-return-gnandi-case-right-effective-remedy.

[116] TEU (n 4) Art 263.

[117] Case C-355/10 *European Parliament v Council of the European Union* EU:C:2012:207.

does not exclude the possibility of review by the European Parliament of these policies and agreements.

The EU Parliament could bring an action in front of the CJEU. The Parliament could ask for an opinion of the Court on the agreements formed with third countries to determine whether they are compatible with the Treaties, as Article 218(11) TFEU outlines. The CJEU could then find that the conclusion of the agreements involved is a delegation of political choices that can only be made by the European legislature, that the Parliament was not provided with an opportunity to consent to the agreements before they were concluded, or that the execution of these agreements violates fundamental rights. Similarly, the EU Parliament could bring a case of annulment under Article 263 TFEU against the Commission or the agencies for concluding agreements without following the procedures laid out in the Treaties in violation of the principle of institutional balance or agreements that violate the EU Charter.

If the Court were to review these policies under a fundamental rights analysis, the Court would need to find that the EU actors were legally responsible for the resulting actions. Under Article 16 of the International Law Commission's articles on the 'Responsibility of International Organizations', an international organisation which aids or assists a State in the commission of an internationally wrongful act by the latter is internationally responsible for doing so if: '(a) The act would, but for the coercion, be an internationally wrongful act of the coerced State or international organization; and (b) The coercing international organization does so with knowledge of the circumstances of the act'.[118] Article 42 of the same International Law Commission articles state, 'no international organization [should] … render aid or assistance in maintaining' a situation in violation of peremptory norms of general international law (*jus cogens*). Analysis by a number[119] of commentators[120] outline the EU and Member States' potential responsibility under international law for the violation perpetuated by third-country nationals.

An action of annulment brought by a privileged litigant is likely to have the most success. Practically, the legal hurdles to establish standing are significantly lower. Politically, one of the institutions bringing suit would represent a significant political shift and mean that the Court would not be acting on its own in curtailing an effective EU tool to slow migration. That being said, this is also an unlikely scenario because of the political capital this action would require. As it currently stands, it would be surprising if an EU institution (most likely the EU Parliament) brought such a claim. To date, calls to review and remedy the cooperation policies have appeared to fall on deaf ears.[121]

[118] UN General Assembly, 'Resolution adopted by the General Assembly on 9 December 2011' (UNGA, 27 February 2012) A/RES/66/100.

[119] Reidy (n 73).

[120] Skordas (n 65).

[121] Human Rights Watch, 'EU: Time to Review and Remedy Cooperation Policies Facilitating Abuse of Refugees and Migrants in Libya' (*Human Rights Watch*, 28 April 2020) www.hrw.org/news/2020/04/28/eu-time-review-and-remedy-cooperation-policies-facilitating-abuse-refugees-and.

Another alternative would be Member States bringing a case against the EU Parliament, the Council or the Commission. In this action, the Member State could bring suit against any of these institutions' actions or failure to act. The most obvious case would be against these institutions, probably focused on the Commission, for failure to conform to fundamental rights. However, a Member State could also sue for failure to comply with institutional balance since EU institutions have in fact concluded and executed agreements with third countries that do not comport with the procedures set out in the Treaties. While these actions would have a higher chance of succeeding, the political realities again mean that it is unlikely they would bring such a case. Few Member States have such a safe pro-migrant majority that bringing a suit would be feasible. The most likely type of litigant in these types of cases is an individual. One option for them would be to bring a case in a national court. There are a number of downsides to this approach. The first is jurisdictional limitations: most Member States will not be able to hear cases against EU policy when the harm occurred in a third country. Some Member States, like Sweden and Germany, have universal jurisdiction over grave human rights violations (eg, crimes against humanity, torture, genocide, etc) due to the conditions in detention camps in places like Libya. This avenue is possible in theory, but unlikely in practice.

Furthermore, an applicant could bring a case against their own Member State for the implementation of a directive (ie, the 'Return Directive')[122] that contravened fundamental rights or the Member State's constitutional laws. These cases are difficult for national court judges due to the opposing policy objectives of effective migration mitigation versus the protection of fundamental rights, coupled with the political sensitivity of this question. National courts, especially those in the periphery countries bearing the brunt of internal migration and border control, have reason to find practices in neighbouring third countries acceptable to relieve pressure from their governments. Even if a case on migration control is decided in favour of third-country nationals at a national level, this could have only minimal impact on greater, European policy. There is not always regular communication between the national courts of Member States, meaning their decisions are not taken up by other Member States. And even in their own countries, their decisions are not always properly implemented by other branches of their governments – sometimes intentionally, sometimes unintentionally. As Madalina Moraru and Galina Cornelisse observed, 'ten years after the entry into force of the Return Directive, incorrect implementation is still widespread across the EU'.[123] More than that, the national courts do not have jurisdiction over interpretation of EU law, in which case they are meant to make a preliminary reference.

[122] Council Directive 2008/115/EC of 16 December 2008 on common standards and procedures in Member States for returning illegally staying third-country nationals [2008] OJ L348/98.

[123] M Moraru, G Cornelisse and P De Bruycker (eds), 'Introduction: Judicial Dialogue on the Return Directive – Catalyst for Changing Migration Governance?' in *Law and Judicial Dialogue on the Return of Irregular Migrants from the European Union* (Oxford, Hart Publishing, 2020) 35.

There are a few complications when it comes to preliminary reference, yet it is one of the more common instances of EU interpretation. One complication is the varying reticence to proceed with a preliminary hearing. Angeliki Papapanagiotou-Leza and Stergios Kofinis point out that in Greek courts, for example, judges do not always utilise preliminary references because they are complex, burdensome and slow.[124] Due to the complex mix of actors in the EU's externalisation migration policy, there is a question whether the CJEU has the competence to rule on the issue.[125] There are no codified rules regarding when the conduct of a Member State may be attributable to the Union. The rule generally used is that an action of a Member State is attributable when the EU has exercised legal decision-making power.[126] Unfortunately, this legal analysis does not take into account the power dynamics between the actors, nor does it work well in cases of complex agreements involving numerous actors in blurred roles. Applying this kind of legal standard to instances of multi-actor agreements, like the EU–Turkey Statement, results in rulings where the Court believes it cannot exercise competence, even though EU institutions and agencies are deeply involved in the execution of the agreement. Accordingly, this has proven a poor method to bring this policy into compliance with fundamental rights principles.

Individuals can also bring cases directly to the CJEU in certain cases. An individual could bring an action of annulment under Article 263(4) TFEU. Any legal individual can bring an action to review the legality of acts of EU institutions, bodies, offices or agencies of the Union intended to produce legal effects.[127] This would allow the Court to review the legality of the EU institutions' and agencies' actions involved in executing policy to externalise migration mitigation. The individual would have to show direct and individual concern or a regulatory act that does not have implementing measures and direct concern to that individual.[128] Due to the Court's narrow reading of individual concern,[129] a harmed asylum seeker would struggle to prove this unless their name were explicitly written in a regulation or decision.[130] Alternatively, it would need to be a legal act that did not have implementing measures, yet the very nature of externalising the acts of

[124] S Sarolea, 'Can the Return Directive Contribute to Protection for Rejected Asylum Seekers and Irregular Migrants in Detention? The Case of Greece' in M Moraru, G Cornelisse and P De Bruycker (eds), *Law and Judicial Dialogue on the Return of Irregular Migrants from the European Union* (Oxford, Hart Publishing, 2020).

[125] M Fink, 'The Action for Damages as a Fundamental Rights Remedy: Holding Frontex Liable' (2020) 21 *German Law Journal* 532.

[126] Compare Case 217/81 *Interagra v Commission* EU:C:1982:155 and Case 175/84 *Krohn v Commission* EU:C:1986:85.

[127] TEU (n 4) Art 263.

[128] ibid.

[129] Case 25-62 *Plaumann & Co v Commission of the European Economic Community* EU:C:1963:17.

[130] K Leube, 'Can the EU Be Held Accountable for Financing Development Projects that Violate Human Rights?' (2017) 48 *Georgetown Journal of International Law* 1243, available at: www.law.georgetown.edu/international-law-journal/wp-content/uploads/sites/21/2018/05/48-4-Can-the-EU-Be-Held-Accountable-for-Financing-Development-Projects-That-Violate-Human-Rights.pdf.

containment entails implementing measures. Moreover, for a case of annulment a litigant would need to bring the case within two months of the legal act being concluded or finding out about it. These standards make it very difficult, if not impossible, for an individual to bring a case in these circumstances.

The case of *Ledra Advertising* arising out of another politically charged policy for the EU – the European Stability Mechanism – is particularly relevant here. The Court had held in *Pringle* that the MoU in which the European Stability Mechanism agreement was concluded was not a measure adopted by an EU institution (and similarly that the Eurogroup statement, raised in *Mallis*, was not intended to produce legal effects). The legal reasoning bears significant similarity to the General Court's ruling on the EU–Turkey Statement. In *Ledra*, the Court held that even though the act could not be annulled, the EU may incur non-contractual liability in an action for damages.

Similar to an action of annulment, an action for damages under Article 340 TFEU can be brought by any legal individual. However, the standing restrictions are significantly easier than a case of annulment – including the fact that an individual has five years as opposed to two months to raise the issue. According to settled case law, to bring this case, a litigant would need to prove (1) an illegal act by an EU institution or body; (2) actual damage; and (3) a causal relation between the illegal act and the damage.[131] The illegality of the EU institution or body could include contravening EU law or a violation of international human rights law.[132] The Court has additionally found that such an action must arise from a breach that is sufficiently serious.[133] In essence, the seriousness of the breach depends on how much discretion the authority enjoys, how clear the line demarcating lawful from unlawful conduct is, and how reprehensible overstepping that line is in a specific case.[134] A key factor here is that the CJEU has not developed a settled analysis specific to fundamental rights for an action for damages.

The first step would be to determine if there was a breach of EU fundamental rights. The Charter ensures that EU institutions and bodies have a positive obligation to uphold fundamental rights. To determine the existence and breach of positive obligations as well as liability for it, the Court would look at the EU body's knowledge or risk of interference with fundamental rights, the possibilities it has to prevent the breach in the specific situation, and the projected effect of measures it could have taken.[135] Damage here would depend on the applicant, but, given the number of individuals who have faced violations of their human rights resulting in physical and mental harm, this should not be a significant hurdle. The causal link is analysed by considering whether the existence of the infringement of Union

[131] Case C-352/98 P *Bergaderm and Goupil v Commission* EU:C:2000:361.
[132] M Jacob and M Kottmann, 'AEUV Art 340' in E Grabitz et al (eds), *Das Recht der Europäischen Union* (Munich, CH Beck, 2016).
[133] Bergaderm and Goupil v Commission (n 131) para 42.
[134] Fink, 'The Action for Damages as a Fundamental Rights Remedy' (n 125).
[135] ibid.

law was a necessary and sufficient condition for the damage to occur.[136] In other words, did the EU's action contribute to the harm? There are different standards used to assess this prong and the one the Court chooses will be essential in whether it is realistic for a harmed party to succeed in this action.

In the assessment of the EU's potential violation of an individual's right to leave, an act of interference should require specific justification to be lawful. Any such 'restriction may be justified in a given case only if there are clear indications of a genuine public interest which outweighs the individual's right to freedom of movement'.[137] Thus, 'a general measure preventing almost the entire population of a State from leaving'[138] cannot be considered necessary. Blanket pullbacks and retention based on nationality grounds – as those demanded by the EU – fail to conform to the principles of proportionality and non-discrimination.[139] Individuals are entitled to a detailed consideration of individual circumstances and other interests at stake. It is important to note that the Court has made it clear that the Charter is applied whenever EU institutions or bodies are acting, regardless of whether that action is internal or external to the EU borders.[140]

In addition, an assessment could be done on the EU's support of detention centres and the prohibition of arbitrary detention. First, it is important to note that this extends to action taken extraterritorially.[141] Combined with the standards of positive obligations and state responsibility, the EU's contributions to detention camps in Libya points to a clear and serious breach. The damages suffered at these detention camps have been well documented, as mentioned above. And the causal link is fairly clear considering the reporting indicating that, but for the money made available to them (by the European institutions), Libyan militias would not perform their operation in the same way.

There is certainly a reasonable claim under the action for damages by an asylum seeker, but the Court would need to set the standards of this action in a way that would be friendly to the applicant. As Melanie Fink writes about a possible case against Frontex, 'The Court would have to broaden the conduct for which Frontex is liable, apply a less stringent approach to the sufficiently serious breach requirement, and reflect on the conditions under which positive obligations give

[136] Joined Cases 64 and 113/76, 167 and 239/78, 27, 28 and 45/79 *Dumortier v Council* EU:C:1979:223 para 21; Case C-419/08 P *Trubowest Handel and Makarov v Council and Commission* EU:C:2010:147 para 53.

[137] *Hajibeyli v Azerbaijan* App no 16528/05 (ECtHR, 10 July 2008) para 63. For a commentary on 'national security' and 'public order' restrictions in this realm, see generally B Rainey, E Wicks and C Ovey, *Jacobs, White, and Ovey: The European Convention on Human Rights*, 5th edn (Oxford, Oxford University Press, 2010).

[138] *Streletz, Kessler and Krenz v Germany* App nos 34044/96, 35532/97 and 44801/98 (ECtHR, 22 March 2001) para 100.

[139] Satvinder Singh Juss (ed), *Research Handbook on International Refugee Law* (Cheltenham, Edward Elgar Publishing, 2019) 99.

[140] *Kadi* (n 113).

[141] *Al-Saadoon and Mufdhi v UK* App no 61498/08 (ECtHR, 2 March 2010); and *Al-Skeini v UK* App no 55721/07 (ECtHR, 7 July 2011).

rise to liability'.[142] With no other suitable opportunity for a harmed asylum seeker to bring a case against the EU's complicity in fundamental rights violations, these adjustments provide reasonable recourse that complies with the Court's ruling in *Gnandi*, which outlined that EU acts must be interpreted in the light of the right to an effective remedy (Article 47 of the EU Charter) and the *non-refoulement* principle (Articles 18 and 19 of the Charter and Article 33 of the Geneva Convention).

VI. Conclusion

In recent years, the EU has taken on more competence in the field of migration and border control. This has been through the expansion of agencies like Frontex, as well as through complex agreements inducing third countries to prevent migrants from fleeing their country of origin or a transit third country. The result has been a deteriorating humanitarian situation just outside EU territory. Due to current legal jurisdiction and frameworks, there is an absence of accountability based on the human rights violations stemming from this migration management policy. More than that, the third countries detaining migrants are using them as bargaining chips to obtain financing from the EU and its Member States. Accordingly, these third countries are able to avoid condemnation for their violations from the EU and come to other negotiations with a stronger hand.

Given the political divides across the continent, it is unlikely that EU institutions will act to correct this current trajectory themselves. The EU's recently proposed 'New Pact on Migration and Asylum' fails to take a different approach. In fact, the Pact appears to emphasise an increase in return and readmission agreements with third countries. Even though the EU recently established a sanction mechanism to combat grave human rights violations, it is unlikely that this will be focused on EU collaborators stemming the flow of migrants entering the Union. The Commission's role as 'guardian of the Treaties' is essential for ensuring the EU's overall performance and accountability. It has so far failed to take adequate steps to apply the Charter's protections to recent migration projects, which has resulted in countless deaths. While the EU Parliament could, in theory, raise concerns about the current policy, this is politically unlikely. This leaves the courts as the arena where hope remains.

Although there has been a myriad of attempts to remedy this situation, few have been successful. Victims of these human rights violations have attempted to bring cases in national courts, the ECtHR, the ICC and even the Court of Auditors. While some of these rulings may produce helpful outcomes, they are slow and burdensome routes to effective judicial remedy. As the role of EU institutions and agencies in migration and border control expands, their actions must comply with EU principles.

[142] Fink, 'The Action for Damages as a Fundamental Rights Remedy' (n 125).

As the CJEU has done in other instances, here the Court has exercised serious restraint in engaging in a dynamic situation at the heart of EU politics. However, by avoiding judicial activism in the face of clear and costly breaches of fundamental rights, the Court is exercising 'judicial passivism'[143] and shying away from its critical role in the EU's ecosystem. Instead of ensuring that EU policy complies with EU principles, the Court's inaction only emboldens policymakers. Indeed, EU actions have only gone further to externalise migration mitigation to third countries, thus avoiding responsibility itself while drastically reducing the number of migrants entering the Union's territory. While this approach is not new, recent years have seen a significant increase in this externalisation of EU migration and border control. Left unchecked and without clear guidance, fear of xenophobic political waves will continue to drive the discussion and policy decisions away from compliance with the EU Charter.

Previous attempts to bring cases before the Court have resulted in criticised judgments on technical matters rather than substance. Judgments arising out of preliminary hearings or cases of annulment are likely to fail for similar reasons. However, the CJEU holds the ability to address this serious breach. Indeed, an action of damages against EU institutions or agencies for action contravening the EU Charter has little case law and the potential to signal the bounds of the problematic externalisation policy. Opening the EU to this kind of liability will ensure that policymakers take into account the impact of their actions not only on the decreasing number of migrants, but on the conditions to which those migrants are subjected. Doing so would mean the Court correctly holding its institutions accountable, without stepping into the realm of political decision-making.

[143] Goldner Lang (n 2).

INDEX

www.ingramcontent.com/pod-product-compliance
Ingram Content Group UK Ltd.
Pitfield, Milton Keynes, MK11 3LW, UK
UKHW020810290926
15470UKWH00003B/1076

9 781509 937332